i-Ready® Classroom
Mathematics

Grade 6 • Volume 2

Kathleen
Cameron

NOT FOR RESALE

978-1-7280-1299-5
©2021–Curriculum Associates, LLC
North Billerica, MA 01862
No part of this book may be reproduced
by any means without written permission
from the publisher.
All Rights Reserved. Printed in USA.
7 8 9 10 11 12 13 14 15   22 21

BTS21

Curriculum Associates

801811

Contents

Rises 2 meters
every second

120 m

ii

Item	Coins Needed
Dance move	175
Costume	850

UNIT 2

Decimals and Fractions

Base-Ten Operations, Division with Fractions, and Volume

Contents (continued)

1 s

5 ft   10 ft   15 ft   20 ft   25 ft

UNIT 4

Ratio Reasoning

Unit Rates and Percent

Contents (continued)

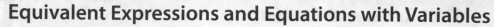

UNIT 5

Algebraic Thinking

Equivalent Expressions and Equations with Variables

UNIT 6

Positive and Negative Numbers

Absolute Value, Inequalities, and the Coordinate Plane

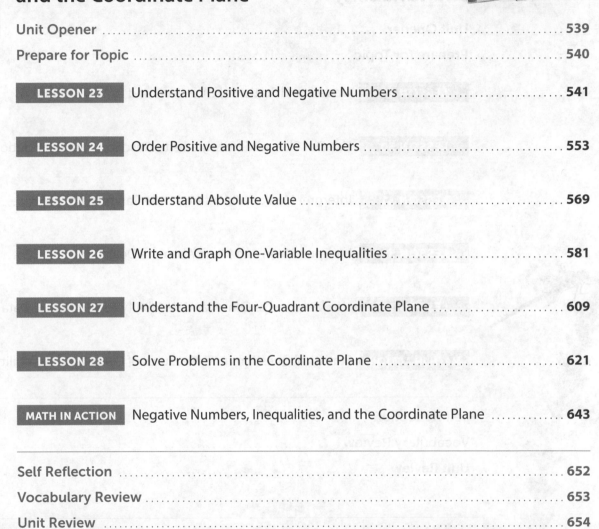

Contents (continued)

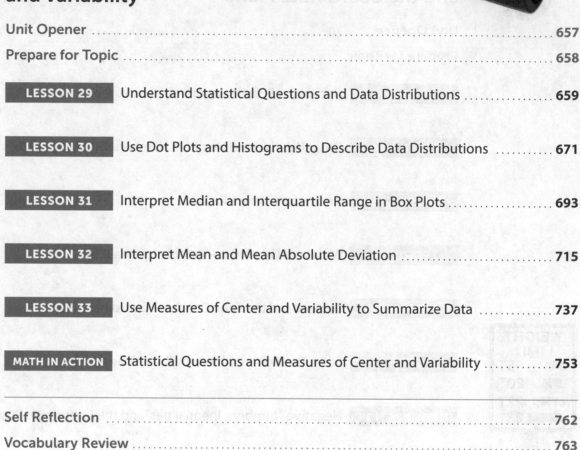

UNIT 7

Statistical Thinking

Data Distributions and Measures of Center and Variability

PEMDAS
Purple Elephants
making drinks
at starbucks

Unit 5

Algebraic Thinking

Equivalent Expressions and Equations with Variables

✓ **Self Check** | Before starting this unit, check off the skills you know below. As you complete each lesson, see how many more skills you can check off!

I can . . .	Before	After
Identify when two expressions are equivalent.	☐	☐
Write equivalent expressions.	☐	☐
Determine whether a number is a solution of an equation and write equations with variables to represent real-world problems.	☐	☐
Solve equations that represent real-world problems.	☐	☐
Identify the independent variable and dependent variable in a relationship between two quantities.	☐	☐
Write an equation to represent the relationship between an independent variable and a dependent variable.	☐	☐
Analyze the relationship between independent and dependent variables.	☐	☐
Use math vocabulary and precise language to describe writing equivalent expressions and solving equations.	☐	☐

➤ **Think about what you know about finding the value of an expression. Without evaluating the expressions, circle the expression with a different value in each row.**

A	$3 \times 2 \times 7$	$7 \times 2 \times 3$	$(3 + 3) \times 7$	$3 + 3 \times 7$	$7 \times (3 + 3)$
B	$4 + 4 + 4$	$2 \times 2 \times 4$	$4 + (2 \times 4)$	$4 + 2 \times 4$	4×3
C	$2 \times 2 \times 2$	4×2	2×4	2^3	2×3
D	5×4	$2 + 3 \times 4$	$(3 \times 4) + 2$	$12 + 2$	$2 + (3 \times 4)$
E	$10 + 15$	$10 + 5 \times 3$	5^2	$2 \times 2 \times 2 \times 2 \times 2$	$5 \times 3 + 10$
F	$2 \times (4 + 7)$	2×11	$2 \times 4 + 7$	$2 \times 2 + 7$	$7 + 2 \times 2$
G					

Meet with a partner and compare your answers. Discuss the answers on which you disagree. You may revise or add to your work. With your partner, add one more set of expressions to the list and circle the expression with a different value.

Dear Family,

This week your student is learning how to write and identify equivalent expressions. **Equivalent expressions** are expressions in different forms that always represent the same value.

For example, the expression 8 + 12 is equivalent to the expression 4(2 + 3) because both expressions represent the same value, 20.

Your student will be learning to solve problems like the one below.

Write an expression equivalent to 1 + 3(x + 1) + x.

➤ **ONE WAY** to write equivalent expressions is to use algebra tiles.

First, represent the given expression with algebra tiles.

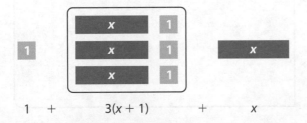

1   +   3(x + 1)   +   x

Then, rearrange the tiles to write an equivalent expression.

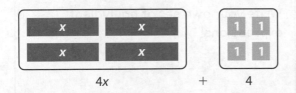

4x   +   4

➤ **ANOTHER WAY** is to use properties of operations.

1 + 3(x + 1) + x

1 + 3(x) + 3(1) + x   ← Distributive property: a(b + c) = ab + ac

1 + 3x + 3 + x   ← Identify pairs of **like terms**.

(3x + x) + (1 + 3)   ← Reorder and regroup so that like terms are together.

4x + 4

Using either method, you can see that 4x + 4 and 1 + 3(x + 1) + x are equivalent expressions.

 Use the next page to start a conversation about equivalent expressions.

Write and Identify Equivalent Expressions

Activity Exploring Equivalent Expressions

➤ **Do this activity together to match equivalent expressions.**

Each expression at the right is equivalent to the expression in either Set 1, Set 2, or Set 3.

Copy each expression into the appropriate box to make three sets of equivalent expressions. Then write your own set of three equivalent expressions.

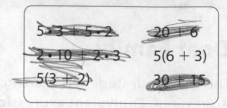

$5 \cdot 3 + 5 \cdot 2$ $20 + 6$

$2 \cdot 10 + 2 \cdot 3$ $5(6 + 3)$

$5(3 + 2)$ $30 + 15$

SET 1

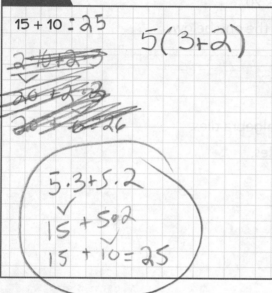

$15 + 10 = 25$

$5(3 + 2)$

$2 \cdot 10 + 2 \cdot 3$

$20 + 2 \cdot 3$

$20 + 6 = 26$

$5 \cdot 3 + 5 \cdot 2$

$15 + 5 \cdot 2$

$15 + 10 = 25$

SET 2

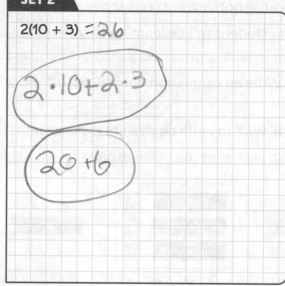

$2(10 + 3) = 26$

$2 \cdot 10 + 2 \cdot 3$

$20 + 6$

SET 3

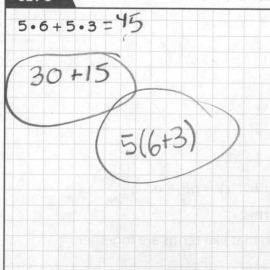

$5 \cdot 6 + 5 \cdot 3 = 45$

$30 + 15$

$5(6 + 3)$

SET 4

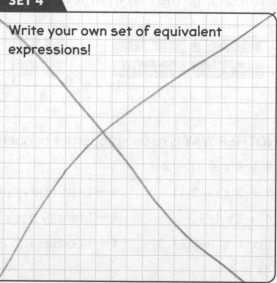

Write your own set of equivalent expressions!

? How do your sets of expressions show examples of the distributive property, $a(b + c) = ab + ac$?

Explore Equivalent Expressions

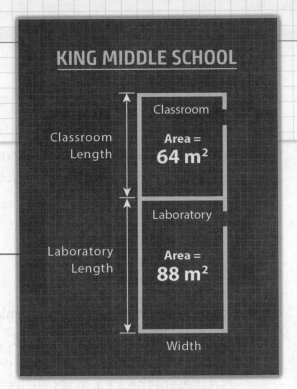

KING MIDDLE SCHOOL

Classroom

Classroom Length

Area = **64 m²**

Laboratory

Laboratory Length

Area = **88 m²**

Width

Previously, you learned how to write and evaluate expressions. In this lesson, you will learn about equivalent expressions.

➤ **Use what you know to try to solve the problem below.**

In the design for a new school, a classroom needs to have the same width as a laboratory. The architect wants the width to be as great as possible. The length and width of each room should be a whole number of meters. What length and width should the architect use for each room?

TRY IT

 Math Toolkit grid paper, sticky notes, unit tiles

Class = 8•8, 2•32, 4•16

Lab = 8•11, 2•44, 4•22

DISCUSS IT

Ask: How did you determine the greatest possible width of the rooms?

Share: I started by . . . Then I . . .

Learning Targets SMP 1, SMP 2, SMP 3, SMP 4, SMP 5, SMP 6
• Apply the properties of operations to generate equivalent expressions.
• Identify when two expressions are equivalent.
• Use the distributive property to express a sum of two whole numbers 1–100 with a common factor as a multiple of a sum of two whole numbers with no common factor.

CONNECT IT

1 Look Back What length and width should the architect use for the classroom and the laboratory? Explain how you know.

2 Look Ahead When two rectangles share a common side, the areas of the rectangles have a common factor.

a. The expressions 36 + 20 and 4(9 + 5) both represent the area, in square feet, of the outer rectangle. They are **equivalent expressions** because they name the same value. Show that these expressions are equivalent by finding the value of each expression.

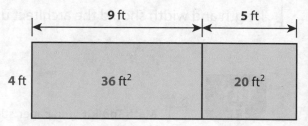

$$36 + 20 = \underline{\hspace{1cm}} \qquad 4(9 + 5) = 4 \times \underline{\hspace{1cm}}$$

$$= \underline{\hspace{1cm}}$$

b. You can also use the distributive property to show that the sum 36 + 20 is equivalent to the product 4(9 + 5). To rewrite 36 + 20 as a product, you can use the greatest common factor (GCF) of 36 and 20 as one of the factors.

The GCF of 36 and 20 is _____.   36 + 20

Rewrite each term using the GCF as a factor.   _____ × 9 + _____ × 5

Use the distributive property.   _____ × (_____ + _____)

c. Rewrite the sum 42 + 35 as a product. Use the GCF of 42 and 35 as one of the factors. Use a sum as the other factor.

3 Reflect How can you use the distributive property to rewrite a sum of two terms as a product of two factors?

Prepare for Writing and Identifying Equivalent Expressions

1 Think about what you know about expressions. Fill in each box. Use words, numbers, and pictures. Show as many ideas as you can.

Word	In My Own Words	Examples
expression		
term		
coefficient		
distributive property		

2 What is the coefficient of n in the expression $n + 15$? Explain how you know.

3 An architect is designing a sandwich shop, as shown in the diagram. The kitchen and dining room will be the same length. The length needs to be as great as possible. The length and width of each room should be a whole number of meters.

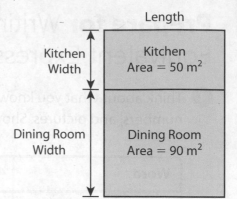

Length

Kitchen Width — Kitchen Area = 50 m²

Dining Room Width — Dining Room Area = 90 m²

a. What length and width should the architect use for the kitchen and for the dining room? Show your work.

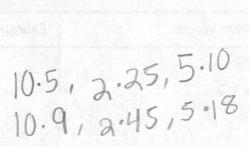

$10 \cdot 5, \ 2 \cdot 25, \ 5 \cdot 10$
$10 \cdot 9, \ 2 \cdot 45, \ 5 \cdot 18$

SOLUTION _____

_____

b. Check your answer to problem 3a. Show your work.

Develop Using the Distributive Property to Write Equivalent Expressions

➤ **Read and try to solve the problem below.**

The Romano family pays for a streaming movie service that costs $8 per month. They want to add a second movie service for *d* dollars per month. Write two expressions for the total cost of both services for 3 months. One expression should be a sum of two terms, and one should be a product of two factors.

TRY IT

 Math Toolkit algebra tiles, grid paper

DISCUSS IT

Ask: What does each part of your two expressions represent?

Share: In my first expression, . . . In my second expression, . . .

➤ **Explore different ways to understand using the distributive property to write equivalent expressions.**

The Romano family pays for a streaming movie service that costs $8 per month. They want to add a second movie service for d dollars per month. Write two expressions for the total cost of both services for 3 months. One expression should be a sum of two terms, and one should be a product of two factors.

Model It

You can use algebra tiles to help you write an algebraic expression.

Each square tile represents $1. Each rectangular tile represents d dollars.

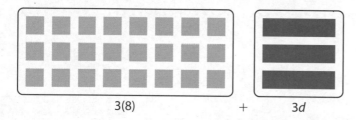

3(8)   +   3d

The tiles show that the expression $24 + 3d$ represents the total cost of both services for 3 months.

Analyze It

You can use the distributive property to find an equivalent expression.

Rewrite the expression $24 + 3d$ as a product of two factors. One factor is a common factor of the two terms.

$24 + 3d$

$3(8) + 3(d)$ ⟵ The GCF of 24 and $3d$ is 3.

$3(8 + d)$

CONNECT IT

➤ **Use the problem from the previous page to help you understand how to use the distributive property to write equivalent expressions.**

1 Look at the expressions 24 + 3d and 3(8 + d). Which expression is a sum of two terms? Which expression is a product of two factors?

2 The tiles in **Model It** are grouped to model the expression 24 + 3d. The same set of tiles is shown at the right. Circle and label groups of tiles to show how the tiles also model the expression 3(8 + d).

3 Equivalent expressions always name the same value. How do the algebra tiles show that 24 + 3d and 3(8 + d) will always have the same value?

4 In **Analyze It**, the distributive property is used to rewrite the sum 24 + 3d as the product 3(8 + d). How do you use the distributive property to rewrite the product 3(8 + d) as the sum 24 + 3d?

5 What are two ways you can use the distributive property to write equivalent expressions?

6 The distributive property applies to differences as well as sums. How could you use the distributive property to rewrite 6x − 6 as a product?

7 **Reflect** Think about all the models and strategies you have discussed today. Describe how one of them helped you better understand how to use the distributive property to write equivalent expressions.

Apply It

➤ **Use what you learned to solve these problems.**

8 **a.** Use the distributive property to rewrite $(5x + 3)(2)$ as a sum of two terms. Show your work.

SOLUTION _____

b. You can use the commutative and associative properties of multiplication to reorder and regroup factors. Explain how you used one or both of these properties in your work for problem 8a.

9 Which expression is equivalent to $63 + 56$?

A $7(9 + 8)$

B $3(60 + 56)$

C $6(3 + 5)$

D $7(9 + 56)$

10 A company sells fruit cups in packs of 4. The packs currently weigh 20 oz. The company plans to reduce the weight of each cup by n oz. The expression $20 - 4n$ represents the new weight, in ounces, of a pack of fruit cups. Rewrite the expression for the new weight as a product of two factors. Show your work.

SOLUTION _____

Practice Using the Distributive Property to Write Equivalent Expressions

➤ **Study the Example showing how to use the distributive property to rewrite a product. Then solve problems 1–6.**

Example

Rewrite the expression $3(7a - 4b)$ as a difference.

You can use the distributive property to rewrite the product.

Multiply $7a$ and $4b$ by 3.

$3(7a - 4b)$

$3 \cdot 7a - 3 \cdot 4b$

Use the associative property.

$(3 \cdot 7)a - (3 \cdot 4)b$

Multiply inside the parentheses.

$21a - 12b$

The difference $21a - 12b$ is equivalent to $3(7a - 4b)$.

---

1. You use the associative property of multiplication to change how factors are grouped. In the Example, why are the factors of the term $3 \cdot 7a$ regrouped as $(3 \cdot 7)a$?

2. Jesse says that the expressions $7(2x + 9)$ and $14x + 9$ are equivalent. Do you agree with Jesse? Explain.

3. Use the greatest common factor of 84 and 48 to write the sum $84 + 48$ as a product. Write a whole number in each blank.

    $84 + 48$

    _____ × (7 + _____)

Vocabulary

distributive property
for any numbers a, b, and c,
$a(b + c) = ab + ac$.

equivalent expressions
two or more expressions in different forms that always name the same value.

greatest common factor (GCF)
the greatest factor two or more numbers have in common.

4 Rewrite the expression $2(3 - 4k)$ as a difference. Show your work.

SOLUTION _____

5 Tell whether each pair of expressions is *Equivalent* or *Not Equivalent*.

	Equivalent	Not Equivalent
a. $5(3t - 6)$ and $15t - 30$	◯	◯
b. $16 + 72n$ and $(2 + 9n)(8)$	◯	◯
c. $4(6a + 8b)$ and $10a + 12b$	◯	◯
d. $7x - 9y$ and $(7x - y)(9)$	◯	◯

6 Kaley plans to increase the amount of food she feeds her puppy each day by x oz. The expression $3x + 18$ represents the total weight of food, in ounces, Kaley will need for her puppy for the next three days.

Increase by x oz per day

a. Rewrite the expression as a product of two factors. Show your work.

SOLUTION _____

b. How many ounces of food did Kaley feed her puppy each day before she increased the amount? Explain how you know.

Develop Combining Like Terms

➤ **Read and try to solve the problem below.**

Ryan is making papel picado as decorations for his aunt's wedding. The receipt shows how much tissue paper he bought. Each small package holds *x* sheets, and each large package holds *y* sheets. Write an expression with exactly three terms to represent the total number of sheets of tissue paper Ryan bought.

PAPER PLUS
Art Supply Store
RECEIPT

ITEM	AMOUNT
• gold tissue paper 2 large packages	$4.44
• blue tissue paper 3 small packages	$2.46
• green tissue paper 1 large package	$2.22
• purple tissue paper 2 small packages	$1.64
• pink tissue paper 4 sheets	$0.84

THANK YOU FOR SHOPPING
IN OUR STORE!

TRY IT

  Math Toolkit algebra tiles, grid paper

$$2y + 3x + 1y + 2x + 4$$

$$2y + 3x + 1y + 2x + 4$$

$$3y \quad 5x + 4$$

DISCUSS IT

Ask: What does each term in your expression represent?

Share: The first term represents . . .

➤ **Explore different ways to combine like terms.**

Ryan is making papel picado as decorations for his aunt's wedding. The table shows how much tissue paper he bought. Each small package holds *x* sheets, and each large package holds *y* sheets. Write an expression with exactly three terms to represent the total number of sheets of tissue paper Ryan bought.

Paper Color	Amount
Gold	2 large packages
Blue	3 small packages
Green	1 large package
Purple	2 small packages
Pink	4 sheets

Picture It

You can draw a picture to help you write an algebraic expression.

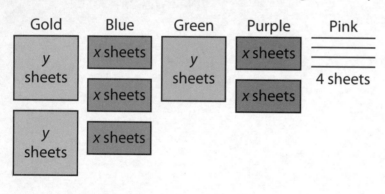

$2y + 3x + y + 2x + 4$

Analyze It

You can use properties of operations to combine terms with the same variable parts.

Identify the **like terms**.	$2y + 3x + y + 2x + 4$
Reorder and regroup the terms.	$(2y + y) + (3x + 2x) + 4$
Rewrite the term *y* as 1*y*.	$(2y + 1y) + (3x + 2x) + 4$
Use the distributive property with each pair of like terms.	$(2 + 1)y + (3 + 2)x + 4$

Papel picado

➤ **Use the problem from the previous page to help you understand how to combine like terms.**

1 Look at **Picture It**. How do the shapes show that an expression for the total number of sheets of tissue paper will have at least three terms?

2 Look at the four equivalent expressions in **Analyze It**.

   a. What are the like terms in the expression $2y + 3x + y + 2x + 4$? Explain.

   b. The commutative property of addition lets you reorder terms. How is this property used to rewrite the expression?

   c. Look at the last expression. Why can you use the distributive property to combine like terms?

3 What expression with exactly three terms can you write to represent the total number of sheets of tissue paper Ryan bought? How are the coefficients of the variable terms related to the coefficients of the variable terms of the original expression?

4 **Reflect** Think about all the models and strategies you have discussed today. Describe how one of them helped you better understand how to combine like terms of an algebraic expression.

Apply It

➤ **Use what you learned to solve these problems.**

⑤ Write an expression equivalent to $12g - 3g + 7$ with exactly two terms. Show your work.

$$(12g - 3g) + 7$$
$$9g + 7$$

SOLUTION _____

⑥ Which expressions are equivalent to $6a - a + 4b$? Select all that apply.

A $10b$

B $9ab$

$6a - a$
$5a + 4b$

C $6 + 4b$

D $5a + 4b$ ⟵circled

E $(6 - 1)a + 4b$ ⟵circled

F $(6 \cdot 1)a + 4b$ ⟵circled

⑦ An athletic store receives an order for 8 blue jerseys, 12 pairs of blue shorts, 10 gold jerseys, and 5 pairs of gold shorts. Each jersey weighs j oz, and each pair of shorts weighs s oz. They are packed in a box that weighs 16 oz when empty. Write an expression with exactly three terms for the total weight, in ounces, of the box. Show your work.

$$8j + 12s + 10j + 5s + 16$$
$$(8j + 10j) + (12s + 5s) + 16$$
$$18j + 17s + 16$$

Item	Quantity
blue jersey	8
blue shorts	12
gold jersey	10
gold shorts	5

SOLUTION _____

Practice Combining Like Terms

➤ **Study the Example showing how to combine like terms. Then solve problems 1–6.**

Example

The Woodworking Club is selling picture frames at the school craft fair. The frames sell for $11 each. Materials for each frame cost $6, and renting a booth costs $36. The expression $11f - 6f - 36$ represents the amount of money the club will make for selling f frames. Rewrite the expression with exactly two terms.

You can use the distributive property to combine like terms.

The terms $11f$ and $6f$ are like terms because both have the variable f.

$11f - 6f - 36$

$(11 - 6)f - 36$

$5f - 36$

The terms of $5f - 36$ are not like terms, so they cannot be combined.

The equivalent expression is $5f - 36$.

---

1 Look at the Example. Suppose the club increases the selling price of a frame to $13. Write an expression with exactly two terms for the amount of money the club will make for selling f frames. Show your work.

SOLUTION _____

2 Which expression is equivalent to $3a + 9a + 7b - b$?

A $12a + 7$

B $12a + 6b$

C $18ab$

D $19a$

$12 + 6b$

Vocabulary

equivalent expressions
two or more expressions in different forms that always name the same value.

like terms
two or more terms that have the same variable factors.

perimeter
the distance around a two-dimensional shape.

3 Neena and Carissa collect trading cards. Neena has 4 packs of castle cards and 5 packs of hero cards. Carissa has 6 packs of castle cards and 4 packs of hero cards. Each castle pack holds *c* cards, and each hero pack holds *h* cards. Write an expression with exactly two terms for the total number of cards Neena and Carissa have. Show your work.

Challenge

SOLUTION _____

4 Write a whole number in each blank to show an expression that is equivalent to $15x + 10$.

$20x -$ ___5___ $\cdot x +$ ___10___

5 Isaiah writes an expression with 5 terms. All 5 terms are like terms. How many terms are in the equivalent expression with the least number of terms? Explain.

We can all turn them into a single term.

$3x + 5x + 7x + 10x + 20x =$

$45x$

6 The length of a rectangle is twice the width *w*. Which expressions represent the perimeter of the rectangle? Select all that apply.

(A) $2w + w + 2w + w$

(B) $2w + 2(2w)$

(C) $2(w + 2w)$

(D) $2(2w)$

(E) $6w$

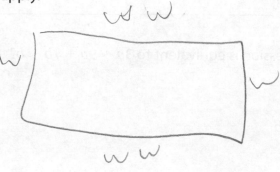

Develop Identifying Equivalent Expressions

➤ **Read and try to solve the problem below.**

Which of these three expressions are equivalent?

$3(x + 2) + 2x$ $2 + 4(x + 1) + x$ $2(3 + 3x) - 2x$

  Math Toolkit algebra tiles, grid paper

DISCUSS IT

Ask: What is another way you could show which expressions are equivalent?

Share: I could also . . .

➤ **Explore different ways to identify equivalent expressions.**

Which of these three expressions are equivalent?

$3(x + 2) + 2x$ $2 + 4(x + 1) + x$ $2(3 + 3x) - 2x$

Model It

You can use algebra tiles to model each expression.

$3(x + 2) + 2x$

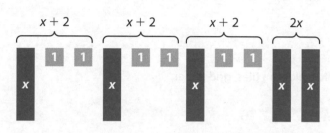

$2 + 4(x + 1) + x$

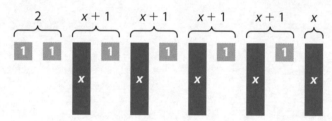

$2(3 + 3x) - 2x$

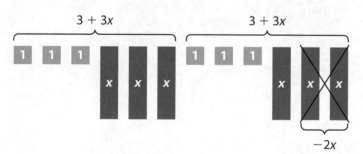

Analyze It

You can use properties of operations to write each expression without parentheses and with the fewest number of terms possible.

$3(x + 2) + 2x$	$2 + 4(x + 1) + x$	$2(3 + 3x) - 2x$
$3 \cdot x + 3 \cdot 2 + 2x$	$2 + 4 \cdot x + 4 \cdot 1 + x$	$2 \cdot 3 + 2 \cdot 3x - 2x$
$3x + 6 + 2x$	$2 + 4x + 4 + x$	$6 + 6x - 2x$
$(3x + 2x) + 6$	$(2 + 4) + (4x + x)$	$6 + (6x - 2x)$
$5x + 6$	$6 + 5x$	$6 + 4x$

➤ **Use the problem from the previous page to help you understand how to identify equivalent expressions.**

1 Look at **Model It**. How do you use tiles to model $3(x + 2) + 2x$?

2 How could rearranging the algebra tiles help you determine which expressions are equivalent?

3 Look at the first group of expressions in **Analyze It**. List the properties of operations that are used to rewrite the expression $3(x + 2) + 2x$.

4 Which of the three expressions are equivalent? Explain how you know.

5 How are properties of operations useful for identifying equivalent expressions?

6 **Reflect** Think about all the models and strategies you have discussed today. Describe how one of them helped you better understand how to solve the **Try It** problem.

Apply It

➤ **Use what you learned to solve these problems.**

7 Two groups of campers carry their water in reusable packs that come in three sizes. The table shows how many packs each group carries. A medium water pack holds 1 liter more than a small pack holds. A large pack holds 2 liters more than a small pack. Do the two groups carry the same amount of water? If not, which group carries more? Use w to represent the number of liters of water a small pack can hold. Show your work.

Size	Group 1	Group 2
small	1	2
medium	3	1
large	2	3

SOLUTION _____

8 Which expressions are equivalent to $8a - 6$? Select all that apply.

A $5a + 6 - 3a$

B $2a + 6(a - 1)$

C $4a + 2(2a - 3)$

D $2 + 3a + 3(a - 2)$

E $11a - a + 2(a - 3)$

9 Are the expressions $3(x + y) + 2y + 10$ and $x + 5y + 2(x + 5)$ equivalent? Show your work.

SOLUTION _____

Practice Identifying Equivalent Expressions

➤ **Study the Example showing how to determine whether expressions are equivalent. Then solve problems 1–5.**

Example

Are the expressions $4(x + 1) - 1$ and $2(x + 1) + 2x$ equivalent?

You can use properties of operations to rewrite the expressions.

$4(x + 1) - 1$	$2(x + 1) + 2x$
$4 \cdot x + 4 \cdot 1 - 1$	$2 \cdot x + 2 \cdot 1 + 2x$
$4x + 4 - 1$	$2x + 2 + 2x$
$4x + (4 - 1)$	$(2x + 2x) + 2$
$4x + 3$	$4x + 2$

No matter what the value of x is, $4x + 3$ will always be 1 more than $4x + 2$. The expressions $4x + 3$ and $4x + 2$ never name the same value.

The expressions $4(x + 1) - 1$ and $2x + 2(x + 1)$ are not equivalent.

1 Explain how the distributive property and the commutative property of addition are used in the Example to show that $2(x + 1) + 2x$ is equivalent to $4x + 2$.

2 Is each expression equivalent to the expression $48a - 36b$? Select *Yes* or *No* for each expression.

$12(3a+a-36b)$

369
$+) -36b$
$12a)$

$48a - 36b$

	Yes	No
a. $30(18a - 6b)$	○	●
b. $12a + 36(a - b)$	●	○
c. $12(3a + a - 3b)$	●	○
d. $4(10a + 2a - 9b)$	●	○

3 An adult ticket to a corn maze costs $4 more than a child ticket. A senior ticket costs $3 more than a child ticket. Amelia's family has 3 children and 2 adults. Manuel's family has 2 children, 1 adult, and 2 seniors. Do the two families pay the same amount for tickets to the maze? If not, who pays more? Use c to represent the cost of a child ticket. Show your work.

Corn maze

SOLUTION _____

4 You can use the commutative property to reorder the terms of an expression. James says that you can use the commutative property to rewrite $5m + 10$ as $10m + 5$. Is James correct? Explain.

No, because

5 Which of these three expressions are equivalent? Show your work.

$7(2 + 3x) - 3x$ $2(6x + 7) + 10x$ $4(3 + 3x) + 2(1 + 3x)$

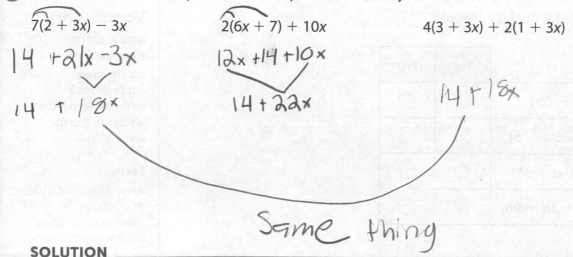

$14 + 21x - 3x$ $12x + 14 + 10x$

$14 + 18x$ $14 + 22x$ $14 + 18x$

Same thing

SOLUTION _____

Refine Writing and Identifying Equivalent Expressions

➤ **Complete the Example below. Then solve problems 1–10.**

Example

Are the expressions $(3x)(x) + 6$ and $x + x + 6 + x$ equivalent?

Look at how you could rewrite the expressions to compare them.

$(3x)(x) + 6$ $x + x + 6 + x$

$3(x \cdot x) + 6$ $(x + x + x) + 6$

$3x^2 + 6$ $3x + 6$

SOLUTION _____

CONSIDER THIS . . .
Are the terms $3x^2$ and $3x$ like terms? Why or why not?

PAIR/SHARE
Explain how you know whether the expressions are equivalent.

Apply It

1 The fine for an overdue library book is $0.75 for the first day and $0.50 for each additional day. Rewrite the expression $0.75 + 0.5(d - 1)$ for the fine as a sum of two terms where d represents the number of days overdue. Show your work.

CONSIDER THIS . . .
How could you use the distributive property to rewrite the expression?

PAIR/SHARE
What would the fine be for a book that is 4 days overdue?

SOLUTION _____

2 Ana and Katrina are buying fruit to bring to their book club meeting. Ana buys 2.4 lb of oranges and 0.8 lb of cherries. Katrina buys 1.8 lb of oranges and 1.3 lb of cherries. Oranges cost r dollars per pound, and cherries cost c dollars per pound. Write an expression with exactly two terms for the total cost of the fruit Ana and Katrina buy. Show your work.

> **CONSIDER THIS . . .**
> The cost of Ana's oranges is equal to the weight of her oranges times the cost per pound.

> **PAIR/SHARE**
> What does each term in your expression represent?

SOLUTION _____

3 Which expression is equivalent to $3(2x + 4y) - y$?

A 17

$6x + 12y - y$

B $6x + 12$

$6x + 11y$

C $3(6xy) - y$

D $6(x + 2y) - y$

Kimani chose C as the correct answer. How might she have gotten that answer?

> **CONSIDER THIS . . .**
> How can you use properties of operations to rewrite $3(2x + 4y) - y$ in a different way?

> **PAIR/SHARE**
> How could you use $x = 1$ and $y = 2$ to check your answer?

4 A park meadow is planted with wildflowers. The Parks Department plans to extend the length of the rectangular meadow by x meters. Which expressions represent the total area, in square meters, after the meadow's length is increased? Select all that apply.

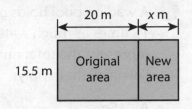

A $310 + x$

B $15.5(20x)$

C $20x + 15.5$

D $15.5x + 310$

E $15.5(20 + x)$

F $35.5 + x$

5 Use the distributive property to write two different expressions equal to 72. Each expression should be the product of a number and a sum. Show your work.

SOLUTION _____

6 Look at each pair of expressions. Select *Equivalent* or *Not Equivalent* for each pair.

	Equivalent	Not Equivalent
a. $f + f + f$ and $3f$	○	○
b. $x^2 + 3y$ and $(x + x) + y \cdot y \cdot y$	○	○
c. $2.5(2n - 4)$ and $5n - 4$	○	○

7 Show how to use the greatest common factor of 84 and 72 to rewrite $84m - 72n$ as a product of two factors. Label the step that shows the distributive property.

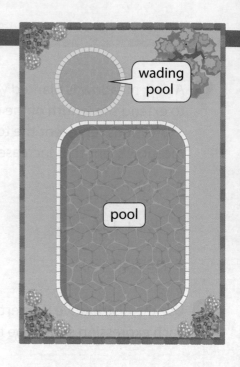

wading pool

pool

8 A wading pool holds *g* gallons of water. A swimming pool holds 15 times as much water as the wading pool. Which expressions represent the total number of gallons of water in both pools? Select all that apply.

A 15*g*

B 16*g*

C 15 + *g*

D 2*g* + 15

E *g* + 15*g*

9 Are the expressions $\frac{1}{2}(4c + 8) + 3c - 2$ and $4c + 2(0.5c + 1)$ equivalent? Show your work.

SOLUTION _____

10 **Math Journal** Brian says that the expressions $2(x + 2)$ and $3(x + 1) + 1$ are equivalent because they name the same value when $x = 0$. Is Brian's reasoning correct? Explain.

✔ End of Lesson Checklist

☐ **INTERACTIVE GLOSSARY** Find the entry for *like terms*. Explain why the terms 5*a* and 5*b* in the expression $5a + 5b + 8$ are not like terms. Label your explanation as a non-example.

☐ **SELF CHECK** Go back to the Unit 5 Opener and see what you can check off.

Dear Family,

This week your student is exploring solutions of equations with variables.

An equation uses an equal sign to show that two expressions have the same value. For example, 4 + 5 and 6 + 3 both equal 9. The equation 4 + 5 = 6 + 3 shows that these two different numerical expressions have the same value.

Sometimes equations have variables that stand for unknown quantities. An equation is true when its two sides have the same value. A value of a variable that makes an equation true is a **solution of an equation**. For example, the equation $x + 3 = 5$ has a solution of 2 because 2 + 3 = 5 is a true statement.

Your student will be learning to model solutions of equations like the one below.

> Show that 3 is a solution of the equation $4 = x + 1$.

➤ **ONE WAY** to show that a number is a solution of an equation is to represent the equation with a bar model.

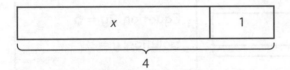

The bar model represents both the equation $4 = x + 1$ and the equation $x = 4 - 1$. The length of the bar labeled x is $4 - 1$, or 3.

➤ **ANOTHER WAY** is to use substitution.

$4 = 1 + x$

$4 = 1 + 3$ ← Substitute 3 for x.

$4 = 4$ ← The equation 4 = 4 is a true statement.

If $x = 3$, then the equation $4 = 1 + x$ is true.

Both representations show that 3 is a solution of the equation $4 = x + 1$.

 Use the next page to start a conversation about solutions of equations.

Activity Exploring Solutions of Equations

➤ **Do this activity together to explore solutions of equations.**

Set 1 and Set 2 each include a bar model that represents the relationship between the two sides of the given equation. The solution of the equation is also shown.

What do you notice in Set 1 and Set 2? Draw your own bar model in Set 3 and then write an equation to match.

SET 1

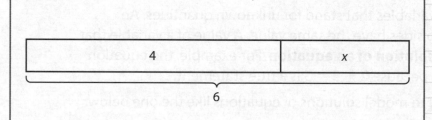

Equation: $4 + x = 6$

Solution: $x = 2$

SET 2

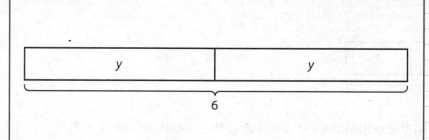

Equation: $2y = 6$

Solution: $y = 3$

SET 3

Draw your own bar model that includes a variable. Then write an equation to match!

? How can a bar model help you find the solution of an equation?

Explore Solutions of Equations

Model It

➤ **Complete the problems about modeling equations.**

1 The equal sign in an equation shows that the expression on the left side has the same value as the expression on the right side.

A bar model can represent the relationship between the two sides of an equation. Circle each equation that the bar model represents.

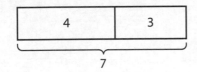

| 4 | 3 |

7

$4 + 3 = 7$ $4 = 12 \div 3$ $3 \cdot 4 = 12$ $4 = 7 - 3$

$7 + 4 = 11$ $7 = 3 + 4$ $7 - 4 = 3$ $7 \div 4 = 1\frac{3}{4}$

2 Write two different equations that each bar model represents.

a.

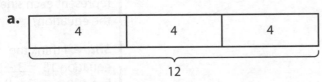

| 4 | 4 | 4 |

12

$12 \div 3 = 4$ $4 + 4 + 4 = 12$

b.

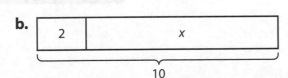

| 2 | x |

10

$2 + x = 10$ $10 - 2 = x$

c.

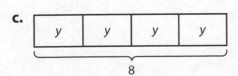

| y | y | y | y |

8

$y + y + y + y = 8$ $4y = 8$

DISCUSS IT

Ask: Why can you use more than one equation to represent the same bar model?

Share: A bar model helps me see . . .

◎ **Learning Target** SMP 2, SMP 3, SMP 7
Understand solving an equation or inequality as a process of answering a question: which values from a specified set, if any, make the equation or inequality true? Use substitution to determine whether a given number in a specified set makes an equation or inequality true.

Model It

➤ **Complete the problems about equations with variables.**

3 Complete the model to represent each equation.

a. $15 = 3 + x$

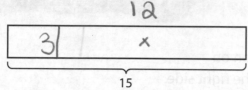

b. $15 = 3 \cdot x$

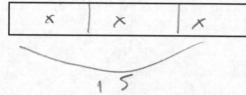

4 An equation is true when its two sides have the same value. A value of a variable that makes an equation true is a **solution of the equation**.

Use your models from problem 3 to find a solution of each equation. Explain your reasoning.

a. $15 = 3 + x$

b. $15 = 3 \cdot x$

DISCUSS IT

Ask: How do your bar models in problem 3 represent each side of the equation?

Share: I think the equation $15 = 3 + x$ has only one solution because . . .

5 **Reflect** Explain what the equation $3x = 6$ means without using the word *equal*. Explain why 2 is a solution of the equation.

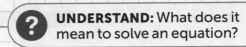

Develop Understanding of Solutions of Equations

Model It: Hanger Diagrams

➤ **Try these two problems about equations and hanger diagrams.**

1 A hanger diagram uses shapes that represent weights to model two expressions. When the expressions have the same value, the hanger is level, or balanced. An unbalanced hanger shows that two expressions do not have the same value. Complete the statements by writing the total weight for each side of the hanger.

a.

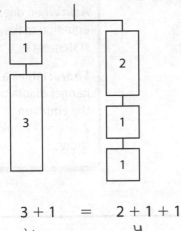

$$3 + 1 \quad = \quad 2 + 1 + 1$$

$$\underline{4} \qquad = \qquad \underline{4}$$

b.

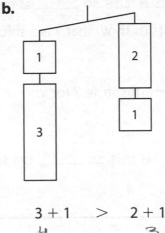

$$3 + 1 \quad > \quad 2 + 1$$

$$\underline{4} \qquad > \qquad \underline{3}$$

> **DISCUSS IT**
>
> **Ask:** How is a hanger diagram different from a bar model? How is it similar?
>
> **Share:** I think the right side of a hanger is lower than the left side when...

2 Use the balanced hanger at the right.

a. Explain why the hanger diagram represents the equation $x + 1 = 3$.

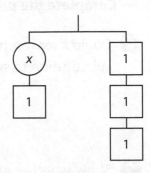

b. Tell whether the hanger would be *balanced* or *unbalanced* if you replaced the x-weight with each of the weights shown below. Explain your reasoning for each weight.

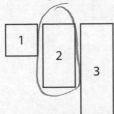

c. Which value in the set {1, 2, 3} is a solution of the equation $x + 1 = 3$?

Model It: Substitution

➤ **Try this problem involving substitution.**

3 An equation with a variable may be true or false, depending on the value of the variable. You can use substitution to decide.

a. Complete the statements to show that 9 is not a solution of $2 + x = 9$.

$$2 + x = 9$$

$2 +$ _____ $= 9$ ⟵ Substitute 9 for x.

_____ $= 9$

The equation ___9___ = ~~9~~ 7 is false, so ___7___ is not a solution of $2 + x = 9$.

b. Complete the statements to show that 7 is a solution of $2 + x = 9$.

$$2 + x = 9$$

$2 +$ _____ $= 9$ ⟵ Substitute 7 for x.

_____ $= 9$

The equation _____ $= 7$ is true, so _____ is a solution of $2 + x = 9$.

> **DISCUSS IT**
>
> **Ask:** When does an equation make a false statement?
>
> **Share:** I think a hanger diagram for the equation $2 + x = 9$ would show . . .

CONNECT IT

➤ **Complete the problems below.**

4 Could x represent a value of 4 in the hanger diagram? Use an equation and substitution to support your answer.

No

$x + x = 6$ $1 + 1 + 1 + 1 + 1 + 1 < 8$

$4 + 4 = 6$

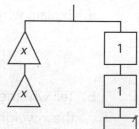

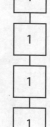

5 Show whether each value in the set {2, 3, 4} is a solution of the equation $x + 2 = 6$.

Practice Identifying Solutions of Equations

➤ **Study how the Example shows using substitution to determine if values in a set include a solution of an equation. Then solve problems 1–6.**

Example

Use substitution to decide whether each value in the set {7, 8, 9} is a solution of the equation $28 = x \cdot 4$.

Substitute each value for x. Compare the values of the two sides of the equation.

Substitute **7** for x.

$28 = x \cdot 4$

$28 = 7 \cdot 4$

$28 = 28$ ⟵ true

Substitute **8** for x.

$28 = x \cdot 4$

$28 = 8 \cdot 4$

$28 = 32$ ⟵ false

Substitute **9** for x.

$28 = x \cdot 4$

$28 = 9 \cdot 4$

$28 = 36$ ⟵ false

When x is 7, the equation is true. So, 7 is a solution of $28 = x \cdot 4$.

When x is 8 or 9, the equation is false. So, 8 and 9 are not solutions of $28 = x \cdot 4$.

1. Suppose the equation $28 = x \cdot 4$ in the Example is written in the form $4x = 28$. Is 7 still a solution? Explain.

   yes. Because it form does not matter

2. Use substitution to determine if 0 is a solution of $5x = 5$.

   No. Anything multiplied by $0 = 0$

3. Lucía says that 35 and 65 are both solutions of the equation $50 = x + 15$. Is Lucía correct? Explain your answer.

   No. X = 35 so 65 cannot be a solution. If it was 65 it would be equal to 80 not 50

Vocabulary

equation
a mathematical statement that uses an equal sign (=) to show that two expressions have the same value.

solution of an equation
a value that can be substituted for a variable to make an equation true.

4 Complete the statements to show the total weight for each side of the hanger.

a.

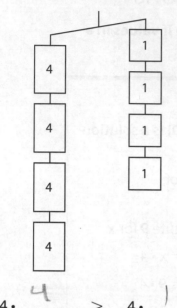

$$4 \cdot \frac{4}{16} > 4 \cdot \frac{1}{4}$$

$$16 > 4$$

b.

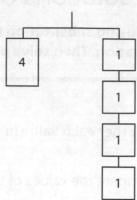

$$\frac{4}{4} = 1 + 1 + 1 + \frac{1}{4}$$

$$\underline{} = \underline{}$$

5 Demarco substitutes a value for x in the equation $\frac{1}{2}x = 4$.

a. How will Demarco know if the value is a solution of the equation?

if the expression of 4, then the value $\frac{1}{2}x$ has a value is that Demarco did

b. Is 8 a solution of the equation? Explain.

Yes if 8 is a subsitute then it would be eanal

6 Use the balanced hanger at the right. Tell whether the hanger will be *balanced* or *unbalanced* when you replace the x-weight with each weight shown below. Explain your reasoning for each weight.

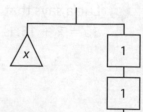

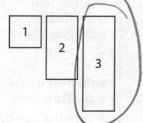

Refine Ideas About Solutions of Equations

Apply It

➤ **Complete problems 1–5.**

1 **Identify** Greg says that x could represent a value of 3 in the hanger diagram. Do you agree? Explain your reasoning.

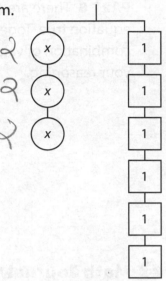

2 **Demonstrate** Write an equation with a solution of 8. Use the variable x and at least three terms in your equation. Explain why 8 is a solution.

3 **Validate** Bianca substitutes a value for x in the equation $4x = 2x + 6$.

   a. How will Bianca know if the value is a solution of the equation?

   b. Is 3 a solution of the equation? Explain your reasoning.

4 Cai writes the equation $a \cdot b = c$.

PART A If a is 4, b is 5, and c is 9, is the equation true? Explain your reasoning.

$$4 \cdot 5 = 9$$

PART B There are many combinations of values for a, b, and c that make the equation true. Together, these values form a solution of the equation. Find a combination of values for a, b, and c that is a solution of the equation. Explain your reasoning.

5 **Math Journal** Mr. Ramírez writes the equation $x + 1 = 7$ and the set {2, 3, 6, 7} on the board. Tell if each value in the set is a solution of the equation and why. What does it mean to solve the equation $x + 1 = 7$?

✓ **End of Lesson Checklist**

☐ **INTERACTIVE GLOSSARY** Find the entry for *solution of an equation*. Add two important things you learned about equations in this lesson.

Dear Family,

This week your student is learning how to write and solve equations that represent real-world situations.

For example, Miguel buys a pack of granola bars that costs $3.26 and a drink. The cashier says his total is $5.25. You can use the equation $3.26 + x = 5.25$, where x is the cost of the drink, to represent this situation.

Subtracting 3.26 from both sides of the equation shows that Miguel's drink costs $1.99.

$$3.26 + x = 5.25$$
$$3.26 + x - 3.26 = 5.25 - 3.26$$
$$x = 1.99$$

Your student will be learning to solve problems like the one below.

> Kendra has $6 to spend on comic books. Each comic book costs $3. Solve the equation $3x = 6$ to find the number of comic books, x, that Kendra can buy.

➤ **ONE WAY** to solve a multiplication equation is to use a hanger diagram.

The hanger diagram shows each side of the equation $3x = 6$ as shapes that represent weights.

The hanger is balanced, so the weight of each x balances the weight of two 1s.

The model shows that $x = 2$.

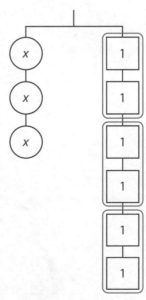

➤ **ANOTHER WAY** is to use the inverse operation, division.

$$3x = 6$$
$$\frac{3x}{3} = \frac{6}{3} \quad \text{Divide both sides by 3.}$$
$$x = 2$$

Using either method, the solution of the equation $3x = 6$ is 2. Kendra can buy 2 comic books.

 Use the next page to start a conversation about equations.

Write and Solve One-Variable Equations

Activity Thinking About Equations Around You

➤ **Do this activity together to investigate equations in the real world.**

Did you know that kids ages 6–17 should get at least 60 minutes of exercise every day? Riding a bike, jumping rope, and dancing are just a few of the ways that you can have fun while exercising!

Suppose you exercise for 15 minutes in gym class and want to ride your bike after school long enough to get a total of 60 minutes of exercise. You can use the equation $15 + x = 60$ to represent this situation, where x is the number of minutes you need to spend bike riding.

? Where else can you use equations to represent relationships in the world around you?

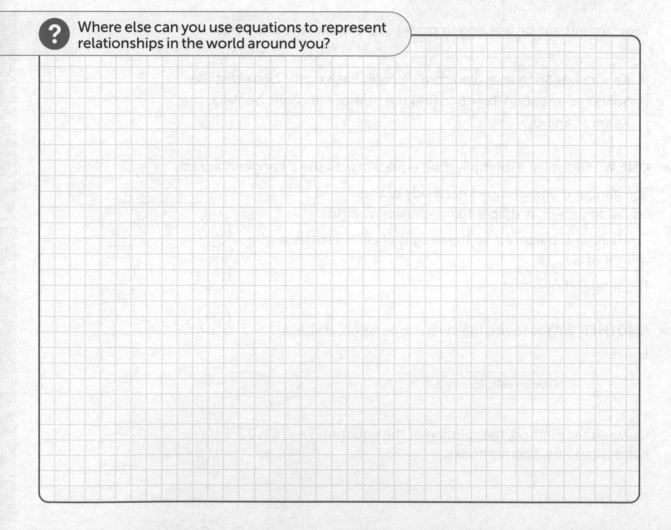

Explore One-Variable Equations

Previously, you learned about solutions of equations. In this lesson, you will learn how to solve addition and multiplication equations in one variable.

➤ **Use what you know to try to solve the problem below.**

What is the value of *x* in the hanger diagram? How do you know?

 TRY IT

✏️ **Math Toolkit** algebra tiles, counters, grid paper

🎯 **Learning Target** SMP 1, SMP 2, SMP 3, SMP 4, SMP 5, SMP 6, SMP 7
Solve real-world and mathematical problems by writing and solving equations of the form $x + p = q$ and $px = q$ for cases in which p, q and x are all nonnegative rational numbers.

CONNECT IT

1 **Look Back** What is the value of *x* in the hanger diagram? Explain how you could find the value of *x*.

2 **Look Ahead** Use the hanger diagram.

a. What expression does the left side of the hanger represent? What expression does the right side of the hanger represent?

b. The hanger is balanced. What does that tell you about the two expressions you wrote in problem 2a? What equation does the hanger diagram represent?

c. Draw two more 1s on each side of the hanger. Why is the hanger still balanced? What equation does the hanger represent now?

d. Suppose you remove three 1s from the right side of the hanger. What should you do to keep the hanger balanced?

3 **Reflect** To keep a hanger diagram balanced, what must you do when adding and removing amounts on the sides of the hanger? Why?

Prepare for Writing and Solving One-Variable Equations

1 Think about what you know about solutions of equations. Fill in each box. Use words, numbers, and pictures. Show as many ideas as you can.

What Is It?	**What I Know About It**

solution of an equation

Examples	**Non-Examples**

2 Circle the equations for which 6 is a solution of the equation.

$4 = x + 2$ $\left(y - 2 = 4\right)$ $\left(6z = 36\right)$ $\left(12 \div w = 6\right)$

$\left(x + 2 = 6\right)$ $56 = 5y$ $\left(8 + z = 14\right)$ $\left(2 = \frac{w}{12}\right)$

3 Look at the hanger diagram.

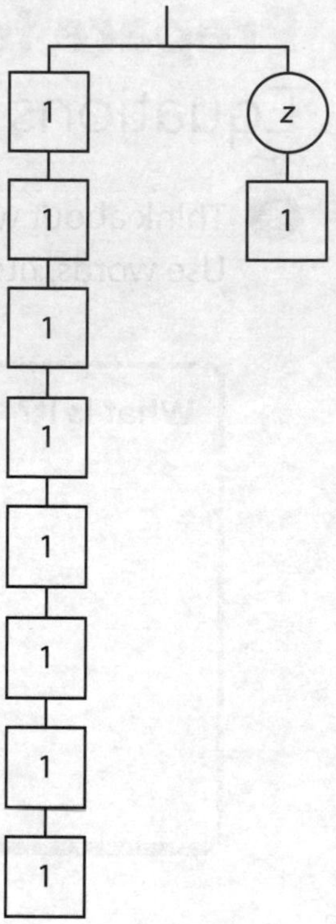

a. What is the value of z in the hanger diagram? Show your work.

7

$1 + z = 8$

SOLUTION _____

b. Check your answer to problem 3a. Show your work.

Develop Solving One-Variable Addition Equations

➤ **Read and try to solve the problem below.**

An animal rescue group in Africa is taking care of 5 injured baby pixie frogs. They plan to release them back into the wild when they are healthy. Each pixie frog needs its own terrarium. One of the rescue volunteers checks and sees that there are only 3 terrariums. Solve the equation $t + 3 = 5$ to find how many more terrariums, t, the rescue center needs.

 TRY IT

 Math Toolkit algebra tiles, counters, grid paper

DISCUSS IT

Ask: What did you do first to solve the problem?

Share: The first thing I did was . . .

➤ **Explore different ways to solve a one-variable addition equation.**

An animal rescue group in Africa is taking care of 5 injured baby pixie frogs. They plan to release them back into the wild when they are healthy. Each pixie frog needs its own terrarium. One of the rescue volunteers checks and sees that there are only 3 terrariums. Solve the equation $t + 3 = 5$ to find how many more terrariums, t, the rescue center needs.

Model It

You can use a hanger diagram to model and solve an addition equation.

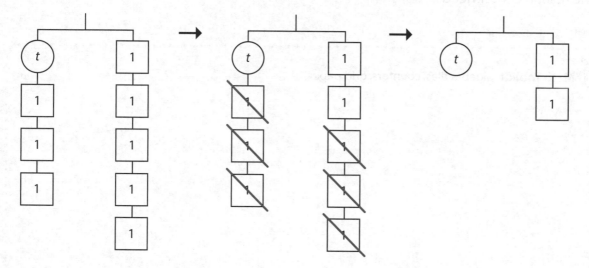

Analyze It

You can use subtraction to solve for a variable in an addition equation.

$$t + 3 = 5$$

$t + 3 - 3 = 5 - 3$ ⬅ Subtract 3 from both sides of the equation.

$$t = 2$$

CONNECT IT

➤ **Use the problem from the previous page to help you understand how to solve a one-variable addition equation.**

1 Look at **Model It**. Why are three 1s removed from each side of the hanger diagram?

2 Look at **Analyze It**. How are the steps for solving the equation similar to the steps for solving the equation with the hanger diagram?

3 How many more terrariums does the rescue center need? How can you use substitution to verify that your answer is correct?

4 How are all the equations below similar to $t + 3 = 5$? Why could you solve each equation by subtracting a number from both sides of the equation?

$$8 + y = 92 \qquad 50 = a + 17 \qquad n + 2.2 = 5 \qquad 12.5 = 7.4 + z$$

5 **Reflect** Think about all the models and strategies you have discussed today. Describe how one of them helped you better understand how to solve one-variable addition equations.

LESSON 21 Write and Solve One-Variable Equations **483**

Apply It

➤ **Use what you learned to solve these problems.**

6 Teresa has some photos on her computer on Monday. On Tuesday, she downloads 24 new photos. Then she deletes 9 photos. She ends up with 33 photos. Explain how the equation $p + 24 - 9 = 33$ represents the situation. Then solve the equation for the variable p and interpret the solution.

$$p+24-9$$
$$33+9 = 42 - 24 = 18$$
$$18 + 24$$

7 What is the solution of the equation $7 + 5 = 4 + y$?

A 6

B 8

C 12

D 16

8 At a local gardening store, a palm tree is 1.2 ft taller than a cactus. The palm tree is 4.9 ft tall. Use the equation $4.9 = c + 1.2$ to find the height in feet, c, of the cactus. Show your work.

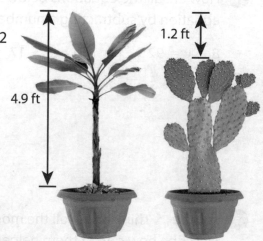

1.2 ft

4.9 ft

SOLUTION _____

Practice Solving One-Variable Addition Equations

➤ **Study the Example showing how to solve a one-variable addition equation. Then solve problems 1–5.**

Example

Cameron buys a stapler. Then he buys 5 notebooks that cost $1.50 each. He spends $13.50 in all. Use the equation $d + 5(1.50) = 13.50$ to find the number of dollars, d, that Cameron spends on the stapler.

$$d + 5(1.50) = 13.50$$

Multiply 1.50 by 5. $\qquad\qquad\qquad\qquad d + 7.50 = 13.50$

Subtract 7.50 from both sides. $\qquad\qquad d + 7.50 - 7.50 = 13.50 - 7.50$

$$d = 6$$

Cameron spends $6 on the stapler.

---

1 **a.** In the Example, why is 7.50 subtracted from both sides of the equation?

subtracting 7.50 from both sides keeps the equation balanced

b. Why can you replace the expression $d + 7.50 - 7.50$ with just the variable d in the last step of solving the equation?

7.50 - 7.50 = 0 + 0

2 Solve the equation $91 = 43 + x$. Show your work.

SOLUTION _____

3) On Monday, Jessica runs on a track at her school. Each day from Tuesday through Friday, she runs $1\frac{1}{2}$ mi in a park. The total distance she runs for the week is 8 mi. Solve the equation $m + 4\left(1\frac{1}{2}\right) = 8$ to find the number of miles, m, Jessica runs on Monday. Show your work.

$4 \cdot 1\frac{1}{2}$

$\frac{4}{1} \cdot \frac{3}{2} = \frac{12}{2} = 6$

$m = 2$

SOLUTION _____

4) What operation can you use on both sides of the equation $100 = 100 + y$ to solve the equation for y? Solve the equation for y. Then explain how to check the solution.

5) Dylan has a pitcher with 1.65 L of orange juice. He pours out 0.2 L of the juice. Then he adds some sparkling water to the pitcher to make orangeade. He ends up with 1.9 L of orangeade. Solve the equation $1.65 - 0.2 + x = 1.9$ to find the amount of sparkling water, x, Dylan adds to the pitcher. Show your work.

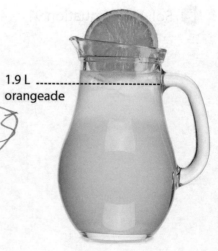
1.9 L orangeade

$1.65 - 0.2 + x = 1.9$

$1.45 + x = 1.9$

$1.45 - 1.45 + x = 1.9 - 1.45$

$x = 0.45$

SOLUTION _____

Develop Solving One-Variable Multiplication Equations

2 packages
8 erasers total

➤ **Read and try to solve the problem below.**

Tamera is buying party favors. She chooses pencil erasers that are shaped like pieces of sushi. Each package she buys contains the same number of erasers. She buys 2 packages and gets a total of 8 erasers. Solve the equation $2x = 8$ to find the number of erasers, x, in each package.

 TRY IT

 Math Toolkit algebra tiles, counters, grid paper

DISCUSS IT

Ask: How is your strategy similar to mine? How is it different?

Share: My strategy is similar because . . . It is different because . . .

LESSON 21 Write and Solve One-Variable Equations   **487**

➤ **Explore different ways to solve a one-variable multiplication equation.**

Tamera is buying party favors. She chooses pencil erasers that are shaped like pieces of sushi. Each package she buys contains the same number of erasers. She buys 2 packages and gets a total of 8 erasers. Solve the equation $2x = 8$ to find find the number of erasers, x, in each package

Model It

You can use a hanger diagram to model and solve a multiplication equation.

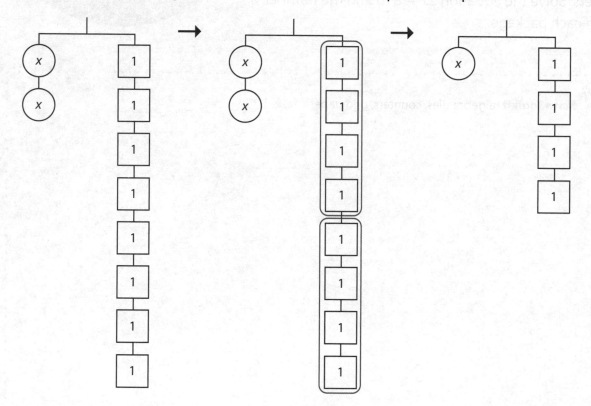

Analyze It

You can use division to solve for a variable in a multiplication equation.

$2x = 8$

$\dfrac{2x}{2} = \dfrac{8}{2}$ ← **Divide** both sides of the equation by 2.

$x = 4$

➤ **Use the problem from the previous page to help you understand how to solve a one-variable multiplication equation.**

1 Look at the second hanger diagram in **Model It**. Why are the 1s separated into two equal groups?

2 Look at **Analyze It**. Why can you use the fractions $\frac{2x}{2}$ and $\frac{8}{2}$ to show dividing both sides of the equation $2x = 8$ by 2?

3 How are the steps for solving the equation similar to the steps for solving the problem with the hanger diagram?

4 How many erasers are in each package? How you can use substitution to check your answer?

5 How is solving $2x = 8$ similar to solving $2 + x = 8$? How is it different?

6 **Reflect** Think about all the models and strategies you have discussed today. Describe how one of them helped you better understand solving one-variable multiplication equations.

Apply It

➤ **Use what you learned to solve these problems.**

7 Four friends go on a camping trip. They decide to share the cost equally. They spend $27.68 on food and $42 to reserve the campsite. You can use the equation $4c = 42 + 27.68$ to find each person's share of the cost.

Campsite $42
Food $27.68

a. What does the variable c represent? Explain how the equation $4c = 42 + 27.68$ represents the situation.

$$\$42 + 27.68 = 69.680$$
$$69.680 \div 4 = \$17.420$$

b. Solve the equation for c and interpret the solution. Show your work.

SOLUTION _____

8 What is the solution of the equation $12\left(\frac{1}{2}\right)y = 2$?

A $\frac{1}{6}$

B $\frac{1}{3}$

C 3

D 6

9 Benjamin ran a total of 21 miles last month. This is 75% of the number of miles he wants to run this month. Solve the equation $0.75m = 21$ to find out how many miles, m, Benjamin wants to run this month. Show your work.

$$.75m = \frac{21}{.75}$$
$$m = 28$$

SOLUTION _____

Practice Solving One-Variable Multiplication Equations

➤ Study the Example showing how to solve a one-variable multiplication equation. Then solve problems 1–5.

Example

Miyako is making potato pancakes. She has $4\frac{3}{4}$ lb of shredded potatoes. She uses $\frac{1}{4}$ lb to make each pancake. Solve the equation $4\frac{3}{4} = \frac{1}{4}p$ to find the number of potato pancakes, p, Miyako can make.

You can divide by the coefficient of the variable to solve the equation for p.

$$4\frac{3}{4} = \frac{1}{4}p$$

$$4\frac{3}{4} \cdot 4 = \frac{1}{4}p \cdot 4 \quad \longleftarrow \text{ To divide by } \frac{1}{4}, \text{ multiply by the reciprocal, 4.}$$

$$\frac{19}{4} \cdot \frac{4}{1} = p$$

$$19 = p$$

Miyako can make 19 potato pancakes.

1 In the Example, why can you replace the expression $\frac{1}{4}p \cdot 4$ on the right side of the equation with just the variable p?

2 Mindy has a piece of string that is $5\frac{1}{2}$ yd long. She cuts it into pieces that are each $\frac{1}{2}$ yd long. Solve the equation $5\frac{1}{2} = \frac{1}{2}x$ to find out how many pieces of string, x, she gets. Show your work.

SOLUTION _____

Hover Copter II

$112.75 + **$8.75 delivery fee**

★ ★ ★ ★

Add to Cart

③ Khalid plans to save the same amount of money each month
for 6 months to buy a remote control helicopter.
The helicopter costs $112.75 plus $8.75 for delivery. Khalid
has a coupon for $18 off the price of the helicopter.

a. Use the equation $6m = 112.75 - 18 + 8.75$ to find out
how much money, m, Khalid should save each month.
Show your work.

SOLUTION _____

b. How much money would Khalid need to save each month if he did not have
the $18 coupon? Explain your reasoning.

④ What operation would you use to solve $10 = 6y$? Explain your reasoning.

⑤ A can of tomato sauce contains 8 oz of sauce. A case contains 12 cans.
Chef Hugo orders some cases of tomato sauce and gets a total of 480 oz of
sauce. Use $12(8)x = 480$ to find out how many cases of tomato sauce Chef Hugo
orders, x. Show your work.

SOLUTION _____

Develop Writing and Solving One-Variable Equations

Hip-Hop Dance-a-thon

Short and Long Routines
combined: 16 minutes

➤ **Read and try to solve the problem below.**

A dance crew is entering a hip-hop dance contest with a short routine and a long routine. The combined length of the two routines must be 16 min. The crew's long routine is 3 times as long as the short routine. Write and solve an equation to find the lengths of the crew's two routines.

TRY IT

Math Toolkit algebra tiles, grid paper, number lines

Short routine ~ x

long routine ~ 3·x   x + 3x = 16

s.r = 4 min.

l.r = 12 min.

➤ **Explore different ways to write and solve a one-variable equation.**

A dance crew is entering a hip-hop dance contest with a short routine and a long routine. The combined length of the two routines must be 16 min. The crew's long routine is 3 times as long as the short routine. Write and solve an equation to find the lengths of the crew's two routines.

Model It

You can use a bar model to show how the quantities in the problem are related.

Let x be the length of the short routine in minutes.

Then the length of the long routine in minutes is $3x$.

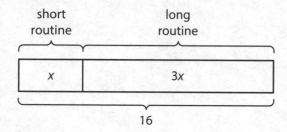

Model It

You can use words to help you write an equation with a variable.

The combined length of the two routines is 16 min.

length of short routine	+	length of long routine	=	total length of routines
↓		↓		↓
x	+	$3x$	=	16

Analyze It

You can use equivalent expressions and an inverse operation to solve an equation.

$$x + 3x = 16$$

$$4x = 16$$

$$\frac{4x}{4} = \frac{16}{4}$$

$$x = ?$$

> **Use the problem from the previous page to help you understand how to write and solve a one-variable equation.**

1 Look at the two **Model Its**. How are they similar?

2 How do the two **Model Its** help you write an equation?

3 Look at the first two equations in **Analyze It**. Why can you replace expression $x + 3x$ with the expression $4x$? Why is this step necessary?

4 What are the lengths of the crew's routines? How can you use substitution to check your answer?

5 How can writing and solving an equation help you solve a real-world problem?

6 **Reflect** Think about all the models and strategies you have discussed today. Describe how one of them helped you better understand how to solve the **Try It** problem.

Apply It

➤ **Use what you learned to solve these problems.**

7 Tyler sells popcorn at the movies. He arrives at work and sees there are some kernels in the popcorn bin. He pours in 4 more cups of kernels to fill the bin. Then he removes 1.5 cups of kernels. Now there are 6 cups of kernels in the bin. Write and solve an equation to find out how many cups of kernels were in the bin when Tyler arrived. Show your work.

$$C + 4 - 1.5 = 6 \text{ cups}$$
$$3.5 + 4 - 1.5 = 6 \text{ cups}$$

SOLUTION _____

8 Colin has 17 fewer baseball cards than Demi. Demi has 28 cards. Which equations can you use to find n, the number of baseball cards Colin has? Select all that apply.

Ⓐ $n = 28 - 17$ Ⓑ $28 = n + 17$

Ⓒ $17 = 28 - n$ ~~Ⓓ $n = 17 + 28$~~

~~Ⓔ $n - 17 = 28$~~   ~~Ⓕ $17 = n - 28$~~

9 Gabe mails two packages. One package weighs $\frac{3}{4}$ as much as the other package. The total weight of the packages is 7 lb. Write and solve an equation to find the weights of the two packages. Show your work.

SOLUTION _____

Name: _____

Practice Writing and Solving One-Variable Equations

➤ **Study the Example showing how to write and solve a one-variable equation. Then solve problems 1–5.**

Example

At the grocery store, Samuel spends $9 on fruits and vegetables. This is 80% of the money he spends in all. How much does Samuel spend?

Let m = the amount in dollars that Samuel spends.

Write an equation.

80% of the money Sam spends is $9.

$$0.8 \cdot m = 9$$

Solve the equation for m.

$$0.8m = 9$$

$$\frac{0.8m}{0.8} = \frac{9}{0.8}$$

$$m = 11.25$$

Samuel spends $11.25.

---

1 There are 12 paperback mysteries on a shelf. This is 40% of the books on the shelf. Write and solve an equation to find the number of books on the shelf. Show your work.

2 Three friends play a game. Jamila has $4\frac{1}{2}$ more points than Carter. Carter has $7\frac{1}{2}$ more points than Aisha. Jamila has 26 points. Write and solve an equation to find the number of points Aisha has. Show your work.

SOLUTION _____

SOLUTION _____

3 At a theme park, the waiting time for the roller coaster is usually 3 times as long as the waiting time for the bumper cars. The park's website says that visitors who go on both rides should expect to wait a total of 30 min. What is the usual waiting time for the bumper cars? Show your work.

Bumper Cars   Roller Coaster

TOTAL ESTIMATED WAIT TIME
30 minutes

SOLUTION _____

4 The length of a rectangle is twice its width. The perimeter of the rectangle is 36 ft. What are the length and width of the rectangle? Show your work.

SOLUTION _____

5 Neva is training for a race. This week, she bikes 5.5 times as far as she runs. Her total distance running and biking this week is 26 mi. How far does Neva run this week? Show your work.

SOLUTION _____

Refine Writing and Solving One-Variable Equations

➤ **Complete the Example below. Then solve problems 1–9.**

Example

At Valley Middle School, $\frac{3}{5}$ of the students study Spanish. There are 96 students who study Spanish. Solve the equation $\frac{3}{5}n = 96$ to find the number of students, n, at the school.

Look at how you could multiply by the reciprocal to solve a multiplication equation.

$$\frac{3}{5}n = 96$$

$$\frac{5}{3} \cdot \frac{3}{5}n = \frac{5}{3} \cdot 96$$

$$1 \cdot n = \frac{5 \cdot 96}{3}$$

$$n = 5 \cdot 32$$

SOLUTION _____

CONSIDER THIS . . .
The product of a number and its reciprocal is 1.

PAIR/SHARE
Why is $\frac{5 \cdot 96}{3}$ equivalent to $5 \cdot 32$?

Apply It

1 The volume of the right rectangular prism is $\frac{1}{2}$ yd³.

What is the height of the prism? Show your work.

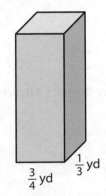

$\frac{3}{4}$ yd $\frac{1}{3}$ yd

CONSIDER THIS . . .
The formulas for the volume of a right rectangular prism are $V = \ell wh$ and $V = Bh$.

PAIR/SHARE
How can you verify that your answer is correct?

SOLUTION _____

2 Yukio has a checking account. On Monday, he writes 3 checks for $65 each. His balance at the end of the day is $330.25. Use an equation with a variable to find Yukio's balance at the start of the day. Show your work.

CONSIDER THIS . . .
When writing checks, your account balance decreases.

SOLUTION _____

3 Carmen and Erin collect cans of food for a food drive. Carmen collects 5 times as many cans of food as Erin. Together, they collect 60 cans of food. Which equation can you solve to find the number of cans of food Erin collects?

A $5x = 60$

B $6x = 60$

C $\frac{1}{5}x = 60$

D $x = 60 \cdot 5$

Jelani chose B as the correct answer. How might he have gotten that answer?

CONSIDER THIS . . .
You can write an equation where one side is an algebraic expression for the total number of cans of food Carmen and Erin collect.

PAIR/SHARE
How can you use estimation to make sure your answer is reasonable?

PAIR/SHARE
How can you find the number of cans of food Carmen collects?

4 Ju-long has 6 guppies in his aquarium. This is 24% of the fish in the aquarium. How many fish are in Ju-long's aquarium? Use an equation with a variable. Show your work.

SOLUTION _____

5 What is the solution of the equation $9\frac{1}{3} = x + 9\frac{1}{3}$?

6 Consider the equation $\frac{2}{5}y = 20$. Tell whether each statement is *True* or *False*.

	True	False
a. You can solve the equation by multiplying both sides by $\frac{5}{2}$.	○	○
b. You can solve the equation by dividing both sides by $\frac{2}{5}$.	○	○
c. The equation has the same solution as $\frac{5}{2}y = 20$.	○	○
d. The equation has the same solution as $\frac{4}{5}y = 40$.	○	○

7 Each day from Monday to Friday, Enrico uses a rideshare scooter to take the same route to and from work. According to the rideshare app, the total distance he rides each week is 13 mi. Explain how to write an equation that Enrico can use to find the distance of one trip to or from work. Show how to solve the equation.

Weekly Total Distance
13 miles

8 Is the value of w the same in both equations shown below? Explain how you can decide without solving the equations.

$$w + 16 = 43 \qquad w + 16 - 7 = 43 - 7$$

9 **Math Journal** Write an equation that you can solve by subtracting 3.2 from both sides of the equation. Then show how to solve the equation and check your solution.

✓ **End of Lesson Checklist**

☐ **INTERACTIVE GLOSSARY** Find the entry for *equation*. Add two important things you learned about equations in this lesson.

☐ **SELF CHECK** Go back to the Unit 5 Opener and see what you can check off.

Analyze Two-Variable Relationships

Dear Family,

This week your student is learning how to analyze the relationship between two quantities that change. The value of one quantity, called the **dependent variable**, depends upon the value of the other quantity, called the **independent variable**.

For example, the equation $d = 1.25t$ represents the distance, d, in miles traveled by a train in t minutes. The **distance** traveled depends on how much **time** has passed.

$$d = 1.25t$$

dependent variable

independent variable

Your student will be learning to solve problems like the one below.

The equation $y = 5x$ represents the total cost, y, in dollars to rent a bicycle for x hours. How much does the total cost increase for each additional hour a person rides the bicycle?

➤ **ONE WAY** to analyze the relationship between two variables is to use a table.

Time (hours), x	Total Cost ($), y
0	0
1	5
2	10
3	15
4	20

Each time the number of hours increases by 1, the total cost increases by $5.

➤ **ANOTHER WAY** is to graph the ordered pairs (x, y).

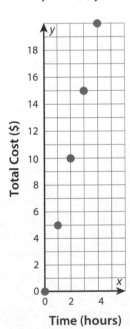

Total Cost ($)

Time (hours)

Using either method, the total cost increases by $5 for each additional hour.

 Use the next page to start a conversation about two-variable relationships.

Activity Thinking About Two-Variable Relationships Around You

➤ **Do this activity together to investigate two-variable relationships in the real world.**

Did you know that the amount of time you spend sleeping can depend on how long it takes you to get to school?

For each minute you spend commuting to school, you can expect to lose an average of 1.3 minutes of sleep. This relationship can be represented with the equation $y = 1.3x$, where x represents commuting time in minutes and y represents minutes of lost sleep.

1 minute of commuting results in 1.3 minutes of lost sleep

? Where else do you see two-variable relationships in the world around you?

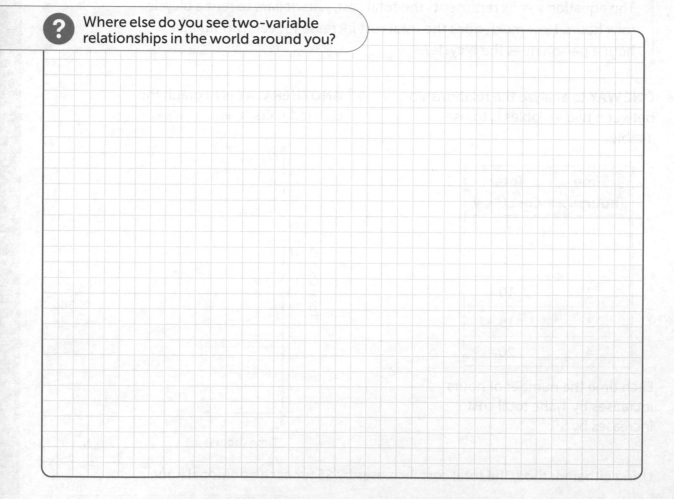

Explore Two-Variable Relationships

Previously, you learned about equations with one variable. In this lesson, you will learn about equations with two variables.

➤ **Use what you know to try to solve the problem below.**

Hiroko makes amigurumi animals for her cousins. The instructions for making an amigurumi fox say to crochet the stitches in a row and then join the ends to make a "round." How can Hiroko use the round number to determine the number of stitches in that round?

Round 1: 6 stitches

Rounds 2 to 7: Increase the number of stitches in the previous round by 6.

 TRY IT

 Math Toolkit connecting cubes, counters, grid paper

 Learning Target   SMP 1, SMP 2, SMP 3, SMP 4, SMP 5, SMP 6, SMP 7
Use variables to represent two quantities in a real-world problem that change in relationship to one another; write an equation to express one quantity, thought of as the dependent variable, in terms of the other quantity, thought of as the independent variable. Analyze the relationship between the dependent and independent variables using graphs and tables, and relate these to the equation.

CONNECT IT

1 **Look Back** How can Hiroko use the number of the round to determine the number of stitches in a round of her fox pattern? Explain how you know.

2 **Look Ahead** In Hiroko's pattern, the number of stitches in a round depends on the round number. An equation in two variables is one way to represent the relationship between two quantities. The value of the **dependent variable** depends on the value of the **independent variable**.

a. A store sells kits for making amigurumi animals. Each kit costs $15. The equation $c = 15k$ can be used to determine the total cost, c, of k kits. In this situation, is c or k the dependent variable? Explain.

b. The equation $k = \frac{c}{15}$ can be used to find the number of kits, k, you can buy with c dollars. In this situation, is c or k the dependent variable? Explain.

c. How are the equations in problems 2a and 2b alike? How are they different?

3 **Reflect** Hiroko and her cousins have $45 to spend on kits. Which equation do you think they would use to find the number of kits they can buy? Why?

Prepare for Analyzing Two-Variable Relationships

1 Think about what you know about variables, expressions, and equations. Fill in each box. Use words, numbers, and pictures. Show as many ideas as you can.

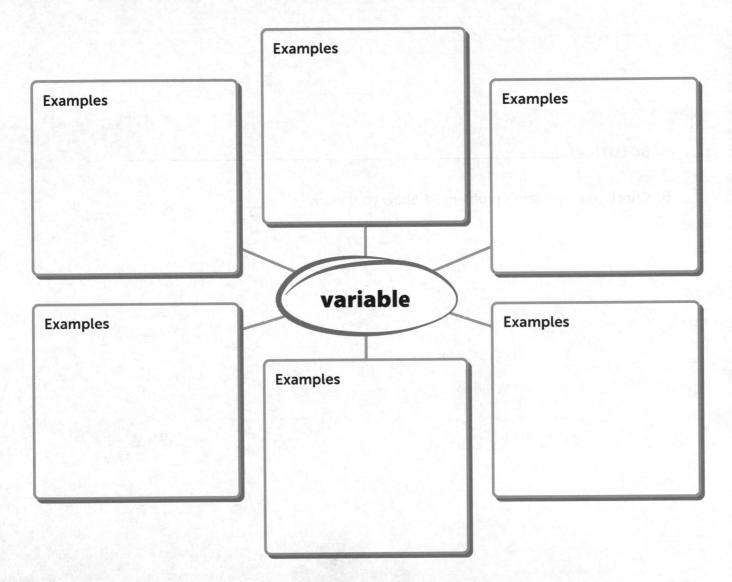

Examples

Examples

Examples

variable

Examples

Examples

Examples

2 Why can the value of the variable *a* in the expression *a* + 2 be any number? Why does the variable *b* in the equation *b* + 2 = 5 have only one value?

3 There are 5 hidden treasures in Level 1 of a smartphone game. Each of the other levels has 1 more hidden treasure than the previous level.

a. How can you use the level number in the game to determine the number of hidden treasures in that level? Show your work.

SOLUTION _____

b. Check your answer to problem 3a. Show your work.

Develop Writing an Equation in Two Variables to Represent a Relationship

MEERKAT HABITAT

Population
8 meerkats

Cost per meerkat
$1.50 per day

➤ **Read and try to solve the problem below.**

An animal reserve is home to 8 meerkats. It costs the reserve $1.50 per day to feed each meerkat. Write an equation with two variables that can be used to determine the total cost of feeding the reserve's meerkats for any number of days.

TRY IT

Math Toolkit counters, grid paper, sticky notes

LESSON 22 Analyze Two-Variable Relationships   **509**

➤ **Explore different ways to write an equation in two variables to represent a relationship.**

An animal reserve is home to 8 meerkats. It costs the reserve $1.50 per day to feed each meerkat. Write an equation with two variables that can be used to determine the total cost of feeding the reserve's meerkats for any number of days.

Model It

You can make a table to look for a relationship between two quantities that vary.

The two quantities are the **number of days** and the
total cost to feed 8 meerkats.

d = number of days

t = total cost ($) to feed 8 meerkats

In each row, the total cost is **12** times the number of days.

Number of Days, d	$(d \times 1.5) \times 8$	Total Cost ($), t
1	$(1 \times 1.5) \times 8$	12
2	$(2 \times 1.5) \times 8$	24
3	$(3 \times 1.5) \times 8$	36
4	$(4 \times 1.5) \times 8$	48

$\times 12$

Model It

You can use words to help you write an equation in two variables.

It costs $1.50 per day to feed 1 meerkat.

$8 \times 1.50 = 12$

So, it costs **$12 per day** to feed 8 meerkats.

Describe how to use the number of days, d, to find the total cost, t.

The **total cost** equals the **cost per day** times the **number of days**.

➤ **Use the problem from the previous page to help you understand how to write an equation in two variables to represent a relationship.**

1 Look at the variables d and t in the first **Model It**. Which variable is the independent variable, and which is the dependent variable? How do you know?

2 The table shows the expression $(d \times 1.50) \times 8$. How does this expression represent finding the total cost to feed 8 meerkats?

3 How is the factor 12 shown below the table related to $(d \times 1.5) \times 8$? What does 12 represent in this situation?

4 Look at the second **Model It**. What equation can you use to find the total cost of feeding the meerkats for any number of days? Use your equation to find the total cost of feeding the meerkats for 1 year, or 365 days.

5 Why is an equation a good model for representing the relationship between an independent variable and a dependent variable?

6 **Reflect** Think about all the models and strategies you have discussed today. Describe how one of them helped you better understand how to write an equation in two variables to represent a relationship.

LESSON 22 Analyze Two-Variable Relationships **511**

Apply It

➤ **Use what you learned to solve these problems.**

7 A company makes frames for photographs. The height of each frame is 2 inches greater than the height of the photo it is designed to hold.

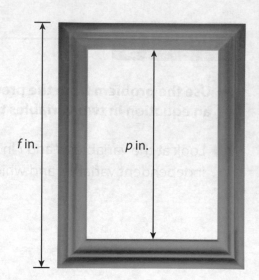

f in.   p in.

a. Write an equation that shows how to find the height, *f*, in inches of a frame designed to hold a photo with a height of *p* inches. Show your work.

SOLUTION _____

b. Which variable is the dependent variable in your equation? How do you know?

8 Snow is falling at a constant rate. The table shows how much snow has fallen since the snow began. Alexis writes the equation $y = x + \frac{1}{4}$ to represent the relationship between the time in hours and the inches of snow. Does her equation correctly model the relationship? Explain.

Time (h), x	Snow (in.), y
1	$1\frac{1}{4}$
2	$2\frac{1}{2}$
3	$3\frac{3}{4}$
4	5

9 A company makes several sizes of phones. For each size, the ratio of the height of the screen to its width is 18 : 9. Write an equation that shows how to find the height in inches of any of the company's phone screens based on the screen's width in inches. Show your work.

SOLUTION _____

Practice Writing an Equation in Two Variables to Represent a Relationship

➤ **Study the Example showing how to write an equation in two variables to represent a relationship. Then solve problems 1–5.**

Example

The total cost of renting a tent is equal to a rental fee plus a cleaning fee of $10. Write an equation with two variables that shows how to find the total cost of renting a tent based on the rental fee.

You can define variables and use them to write an equation that represents the relationship between the rental fee and the total cost.

r = rental fee in dollars

t = total cost in dollars

The **total cost** is equal to the **rental fee** plus $10.

$$t \qquad = \qquad r \qquad + \quad 10$$

The equation $t = r + 10$ can be used to find the total cost of renting a tent.

---

1 Which variable is the independent variable in the Example? Which is the dependent variable? Explain how you know.

2 The total weight of a delivery truck is equal to the weight of the empty truck plus the weight of the packages. The truck weighs 8,200 lb when empty. Write an equation that shows how to use the total weight of the truck to find the weight of the packages. Show your work.

Vocabulary

dependent variable
a variable whose value depends on the value of a related independent variable.

....

independent variable
a variable whose value is used to find the value of another variable.

SOLUTION _____

3   A scientist is studying the digging behavior of black-footed ferrets.

   a. One ferret digs 465 cubic centimeters of soil from a burrow
      in 5 minutes. Based on this digging rate, write an equation
      that can be used to predict the amount of soil, s, in cubic
      centimeters the ferret can dig from a burrow in m minutes.
      Show your work.

   SOLUTION _____

   b. Which variable is the dependent variable in your equation? Explain.

4   There are 80 Calories in every 4-ounce serving of grapes. Which equation can be
   used to determine the number of Calories, y, in x ounces of grapes?

   A $y = 20x$ B $y = x + 20$

   C $y = 0.05x$ D $y = 84 - x$

5   A family's dishwasher uses the same number gallons of water for each
   load. The table shows how many gallons of water, g, the dishwasher
   uses for n loads of dishes. What equation can you use to represent the
   relationship shown in the table? Show your work.

Dishwasher Water Use	
Number of Loads, n	Gallons Used, g
4	18.0
5	22.5
6	27.0
7	31.5

   SOLUTION _____

Develop Analyzing the Relationship Between Two Variables

➤ **Read and try to solve the problem below.**

A restaurant sells party packs with a combination of samosas and pakoras. Customers ordering online enter the number of samosas they want. The ordering system uses the equation $p = 10 - s$ to determine the number of pakoras, p, for a party pack with s samosas. How does the number of pakoras in a party pack change when the number of samosas in the pack increases by 1?

TRY IT

Math Toolkit grid paper, two-color counters

➤ **Explore different ways to analyze the relationship between two variables.**

A restaurant sells party packs with a combination of samosas and pakoras. Customers ordering online enter the number of samosas they want. The ordering system uses the equation $p = 10 - s$ to determine the number of pakoras, p, for a party pack with s samosas. How does the number of pakoras in a party pack change when the number of samosas in the pack increases by 1?

Model It

You can make a table to analyze the relationship between two variables.

Number of Samosas, s	$10 - s$	Number of Pakoras, p
0	$10 - 0$	10
1	$10 - 1$	9
2	$10 - 2$	8
3	$10 - 3$	7

Model It

You can make a graph to analyze the relationship between two variables.

Graph values from the table to show ordered pairs of the form (s, p).

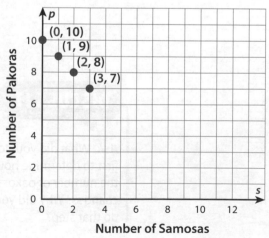

Party Pack Combinations

➤ **Use the problem from the previous page to help you understand how to analyze the relationship between two variables.**

1 Look at the first **Model It**. Explain why *s* is the independent variable and *p* is the dependent variable in this situation.

2 Compare each row of the table to the row below it. How does the number of pakoras change when the number of samosas in a party pack increases by 1?

3 Look at the second **Model It**. How does the graph show the same pattern as the table? Continue this pattern by plotting additional ordered pairs on the graph.

4 Why can the number of samosas never be greater than 10?

5 How can a table and a graph help you analyze the relationship between the independent and dependent variables in an equation?

6 **Reflect** Think about all the models and strategies you have discussed today. Describe how one of them helped you better understand how to analyze the relationship between two variables.

Apply It

➤ **Use what you learned to solve these problems.**

7 A filter cleans the water in Santo's turtle tank. The equation $y = 2.5x$ models the relationship between the amount of water, y, in gallons that passes through the filter in x minutes.

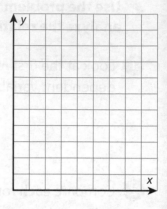

a. Graph the relationship. Include a title on each axis.

b. How does the graph show the rate at which water passes through the filter? How is this rate related to the equation?

8 Muna and her father share the same birthday. The equation $m = f - 32$ relates Muna's age, m, to her father's age, f, in years.

a. Use the equation to complete the table.

b. How much older is Muna's father than she is? How do the table and the equation each show this information?

Father's Age (yr), f	Muna's Age (yr), m
35	
	5
	9
44	

9 The equation $c = 8t$ can be used to determine the total cost, c, in dollars for t tickets to the school musical.

a. Identify the independent variable and the dependent variable.

b. How does the total cost change when the number of tickets increases by 5? Show your work.

SOLUTION _____

Practice Analyzing the Relationship Between Two Variables

➤ **Study the Example showing how to analyze relationships between two variables. Then solve problems 1–4.**

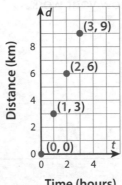

Example

The equation $d = 3t$ represents the distance, d, in kilometers that lava travels in t hours after a volcano erupts. How does the distance the lava travels change for each additional hour that passes?

You can use a table and a graph to analyze the relationship.

The distance the lava travels depends on how much time has passed. So, t is the independent variable, and d is the dependent variable.

Time (h), t	$3t$	Distance (km), d
0	3 • 0	0
1	3 • 1	3
2	3 • 2	6
3	3 • 3	9

Each time the value of t increases by 1, the value of d increases by 3.

With each additional hour, the distance the lava travels increases by 3 km.

1 Choose one point on the graph in the Example and explain what the point represents in the context of the situation.

2 The equation $y = x + 8$ represents the length, y, in inches of a sleeping bag for a person who is x inches tall. Which ordered pair does not belong on the graph?

A (64, 72)   **B** (70, 78)

C (72, 80)   **D** (74, 66)

3 The equation $w = 20n$ models the total weight of honey, w, in pounds that a beekeeper expects to collect from n hives.

a. Graph the relationship modeled by the equation. Include a title on each axis.

b. How does the graph show the expected rate of pounds of honey per hive? How is this rate related to the equation?

c. How many pounds of honey can the beekeeper expect to collect from 6 hives? Show your work.

SOLUTION _____

4 An online company sells watches with different prices. The ordering system uses the equation $c = p + 7.50$ to determine the total cost, c, including shipping for a watch with a price of p dollars.

a. Identify the independent variable and the dependent variable.

b. Use the equation to complete the table.

c. How does the total cost change when the price of a watch decreases by \$1? Show your work.

Price of Watch (\$), p	Total Cost (\$), c
14.00	
	26.50
21.00	
	35.50

SOLUTION _____

Refine Analyzing Two-Variable Relationships

➤ **Complete the Example below. Then solve problems 1–8.**

Example

The equation $c = 6 + 2.5t$ represents the total cost, c, to rent skates and skate at a skating rink for t hours. How much does the total cost increase for each hour a person skates?

Look at how you could use a table to analyze the relationship.

Time (h), t	$6 + 2.5t$	Total Cost ($), c
1	$6 + 2.5(1)$	8.5
2	$6 + 2.5(2)$	11
3	$6 + 2.5(3)$	13.5
4	$6 + 2.5(4)$	16

+1 ⤵ ... +2.5

SOLUTION _____

Apply It

1 One trading game card has a mass of 1.71 g. Each pack of trading game cards contains 16 cards. Write an equation with two variables that shows how to find the total mass in grams of the cards in any number of packs of trading game cards. Show your work.

SOLUTION _____

2 The equation $d = 6.5t$ represents the distance, d, in meters Conan runs in t seconds. By how much does Conan's distance increase for each additional 30 seconds that he runs? Show your work.

SOLUTION _____

3 An electronics store offers an accidental damage plan for all laptops. The table shows how the cost of several laptops changes if the damage plan is included. Based on the table, which equation can be used to determine the total cost of a laptop and damage plan based on the laptop's cost without the plan?

Laptop Cost without Plan ($), x	Laptop Cost with Plan ($), y
296	370
456	530
619	693
779	853

A $y = 0.80x$

B $y = 1.25x$

C $y = x + 74$

D $y = x + 160$

Jaime chose B as the correct answer. How might he have gotten that answer?

4 The graph shows how the amount of wheat seeds a farmer needs depends on the number of acres the farmer is going to plant.

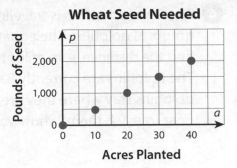

Wheat Seed Needed

a. Write an equation that shows how to find p, the number of pounds of wheat seeds needed to plant a acres. Show your work.

SOLUTION _____

b. Write an equation that shows the number of acres, a, the farmer can plant with p pounds of wheat seeds. Explain how you determined your equation.

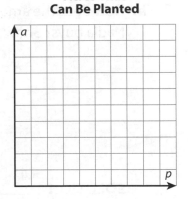

Acres That Can Be Planted

c. Graph your equation from problem 4b. How are the two graphs that relate a and p similar? How are they different?

5 Workers are preparing an athletic field by mixing soil and sand in the correct ratio. The table shows the volume of sand to mix with different volumes of soil. Which statement is correct?

A   For 1,425 m³ of soil, the workers should use 375 m³ of sand.

B   The ratio of the volume of soil to the volume of sand is 1 : 4.

C   A graph of the relationship includes the point (900, 225).

D   The equation $y = 4x$ models the relationship.

Volume of Soil x, (m³)	Volume of Sand y, (m³)
1,100	275
1,200	300
1,300	325
1,400	350

6 A team of scientists is traveling by boat to study a pod, or group, of dolphins. The equation $y = 0.2x$ can be used to find the distance, y, in miles the boat travels in x minutes. The dolphins are currently 8.4 mi from the boat. If the dolphins stay where they are, how long will it take the boat to reach them? Show your work.

SOLUTION _____

7 Nadia has a $15 gift card to an online music store. Each song at the store costs $0.99. The equation $m = 15 - 0.99s$ represents the amount of money, m, Nadia has left on the gift card after buying s songs.

a. The independent variable is _____ and the dependent variable is _____ .

b. How does the amount of money left on the card change for each extra song Nadia buys? Show your work.

SOLUTION _____

8 **Math Journal** Write a word problem that can be solved using an equation in two variables. Explain how to solve your problem.

✓ **End of Lesson Checklist**

☐ **INTERACTIVE GLOSSARY** Find the entry for *dependent variable*. Tell how dependent variables and independent variables are different.

☐ **SELF CHECK** Go back to the Unit 5 Opener and see what you can check off.

Math IN Action

SMP 1 Make sense of problems and persevere in solving them.

Study an Example Problem and Solution

➤ **Read this problem involving writing and solving an equation. Then look at one student's solution to this problem on the following pages.**

New Uniforms

The cheerleaders, marching band, football team, and school mascot purchase new uniforms. The packing slip shows the total amount each team pays and provides information about tax and shipping charges.

Choose one type of uniform. Write and solve an equation to find the price of one uniform before shipping and tax.

Some marching bands have fewer than 20 members, and some have more than 500!

Packing Slip

A★Team UNIFORM COMPANY

	Quantity	Total Paid (includes shipping and tax)	Shipping Method*	Sales Tax
Football Uniforms	60	$9,420.84	Overnight	7% of cost of items
Band Uniforms	75	$14,131.26	Ground	7% of cost of items
Cheerleading Uniforms	25	$2,355.21	2-Day	7% of cost of items
Mascot Uniform	1	$1,273.97	Flat Rate	7% of cost of items

*The shipping charges for band, cheerleading, and football uniforms is a fraction of the cost of the items:

Ground Shipping: $\frac{1}{10}$ of the cost of the items

2-Day Shipping: $\frac{3}{20}$ of the cost of the items

Overnight Shipping: $\frac{1}{4}$ of the cost of the items

The **flat-rate** shipping charge for the mascot uniform is $34.49.

One Student's Solution

First, I need to choose a type of uniform. I can also make an estimate.

The total amount spent on cheerleading uniforms is $2,355.21, which is about $2,500. Since 2,500 ÷ 25 = 100, each uniform costs about $100, including tax and shipping. Tax and shipping increase the price, so each uniform must cost less than $100.

Now, I will draw a diagram to show how quantities in the problem are related.

First, I can show the cost to buy one cheerleading uniform with 2-day shipping. I will use the variable c to represent the price of one cheerleading uniform.

> **NOTICE THAT...**
> It can be helpful to write 7% as a fraction or decimal before multiplying by c.
> $7\% = \dfrac{7}{100} = 0.07$

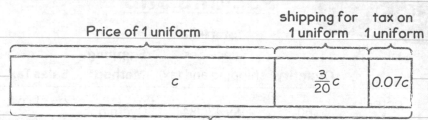

| | shipping for 1 uniform | tax on 1 uniform |
| Price of 1 uniform | | |

total cost for 1 uniform

I know the total cost for one uniform is $c + \dfrac{3}{20}c + 0.07c$.

Next, I need to multiply that expression by 25 since 25 cheerleading uniforms are purchased.

I can use words to help write my equation.

> **NOTICE THAT...**
> You would need to make 25 copies of the diagram to model the equation.

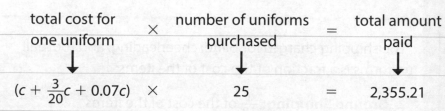

total cost for one uniform	×	number of uniforms purchased	=	total amount paid
↓		↓		↓
$(c + \dfrac{3}{20}c + 0.07c)$	×	25	=	2,355.21

Then, I can use equivalent expressions and inverse operations to solve the equation.

$$(c + \frac{3}{20}c + 0.07c) \times 25 = 2{,}355.21$$

$$(c + 0.15c + 0.07c) \times 25 = 2{,}355.21$$

$$(1.22c) \times 25 = 2{,}355.21$$

$$30.5c = 2{,}355.21$$

$$\frac{30.5c}{30.5} = \frac{2{,}355.21}{30.5}$$

$$c = 77.22$$

NOTICE THAT . . .
It makes sense to use decimals in this problem because the variable c represents an amount of money.

So, the price of one cheerleading uniform is $77.22 before taxes and 2-day shipping charges are added.

I can compare this to my estimate to check if it is reasonable. Because $77.22 is less than $100, my answer makes sense.

Finally, I can check my answer by substituting it into my original equation.

$$(c \quad + \quad \frac{3}{20}c \quad + \quad 0.07c) \quad \times 25 = 2{,}355.21$$

$$(77.22 + \frac{3}{20} \cdot 77.22 + 0.07 \cdot 77.22) \times 25 = 2{,}355.21$$

$$(77.22 + \quad 11.583 \quad + \quad 5.4054) \quad \times 25 = 2{,}355.21$$

$$94.2084 \qquad\qquad \times 25 = 2{,}355.21$$

$$2{,}355.21 = 2{,}355.21 \longleftarrow \text{true}$$

NOTICE THAT . . .
If 77.22 is a solution of the equation, the equation should be true when 77.22 is substituted for c.

Try Another Approach

➤ **There are many ways to solve problems. Think about how you might solve the New Uniforms problem in a different way.**

New Uniforms

The cheerleaders, marching band, football team, and school mascot purchase new uniforms. The packing slip shows the total amount each team pays and provides information about tax and shipping charges.

Choose one type of uniform. Write and solve an equation to find the price of one uniform before shipping and tax.

<table>
<tr><td colspan="6">**Problem-Solving Checklist** ✓</td></tr>
<tr><td>☐ Tell what is known.</td></tr>
<tr><td>☐ Tell what the problem is asking.</td></tr>
<tr><td>☐ Show all your work.</td></tr>
<tr><td>☐ Show that the solution works.</td></tr>
</table>

Packing Slip

A★Team UNIFORM COMPANY

	Quantity	Total Paid (includes shipping and tax)	Shipping Method*	Sales Tax
Football Uniforms	60	$9,420.84	Overnight	7% of cost of items
Band Uniforms	75	$14,131.26	Ground	7% of cost of items
Cheerleading Uniforms	25	$2,355.21	2-Day	7% of cost of items
Mascot Uniform	1	$1,273.97	Flat Rate	7% of cost of items

*The shipping charges for band, cheerleading, and football uniforms is a fraction of the cost of the items:

Ground Shipping: $\frac{1}{10}$ of the cost of the items

2-Day Shipping: $\frac{3}{20}$ of the cost of the items

Overnight Shipping: $\frac{1}{4}$ of the cost of the items

The **flat-rate** shipping charge for the mascot uniform is $34.49.

Plan It

➤ **Answer these questions to help you start thinking about a plan.**

   a. How can you use properties of operations to rewrite your equation in a simpler way?

   b. What operations will you need to perform in order to solve your equation? How do you know?

Solve It

➤ **Find a different solution for the New Uniforms problem. Show all your work on a separate sheet of paper. You may want to use the Problem-Solving Tips to get started.**

PROBLEM-SOLVING TIPS

 Math Toolkit algebra tiles, counters, grid paper, sticky notes

Key Terms

like terms	coefficient	commutative property
variable	distributive property	associative property
expression	solution of an equation	inverse operations

Models You may want to use . . .

- properties of operations to find an equivalent expression.

- a bar model, hanger diagram, or algebra tiles to help you write and solve the equation.

- inverse operations to solve the equation.

- substitution to check that your answer is a solution to the equation.

Reflect

Use Mathematical Practices As you work through the problem, discuss these questions with a partner.

- **Use Structure** What does each term in your equation represent?

- **Reason Mathematically** Could the equation you wrote have the same solution as your partner's? How do you know?

Discuss Models and Strategies

➤ **Read the problem. Write a solution on a separate sheet of paper. Remember, there can be lots of ways to solve a problem.**

Track and Field Training

A coach plans workouts for several groups of athletes on the track and field team. Read the coach's plans for how each group should complete a 400-meter lap around the track.

Choose one group and make a table and a graph to analyze the relationship between distance, *d*, and time, *t*, for that group. Then write an equation that models the relationship.

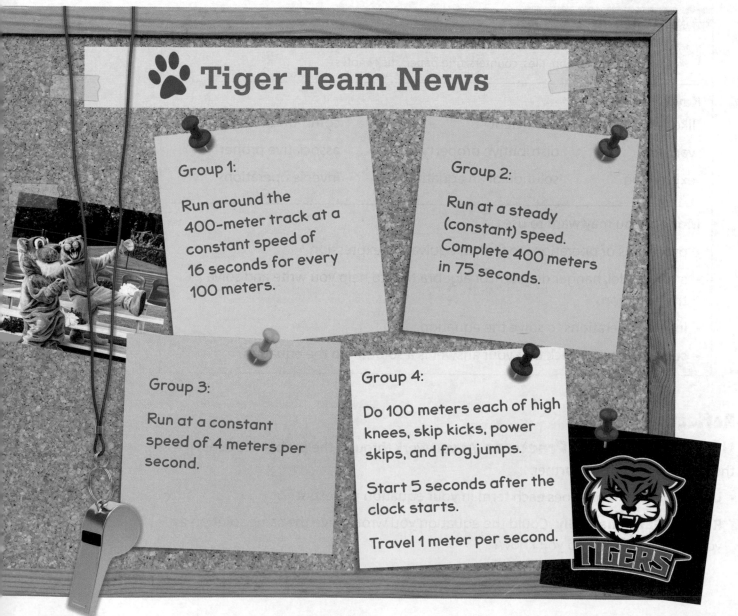

Tiger Team News

Group 1:

Run around the 400-meter track at a constant speed of 16 seconds for every 100 meters.

Group 2:

Run at a steady (constant) speed. Complete 400 meters in 75 seconds.

Group 3:

Run at a constant speed of 4 meters per second.

Group 4:

Do 100 meters each of high knees, skip kicks, power skips, and frog jumps.

Start 5 seconds after the clock starts.

Travel 1 meter per second.

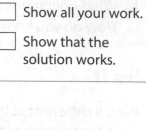

Plan It and Solve It

➤ **Find a solution to the Track and Field Training problem.**

Write a detailed plan and support your answer. Be sure to include:

- a table and a graph that show the relationship between d and t.

- an equation that models the relationship.

PROBLEM-SOLVING TIPS

 Math Toolkit algebra tiles, counters, grid paper, sticky notes

Key Terms

dependent variable	equation	unit rate
independent variable	rate	ratio
term	coefficient	ordered pair

Models You may want to use . . .

- your table or graph to analyze the relationship between d and t.

- words to help you write an equation in two variables.

- a bar model or hanger diagram to help you write an equation in two variables.

Reflect

Use Mathematical Practices As you work through the problem, discuss these questions with a partner.

- **Make Sense of Problems** Which variable is the dependent variable and which is the independent variable? Explain.

- **Be Precise** How will you scale the axes on your graph? Why?

The word *mascot* originates from the French term *mascotte,* which means lucky charm.

Persevere On Your Own

➤ **Read the problem. Write a solution on a separate sheet of paper.**

Practice Schedules

Teams can practice before school, after school, and on Saturday. Read the schedule of practice times below.

Choose two teams. Write an expression to represent the amount of time, in minutes, each team practices in a week. Then determine if the two teams practice the same amount each week.

Sports Practice Schedule 🐾 Go Tigers!

Monday	Tuesday	Wednesday	Thursday	Friday	Saturday**
Before School					
Soccer ⚽	Soccer ⚽	Soccer ⚽		Soccer ⚽	Soccer ⚽
	Swim 🏊	Swim 🏊	Swim 🏊		
					Field Hockey 🏑
	Basketball 🏀	Field Hockey 🏑	Basketball 🏀	Field Hockey 🏑	
					Volleyball 🏐
After School*					
Basketball 🏀	Volleyball 🏐	Basketball 🏀	Volleyball 🏐	Basketball 🏀	
Baseball ⚾	Baseball ⚾	Baseball ⚾	Baseball ⚾	Swim 🏊	
Field Hockey 🏑			Swim 🏊		

* After-school practices are $\frac{1}{2}$ hour longer than before-school practices.

** Saturday practices are twice as long as after-school practices.

Solve It

➤ **Find a solution to the Practice Schedules problem.**

- Choose two teams.
- Choose and define a variable for the unknown value.
- Write an expression to represent the total amount of time, in minutes, each team practices per week.
- Determine whether the expressions are equivalent.

Reflect

Use Mathematical Practices After you complete the problem, choose one of these questions to discuss with a partner.

- **Persevere** What strategies did you use to compare the two expressions you wrote?
- **Critique Reasoning** Do you agree with your partner's answer? Why or why not?

A common soccer ball design is made up of 12 faces that are pentagons, 20 faces that are hexagons, 60 vertices, and 90 edges.

Self Reflection

In this unit you learned to . . .

Skill	Lesson
Identify when two expressions are equivalent.	**19**
Write equivalent expressions.	**19**
Determine whether a number is a solution of an equation and write equations with variables to represent real-world problems.	**20, 21**
Solve equations that represent real-world problems.	**21**
Identify the independent variable and dependent variable in a relationship between two quantities.	**22**
Write an equation to represent the relationship between an independent variable and a dependent variable.	**22**
Analyze the relationship between independent and dependent variables.	**22**
Use math vocabulary and precise language to describe writing equivalent expressions and solving equations.	**19–21**

Think about what you have learned.

➤ **Use words, numbers, and drawings.**

1 Two things I learned in math are . . .

2 I am proud that I can . . .

3 I would like to learn more about how to . . .

Vocabulary Review

➤ Review the unit vocabulary. Put a check mark by items you can use in speaking and writing. Look up the meaning of any terms you do not know.

Math Vocabulary		Academic Vocabulary
☐ dependent variable	☐ like terms	☐ algebraic
☐ equivalent expressions	☐ solution of an equation	☐ depend on
☐ independent variable	☐ variable	☐ substitute
☐ inverse operation		☐ verify

➤ Use the unit vocabulary to complete the problems.

1 A student is buying thank you cards. Each thank you card costs $2. The equation $t = 2c$ represents the total cost, t, this student will spend to buy c cards. Which variable is the independent variable in the equation? Which is the dependent variable? Explain how you know.

2 What is a solution of an equation? Explain one way to check a solution of an equation. Use at least four math or academic vocabulary terms in your explanation. Underline each term you use.

3 Explain one way each pair of terms is related.

a. *like terms* and *equivalent expressions*

b. *variable* and *algebraic*

➤ **Use what you have learned to complete these problems.**

1 Write an expression equivalent to $15k + 6 - 9k - 8$ with exactly two terms. Show your work.

SOLUTION _____

2 The volume of the right rectangular prism is $\frac{5}{12}$ ft³. What is the height of the prism? Show your work.

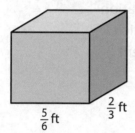

$\frac{5}{6}$ ft $\frac{2}{3}$ ft

SOLUTION _____

3 Which expression is equivalent to $6(x + 3y)$?

A $x + 3y$ **B** $6 + 3y$ **C** $6x + 3y$ **D** $6x + 18y$

4 Find whole numbers to show products that are equivalent to the difference $144 - 24$. Write your answers in the blanks.

$144 - 24$

$12 \times$ _____ $- 12 \times$ _____

$12 ($ _____ $-$ _____ $)$

5 Rico plays the flute and the clarinet. Today, he plays the flute 8.2 times as long as he plays the clarinet. His total time spent playing the flute and the clarinet today is 46 min. How many minutes does Rico play the flute today? Show your work.

SOLUTION _____

6 Which value in the set {2, 12, 24, 36} is a solution of the equation $x - 24 = 12$?

A 2   **B** 12

C 24   **D** 36

7 An office buys a new copy machine. The graph models the number of pages, y, that can be printed in x minutes. Use the graph to find the rate at which the copy machine prints pages. How is this rate related to the equation that represents the graph? Show your work.

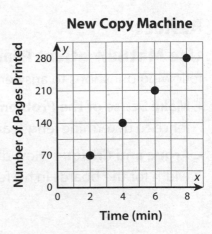

New Copy Machine

Number of Pages Printed vs *Time (min)*

SOLUTION _____

_____

_____

Performance Task

➤ **Answer the questions and show all your work on separate paper.**

Cody is having a rectangular wooden fence built. The fencing company just built a rectangular fence for Cody's neighbor and can adjust its plans for Cody's fence. Cody knows the following information about the fences and the company's plans.

- Cody's fence must have sides that are twice as long as the sides of his neighbor's fence.

- His neighbor's fence contains an area of 887.5 ft^2.

- The length of his neighbor's fence is 12.5 ft.

- The fencing company can use boards that have widths of either 0.33 ft, 0.5 ft, or 0.75 ft. All the boards in the fence must be the same size, and only a whole number of boards can be used.

- The fencing company charges $2.00 per board for the first 100 boards and $1.50 for each additional board.

Help Cody understand the plans for his fence. First, determine the length and width of Cody's fence. Then choose a board width so that the fencing company will use a whole number of boards. Finally, find out how much his fence costs. Write an equation that relates the number of boards Cody needs for his fence, b, to the total cost in dollars, c.

Reflect

Use Mathematical Practices After you complete the task, choose one of the following questions to answer.

- **Make Sense of the Problem** How did you use the information about the neighbor's fence to determine length and width of Cody's fence?

- **Argue and Critique** How did you check to make sure that Cody chose the best width for the boards in his fence?

✓ **Self Check**

Before starting this unit, check off the skills you know below.
As you complete each lesson, see how many more skills you can check off!

I can . . .	Before	After
Plot integers and rational numbers on number lines to represent real-world contexts.	☐	☐
Compare and order positive and negative numbers.	☐	☐
Determine whether a number is a solution of an inequality.	☐	☐
Write and graph inequalities to represent real-world contexts.	☐	☐
Plot ordered pairs in all four quadrants of the coordinate plane.	☐	☐
Use absolute value to find the distance between points on a horizontal or vertical line.	☐	☐
Solve problems about polygons in the coordinate plane.	☐	☐
Listen carefully during discussion in order to understand and explain another person's ideas.	☐	☐

Prepare for Absolute Value and Inequalities

➤ **Think of an example of each type of number. Label its approximate location on the number line. The first one is done for you as an example.**

> **a.** fraction less than 1
> **b.** even number greater than 5
> **c.** decimal between 3 and 4
> **d.** fraction equal to 8
>
> **e.** fraction between $2\frac{1}{2}$ and 3
> **f.** multiple of 3
> **g.** decimal equal to $6\frac{1}{10}$
> **h.** whole number 2 units away from 3

a. $\frac{1}{3}$ is a fraction less than 1.

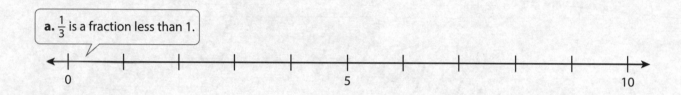

Write something that you know about whole numbers, decimals, and fractions.
See how many ideas you can write.

Whole Numbers	Decimals	Fractions

Dear Family,

This week your student is learning about positive and negative numbers. **Positive numbers** have a value greater than 0. **Negative numbers** have a value less than 0.

Every positive number and negative number has an opposite. **Opposite numbers** are numbers that are the same distance from 0, but in opposite directions.

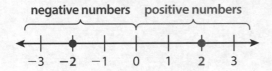

negative numbers   positive numbers

$$-3 \quad -2 \quad -1 \quad 0 \quad 1 \quad 2 \quad 3$$

The numbers 2 and −2 are opposites.

The positive number 2 is sometimes written as +2.

All whole numbers and their opposites are called **integers**. Every integer is also a **rational number**, meaning that it can be written as a positive or negative fraction with a whole-number numerator and denominator.

Your student will be modeling rational numbers like the ones below.

Show $1\frac{1}{2}$ and its opposite on a number line.

➤ **ONE WAY** to show a number and its opposite is to use a horizontal number line.

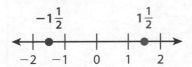

$$-1\frac{1}{2} \qquad 1\frac{1}{2}$$
$$-2 \quad -1 \quad 0 \quad 1 \quad 2$$

➤ **ANOTHER WAY** is to use a vertical number line.

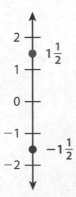

Both models show that $1\frac{1}{2}$ and its opposite, $-1\frac{1}{2}$, are the same distance from 0 and in opposite directions.

 Use the next page to start a conversation about positive and negative numbers.

Activity Thinking About Positive and Negative Numbers Around You

Mount Everest
+29,029 ft

➤ **Do this activity together to investigate positive and negative numbers in the real world.**

Mount Everest is the highest mountain in the world. It reaches a height of about 29,029 feet above sea level. The Dead Sea is the lowest point on land in the world. Its shore is about 1,410 feet below sea level. A point's position above or below a given level, such as sea level, is called its elevation. Positive and negative numbers can be used to represent elevations.

This means that Mount Everest has an elevation of +29,029 feet and the Dead Sea has an elevation of −1,410 feet.

Dead Sea
−1,410 ft

? Where else do you see positive and negative numbers used in the world around you?

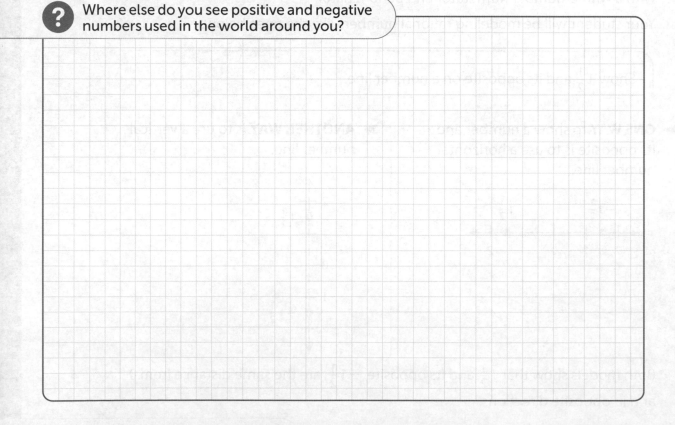

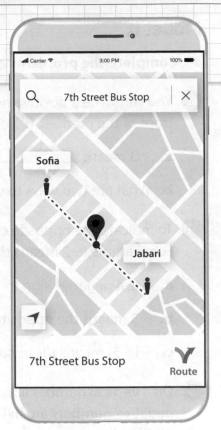

? **UNDERSTAND:** What are positive and negative numbers?

Explore Positive and Negative Numbers

Model It

➤ **Complete the problems about opposite numbers.**

1 Jabari and Sofia get off the bus at the 7th Street bus stop. Jabari walks 3 blocks to the right and Sofia walks 3 blocks to the left. Think of the bus stop as 0 on the number line. Jabari ends up 3 units to the right of 0. Draw tick marks, arrows, and a point on the number line to show where Sofia ends up.

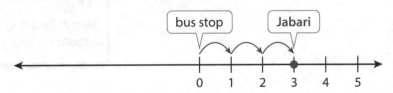

2 In problem 1, Jabari and Sofia walk in opposite directions from the bus stop. **Opposite numbers** are the same distance from 0 on the number line, but on opposite sides of 0.

a. Are numbers to the right of 0 on the number line *less than 0* or *greater than 0*?

b. Numbers greater than 0 are **positive numbers**. Numbers less than 0 are **negative numbers**. The number 0 is neither positive nor negative. Look at the number line. How are negative numbers similar to positive numbers? How are they different?

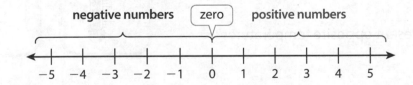

DISCUSS IT

Ask: How do you know that 1 and −1 are opposites?

Share: I would label Sofia's position on the number line as −3 because . . .

◎ **Learning Targets**   SMP 2, SMP 3, SMP 7
• Understand that positive and negative numbers describe quantities having opposite directions or values.
• Recognize opposite signs of numbers as indicating locations on opposite sides of 0 on the number line; recognize that the opposite of the opposite of a number is the number itself and that 0 is its own opposite.
• Find and position integers and other rational numbers on a horizontal or vertical number line diagram.

LESSON 23 Understand Positive and Negative Numbers   **543**

Model It

➤ **Complete the problems about positive and negative numbers.**

3 You can write a positive number two ways. You can write a positive sign (+) in front of the number, or you can write the number without the sign.

   a. +3 means _____.

   b. What are two ways to write *positive 40*?

4 To indicate the opposite of a number, use a negative sign (−). For example, −2 means *the opposite of 2* or *negative 2*.

   a. Use a negative sign to write *negative 3*.

   b. −3 means the opposite of _____.

   c. −(−5) means *the opposite of −5*. So, −(−5) is _____.

> **DISCUSS IT**
>
> **Ask:** Why is 8 the opposite of −8?
>
> **Share:** Zero is its own opposite because . . .

5 On a vertical number line, positive numbers are above 0 and negative numbers are below 0. A thermometer is like a vertical number line.

   a. Complete the scale on each thermometer.

   b. On a Celsius thermometer, 0° represents the freezing point of water. Does the thermometer on the left show a temperature *less than* or *greater than* the freezing point of water?

   c. Does the thermometer on the right show a temperature *less than* or *greater than* the freezing point of water?

   d. Why do 20°C and −20°C represent opposite temperatures?

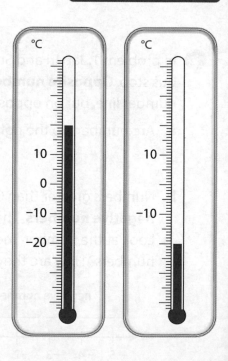

6 **Reflect** Is −25 a positive number or a negative number? Explain how you know. Find the opposite of −25 and explain how you found your answer.

Name:

Prepare for Understanding Positive and Negative Numbers

1 Think about what you know about whole numbers. Fill in each box. Use words, numbers, and pictures. Show as many ideas as you can.

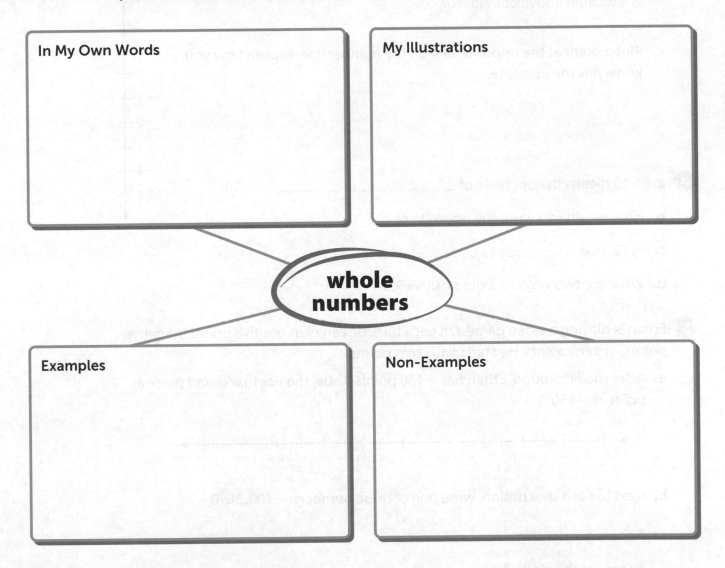

In My Own Words

My Illustrations

whole numbers

Examples

Non-Examples

2 Circle the whole numbers. Explain your reasoning.

9          $\frac{4}{4}$ 1.00000

➤ **Complete problems 3–5.**

3 Look at the point at 4 on the number line.

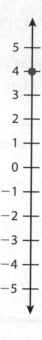

a. How many units is 4 from 0?

b. Is 4 located above or below 0?

c. Plot a point at the opposite of 4 on the number line. Explain how you know it is the opposite.

4 **a.** −10 means the opposite of _____ or _____ 10.

b. How would you write the opposite of 7?

c. +12 means _____.

d. What are two ways to write positive 9?

5 Ethan is playing a video game. On each turn, he can earn positive points, negative points, or zero points. He starts with zero points.

a. After the first round, Ethan has −150 points. Label the tick marks and place a point at −150.

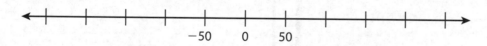

b. Next to each description, write one of these numbers: −100, 50, 0.

A score greater than 0: _____

A score at the start of the game: _____

A score less than 0: _____

c. What is the opposite of −150? Where is this value on the number line? Explain how you know.

> **Vocabulary**
>
> **opposite numbers**
> numbers that are the same distance from 0 on the number line but in opposite directions. Opposite numbers have the same numeral, but opposite signs.

Develop Understanding of Positive and Negative Numbers

Model It: Horizontal Number Lines

➤ **Try these two problems about positive and negative numbers.**

1 All the whole numbers and their opposites are called **integers**.

   a. Identify the value of each integer *a, b, c,* and *d* on the number line.

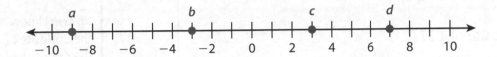

   b. Which of the integers *a, b, c,* and *d* are opposite numbers? Explain.

   c. Which of the integers *a, b, c,* and *d* are less than 0? Explain.

2 Like whole numbers, fractions also have opposites. Fractions that are quotients of whole numbers are called **rational numbers**. Opposites of these fractions are also rational numbers.

   a. Plot points at $-\frac{3}{2}$ and its opposite on the number line. How do you know where to locate the points?

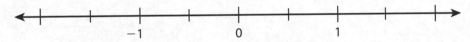

   b. Lupita wants to place points at 0.75 and its opposite on the number line in problem 2a. Explain how Lupita can place each point.

> **DISCUSS IT**
>
> **Ask:** Why are whole numbers also rational numbers?
>
> **Share:** I think decimals like 0.75 and −1.5 are rational numbers because . . .

Model It: Vertical Number Lines

➤ **Try these two problems about rational numbers on a vertical number line.**

3 **a.** Use a rational number to label each point on the number line.

   b. What is the opposite of each number you wrote on the number line?

   c. Plot points at −1.75 and −$\frac{3}{4}$.

4 **a.** What is the opposite of 1.5?

   b. What is the opposite of the opposite of 1.5? Explain.

DISCUSS IT

Ask: How is a fraction like its opposite? How is it different?

Share: I know the opposite of the opposite of a number is always . . . because . . .

CONNECT IT

➤ **Complete the problems below.**

5 How is locating −2.5 on a horizontal number line similar to locating it on a vertical number line? How is it different?

6 Is the opposite of 1$\frac{1}{4}$ *less than 0* or *greater than 0*? Explain how you know. Show both numbers on a number line in your response.

Name:

Practice Locating Positive and Negative Numbers

➤ **Study how the Example shows locating positive and negative numbers on a number line. Then solve problems 1–6.**

Example

Plot each rational number as a point on the number line.

$1\frac{1}{2}$ $\qquad$ $-1\frac{1}{4}$ $\qquad$ $-\frac{1}{2}$

The positive number $1\frac{1}{2}$ is located $1\frac{1}{2}$ units to the right of 0.

The negative number $-\frac{1}{2}$ is located $\frac{1}{2}$ unit to the left of 0.

The negative number $-1\frac{1}{4}$ is located $1\frac{1}{4}$ units to the left of 0.

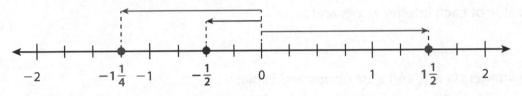

1 Draw a horizontal number line in the space below. Plot and label a point for the opposite of each number in the Example.

2 **a.** What is the opposite of -26? How many units away from 0 is its location on a horizontal number line, and in which direction?

b. What is the opposite of 26? How many units away from 0 is its location on a horizontal number line, and in which direction?

c. What number is the opposite of the opposite of -26? Explain.

Vocabulary

integers
the set of whole numbers and their opposites.

rational number
a number that can be expressed as the fraction $\frac{a}{b}$ or the opposite of $\frac{a}{b}$ where a and b are whole numbers and $b \neq 0$.

3 **a.** Use a rational number to label each point on the number line.

b. What is the opposite of each number you wrote on the number line?

c. Plot points at −0.5 and −1.5.

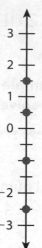

4 Look at the points on the number line.

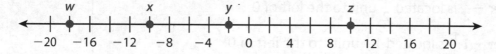

a. Identify the value of each integer *w*, *x*, *y*, and *z*.

b. Which of the integers *w*, *x*, *y*, and *z* are opposites? Explain.

c. Which of the integers *w*, *x*, *y*, and *z* are less than 0? Explain.

5 Use a horizontal or vertical number line. Plot points at $\frac{7}{10}$ and its opposite. Label each point with its value.

6 Akio says −4 has the same value as 4 because they are both 4 units away from 0. Explain why Akio is incorrect.

Refine Ideas About Positive and Negative Numbers

Apply It Math Toolkit number lines

➤ Complete problems 1–5.

1 **Identify** On the number line, the letters *a, b, c,* and *d* represent integers.

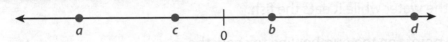

a. Which letters represent negative integers? How do you know?

b. Which letters appear to represent opposite integers? Explain your reasoning.

2 **Interpret** To complete the table, write a number to represent each situation. Write the number's opposite and tell what it means. Explain the meaning of 0.

Situation	Number	Opposite	Meaning of Opposite	Meaning of 0
a. You owe $25.	-25	25	you earn $25	You do not owe or earn any money.
b. A team gains 20 yards in a football game.	20	-20	A team loses 20 yards in a football game.	You don't gain or lose any yards
c. A stock price falls 4.26 points.	-4.26	4.26	A stock price increased value	A stock price stays the same.

3 **Critique** Estela says she plotted two points that represent opposite numbers. Describe Estela's error. How could she correct her graph by moving one point?

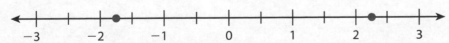

4 *Elevation* describes a location above or below a given point, such as sea level. Positive and negative numbers are used to represent elevations. In this problem, you can think of the surface of the water as representing sea level.

- A pelican is flying 7 ft above sea level.

- Then the pelican dives into the water and grabs a fish at an elevation of $-1\frac{1}{2}$ ft.

- Then the pelican floats on the water while it eats the fish.

PART A Plot and label three points on the number line to show the pelican's elevation when *flying*, *diving*, and *floating*.

PART B Why does it makes sense to let 0 represent sea level?

PART C You can describe the elevation of the fish as $-1\frac{1}{2}$ ft or as $1\frac{1}{2}$ ft below sea level. Explain why one description uses a negative number and the other description uses a positive number.

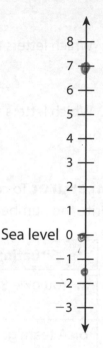

5 **Math Journal** You can use positive and negative numbers to represent gaining and losing points in a game. Plot a point on a number line to represent a loss of 9 points. Then plot a point at the opposite of that number. Label each point with its value. What does the opposite number mean in this situation?

✔ End of Lesson Checklist

☐ **INTERACTIVE GLOSSARY** Find the entry for *negative numbers*. Give three examples of when you would use negative numbers.

Dear Family,

This week your student is learning how to compare positive and negative numbers. The farther to the left a number is located on a horizontal number line, the lesser the value of that number.

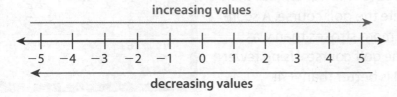

increasing values

−5 −4 −3 −2 −1   0   1   2   3   4   5

decreasing values

You can write an inequality to show which of two numbers has the greater or lesser value. For example, $2 > -3$ means that 2 is greater than −3.

Your student will be learning to solve problems like the one below.

> A town well extends to an elevation of 255 ft below ground level. Jesse's house well extends to an elevation of −260 ft. Which well is deeper?

➤ **ONE WAY** to compare the elevations is to use words to describe their relationship in context.

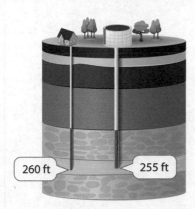

260 ft   255 ft

A point 260 ft underground is deeper than a point 255 ft underground.

➤ **ANOTHER WAY** is to use symbols to write an inequality.

Look at the positions of −260 and −255 on a vertical number line.

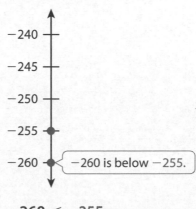

−240

−245

−250

−255

−260 −260 is below −255.

$-260 < -255$

Both models show that Jesse's well is deeper than the town well.

 Use the next page to start a conversation about positive and negative number comparisons.

Activity Thinking About Comparing Positive and Negative Numbers Around You

➤ **Do this activity together to investigate comparing positive and negative numbers in the real world.**

Did you know when you play golf, the lowest score wins? In fact, your final score could even be negative!

A score of −4 means a person used four fewer strokes than was expected in order to complete the golf course. A score of +4 means a person used four more strokes than was expected in order to complete the golf course. Using fewer strokes is better, so a score of −4 is better than +4!

DUSTY HILLS GOLF COURSE

SCORE CARD

Hole	Par	Strokes	Score
1	4	3	−1
2	4	4	−1
3	5	5	−1
4	6	7	0
5	4	6	+2
6	5	5	+2
7	5	6	+3
8	6	6	+3
9	4	5	+4

? Where else do you compare positive and negative numbers in the world around you?

Explore Ordering Positive and Negative Numbers

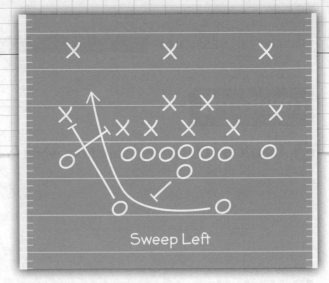

A diagram of a football play

Previously, you learned about positive and negative numbers. In this lesson, you will learn about ordering and comparing positive and negative numbers.

➤ **Use what you know to try to solve the problem below.**

A youth football team tries several different plays. The goal of each play is to gain yards. The coach records the result of each play. List the plays from worst to best.

Name of Play	Wedge	Hook	Flag	Draw	Sweep	Toss
Result: Yards Gained (+) or Lost (−)	−3	+4	−5	+2	0	−4

 TRY IT

 Math Toolkit algebra tiles, number lines, two-color counters

DISCUSS IT

Ask: What did you do first to decide which play is the worst?

Share: The first thing I did was . . .

 Learning Targets SMP 1, SMP 2, SMP 3, SMP 4, SMP 5, SMP 6
• Interpret statements of inequality as statements about the relative position of two numbers on a number line diagram.
• Write, interpret, and explain statements of order for rational numbers in real-world contexts.

CONNECT IT

1 Look Back List the plays from worst to best. Explain how you know.

2 Look Ahead The goal of a football play is to gain yards. The more yards gained or the fewer yards lost, the better the play is. Number lines can be used to help make these types of comparisons with positive and negative numbers.

a. Look at the horizontal number line. Point *D* is farther to the right from 0 than point *C*. Which point represents a greater number?

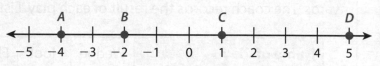

b. Point *A* is farther to the left from 0 than point *B*. Which point represents a greater number?

c. Look at the vertical number line. Point *G* is farther down from 0 than Point *F*. Which point represents a greater number?

d. Point *E* is above Point *F*. Which point represents a lesser number? What is always true when comparing a negative number and a positive number?

3 Reflect How do the values change on a horizontal number line as you move left? How do the values change on a vertical number line as you move up?

Prepare for Ordering Positive and Negative Numbers

1 Think about what you know about positive and negative numbers. Fill in each box. Use words, numbers, and pictures. Show as many ideas as you can.

Word	In My Own Words	Example
positive numbers		
negative numbers		
rational numbers		
inequality		

2 Choose a negative rational number. Write an inequality using the symbol > to compare your number to 0. Explain your thinking.

3 Some friends play history trivia. Players gain 1 point for a correct answer. Players lose 1 point for an incorrect answer. The player with the greatest score wins. The players' scores are shown in the table.

Player	Score
Brett	−7
Ellema	−1
Felipe	+3
Jennifer	0
Kamal	+2
Riley	−5

a. List the players from worst score to best score. Show your work.

SOLUTION _____

b. Check your answer to problem 3a. Show your work.

Susan B. Anthony was born in 1820.

Develop Comparing Positive and Negative Numbers

Oshkosh
Current Temperature
2.5°F

Appleton
Current Temperature
−3.5°F

Green Bay
Current Temperature
−5.0°F

➤ **Read and try to solve the problem below.**

On a winter day, Adnan looks up the current temperatures in three nearby cities. Adnan chooses two of the temperatures and writes a comparison. What are all the possible comparisons he can write? You can use words and/or symbols.

TRY IT

Math Toolkit graph paper, number lines

➤ **Explore different ways to compare positive and negative numbers.**

On a winter day, Adnan looks up the current temperatures in three nearby cities. The temperatures are 2.5°F, −3.5°F, and −5°F. Adnan chooses two of the temperatures and writes a comparison. What are all the possible comparisons he can write? You can use words and/or symbols.

Model It

You can use a number line to compare positive and negative numbers.

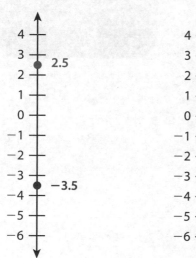 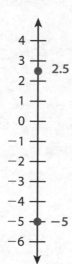 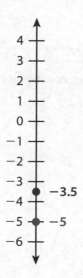

Model It

You can write an inequality to compare positive and negative numbers.

$2.5 > -3.5$ $2.5 > -5$ $-3.5 > -5$

Analyze It

You can use words to interpret the meaning of an inequality in a real-world situation.

2.5°F is warmer than −3.5°F.

2.5°F is warmer than −5°F.

−3.5°F is warmer than −5°F.

CONNECT IT

➤ **Use the problem from the previous page to help you understand how to compare positive and negative numbers.**

1 Look at the two **Model Its**. How can you use a number line to help you write an inequality?

2 Look at **Analyze It**. How can the inequalities help to determine which of two temperatures is warmer?

3 Use the symbol $<$ to rewrite the comparison between $-3.5°F$ and $2.5°F$. Then interpret the meaning of the inequality using the words *colder than*.

4 What are all the possible inequality statements Adnan might write? Use $<$ and $>$.

5 When given a pair of numbers in a real-world situation, how can you compare the numbers using $<$ and $>$? How can an inequality help you interpret the comparison in the real-world situation?

6 **Reflect** Think about all the models and strategies you have discussed today. Describe how one of them helped you better understand how to compare positive and negative numbers.

Apply It

➤ **Use what you learned to solve these problems.**

7 Plot and label the numbers −6.5 and −8.5 on the number line. Then write an inequality using the symbol > to compare the two numbers.

-8.5 -6.5

SOLUTION _____

-6.5 > -8.5
-8.5 < -6.5

8 Which of the following statements are true? Select all that apply.

A 4 > −17 because 4 is to the right of −17 on a horizontal number line.

B 4 > −17 because 4 is to the left of −17 on a horizontal number line.

C 4 > −17 because −17 is to the right of 4 on a horizontal number line.

D 4 > −17 because 4 is above −17 on a vertical number line.

E 4 > −17 because 4 is below −17 on a vertical number line.

F 4 > −17 because −17 is below 4 on a vertical number line.

I love Sharks

9 Notah is studying ocean animals. He learns that the sixgill shark can dive to an elevation of about −8,200 ft relative to sea level and the elephant seal can dive to an elevation of about −7,800 ft. Write an inequality to compare these elevations. Which animal can dive to a lower elevation? Show your work.

A sixgill shark

0 — sea level

−7,800 — Elephant seal
−8,200 — sixgill shark

−7,800 > −8,200

SOLUTION _____

Sixgill shark can dive lower.

Name:

Practice Comparing Positive and Negative Numbers

➤ **Study the Example showing how to compare two negative numbers. Then solve problems 1–5.**

Example

The table shows the amount of money Savanna either withdraws (−) or deposits (+) into her bank account over 5 weeks. Write an inequality to compare the withdrawals for Week 2 and Week 3.

Week	Week 1	Week 2	Week 3	Week 4	Week 5
Amount	+$40	−$40	−$60	+$100	−$80

Plot the amounts on a number line.

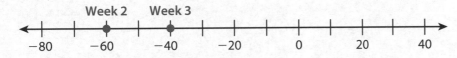

−60 is to the left of −40. So, −60 < −40.

1 **a.** Compare the two amounts in the Example using the symbol >.

b. Does using > for the inequality change which amount represents withdrawing more money? Explain.

2 Write an inequality that compares the value of point A and the value of point B. Show your work.

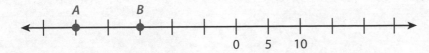

> **Vocabulary**
>
> **inequality**
> a mathematical statement that uses an inequality symbol to show the relationship between values of expressions.

SOLUTION _____

3 The typical level of a low tide at a beach is the 0 point on a number line. Each day's high and low tides are measured relative to the typical low tide. On Monday morning, low tide is at −0.8 ft. On Tuesday morning, low tide is at −0.4 ft.

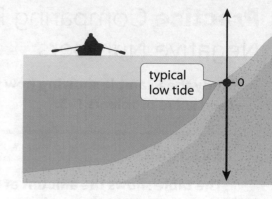

a. Write an inequality to compare the low tides on Monday and Tuesday mornings. Show your work.

$$-0.4 > -0.8$$

SOLUTION _____

b. Which day has a higher low tide? Explain.

4 Consider the inequality $-3 < -2\frac{1}{2}$. What does the inequality tell you about the location of -3 compared to the location of $-2\frac{1}{2}$ on a horizontal number line? Use *to the right* and *to the left* in your answer.

5 In golf, the winner is the person with the lowest score. At the end of a round of golf, Jada's score is positive. Isabel's score is negative. Can you determine who wins? If so, tell who wins and why. If not, explain why not.

Refine Ordering Positive and Negative Numbers

➤ **Complete the Example below. Then solve problems 1–9.**

CONSIDER THIS . . .
You can write all the rational numbers as fractions or write them all as decimals.

Example

Order the following rational numbers from least to greatest.

$$\frac{1}{4}, -1.25, -\frac{3}{4}, 0.5, 1, -\frac{3}{2}$$

Look at how you could use a number line to order rational numbers.

Write the decimals as fractions.

$$-1.25 = -1\frac{1}{4}$$

$$0.5 = \frac{1}{2}$$

Plot the numbers on a number line.

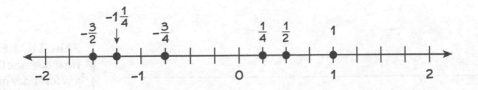

SOLUTION _____

PAIR/SHARE
How would the order change if you changed $-\frac{3}{2}$ to $\frac{3}{2}$?

Apply It

1 Write two inequalities that compare the value of point P and the value of point Q. Show your work.

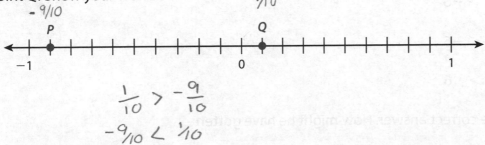

$$\frac{1}{10} > -\frac{9}{10}$$

$$-\frac{9}{10} < \frac{1}{10}$$

CONSIDER THIS . . .
What does each tick mark on the number line represent?

PAIR/SHARE
What inequality can you write to compare the value of point P to -1?

SOLUTION _____

2 A vending machine in a cafeteria sells sandwiches. The machine is restocked once during the day. At the end of each day, a cafeteria worker records how many more (+) or fewer (−) sandwiches are in the machine than there were at the start of the day. The table shows the changes for one week.

Day	Change in Number of Sandwiches
Monday	−3
Tuesday	+4
Wednesday	−5
Thursday	−2
Friday	0

Write an inequality to compare the changes for Monday and Thursday. Tell what your inequality means in terms of the situation. Show your work.

> **CONSIDER THIS...**
> The number of sandwiches at the end of a day is the result of some sandwiches being sold and the machine being restocked with more sandwiches.

SOLUTION _____

_____

> **PAIR/SHARE**
> What does the 0 in the row for Friday mean in this situation?

3 An elevation of −4 m is higher than an elevation of −8 m. An elevation of −8 m is lower than an elevation of −6 m. Which set of inequalities correctly expresses these relationships?

A $-4 < -8$ and $-8 < -6$

B $-4 < -8$ and $-8 > -6$

C $-4 > -8$ and $-8 < -6$

D $-4 > -8$ and $-8 > -6$

Anders chose B as the correct answer. How might he have gotten that answer?

> **CONSIDER THIS...**
> How can you plot the elevations on a vertical number line or a horizontal number line to help write the inequalities?

> **PAIR/SHARE**
> What is a different way you can write the correct pair of inequalities?

4 Sea level has an elevation of 0 ft. Lake Eyre is the lowest point in Australia. It has an elevation of −15 m relative to sea level. Which of the following U.S. locations, if any, have a lower elevation than Lake Eyre? Explain.

Lake Eyre, Australia

Location	Elevation (m)
Death Valley, California	−86
New Orleans, Louisiana	−2.4
Imperial, California	−18
Ouachita River, Arkansas	17

5 Doug says that −7 > −5 because 7 > 5. Do you agree? Explain.

6 Tell whether each statement about the points on the number line is *True* or *False*.

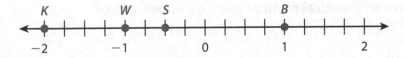

	True	False
a. The value of point K is greater than −1.	○	●
b. The value of point B is greater than the value of point W.	●	○
c. The value of point S is less than 1.	●	○
d. The value of point W is less than −0.5.	●	○

7 Order the following rational numbers from least to greatest. Show your work.

$-1.5, \dfrac{3}{4}, -\dfrac{1}{4}, -1.75, -1, 1.5$

SOLUTION

8 Lilia wants to replace both question marks with the same number so that the inequalities correctly compare the numbers.

$? > -5$ and $? < 2$

Which of these numbers could Lilia use? Select all that apply.

A -7

B -4

C -2

D 0

E 1

F 5

9 **Math Journal** Choose two of the rational numbers shown below. Write two inequalities to compare the numbers, using $<$ and $>$. Then describe the location of one number compared to the other on a vertical number line. Use *above* and/or *below* in the description.

$-\dfrac{3}{4}$ -1.5 $\dfrac{1}{4}$ $-1\dfrac{1}{4}$ -0.5

✓ **End of Lesson Checklist**

☐ **INTERACTIVE GLOSSARY** Write a new entry for *interpret*. Write at least one synonym for *interpret*.

☐ **SELF CHECK** Go back to the Unit 6 Opener and see what you can check off.

Dear Family,

This week your student is learning about absolute value. The **absolute value** of a number is its distance from 0 on the number line.

The symbol |5| is read as *the absolute value of 5*.

|5| = 5 because the distance from 5 to 0 is 5 units.

|−5| = 5 because the distance from −5 to 0 is 5 units.

This means |5| = |−5|.

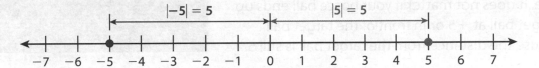

Your student will be comparing absolute values such as the ones below.

Use <, >, or = to compare the absolute values of −6 and −4.

➤ **ONE WAY** to compare absolute values is by using a number line.

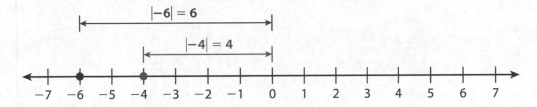

It is a greater distance from −6 to 0 than it is from −4 to 0.

|−6| > |−4|

➤ **ANOTHER WAY** is to interpret the absolute values in a real-world situation.

Think of −6 and −4 as representing debts of $6 and $4.

Since |−6| = 6 and |−4| = 4, the absolute values of −6 and −4 represent the amounts owed, $6 and $4.

A person with a debt of $6 owes more money than a person with a debt of $4.

|−6| > |−4|

Using either model, you can see that |−6| > |−4|.

 Use the next page to start a conversation about absolute value.

Activity Thinking About Absolute Value Around You

➤ **Do this activity together to investigate absolute value in the real world.**

Bocce is a game where players throw bocce balls to get as close to a smaller target ball as possible. It does not matter if your bocce ball rolls past the target ball or if it stops before. Either way, you measure the distance from your bocce ball to the target ball.

In this way, playing bocce is like using absolute value. You can think about the target ball as the 0 point on a number line. It does not matter if your bocce ball ends up past the target ball at $+5$ or in front of the target ball at -5, because the distance from the target ball is still 5.

? Where else do you see absolute value in the world around you?

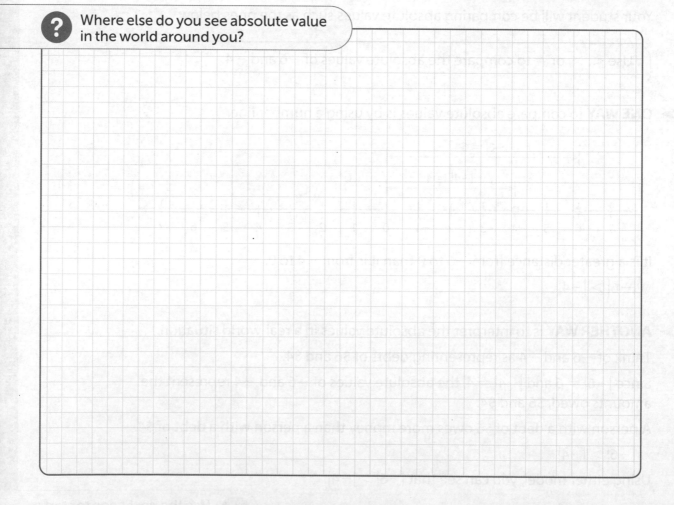

Explore Absolute Value

Drone

Sea cave

Model It

➤ **Complete the problems about distance from 0.**

1 A scientist standing on the deck of a boat uses a drone, and a scuba diver uses a camera to explore a sea cave. The table shows the elevations of four objects relative to sea level.

Object	Camera	Cave floor	Drone	Boat deck
Elevation	−20 ft	−30 ft	20 ft	5 ft

a. Use the number line to show the elevations of the objects from the table. Label each object at its elevation.

b. Are any of the objects the same distance from sea level? If so, how far from sea level are they?

c. Another object is 3 ft from sea level. Is the object's elevation *positive*, *negative*, or could it be *either*? Explain.

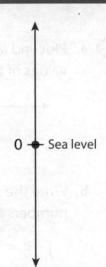

0 ◆ Sea level

2 The **absolute value** of a number is its distance from 0. The notation |−3| is read as *the absolute value of −3* and represents the distance of −3 from 0.

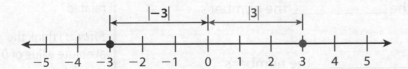

|3| = _____ because the distance from 0 to 3 is _____ units.

|−3| = _____ because the distance from 0 to −3 is _____ units.

DISCUSS IT

Ask: How is absolute value related to zero on the number line?

Share: I think two numbers will have the same absolute value when . . .

◎ **Learning Targets** SMP 2, SMP 3, SMP 7
• Understand the absolute value of a rational number as its distance from 0 on the number line; interpret absolute value as magnitude for a positive or negative quantity in a real-world situation.
• Distinguish comparisons of absolute value from statements about order.

Model It

➤ **Complete the problems about absolute value.**

3 **a.** Plot and label the numbers 3, 4, 5, and 6 on the number line. Do the values of the numbers *increase* or *decrease* as the numbers go from 3 to 6?

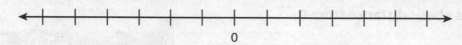

0

b. Write the absolute value of each number. Do the absolute values of the numbers *increase* or *decrease* the numbers go from 3 to 6?

$|3| = $ _____ $|4| = $ _____ $|5| = $ _____ $|6| = $ _____

4 **a.** Plot and label the numbers −3, −4, −5, and −6 on the number line. Do the values of the numbers *increase* or *decrease* as the numbers go from −3 to −6?

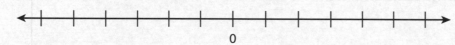

0

b. Write the absolute value of each number. Do the absolute values of the numbers *increase* or *decrease* as the numbers go from −3 to −6?

$|-3| = $ _____ $|-4| = $ _____ $|-5| = $ _____ $|-6| = $ _____

5 Write *lesser* or *greater* to complete each statement.

a. The farther a number is from 0, the _____ the number's absolute value.

b. The closer a number is to 0, the _____ the number's absolute value.

6 **Reflect** Is the absolute value of a number ever negative? Explain your reasoning.

> **DISCUSS IT**
>
> **Ask:** How are distance and absolute value related?
>
> **Share:** I think the absolute value of 0 is ... because ...

Name:

Prepare for Understanding Absolute Value

1 Think about what you know about opposite numbers. Fill in each box.
   Use words, numbers, and pictures. Show as many ideas as you can.

In My Own Words	My Illustrations

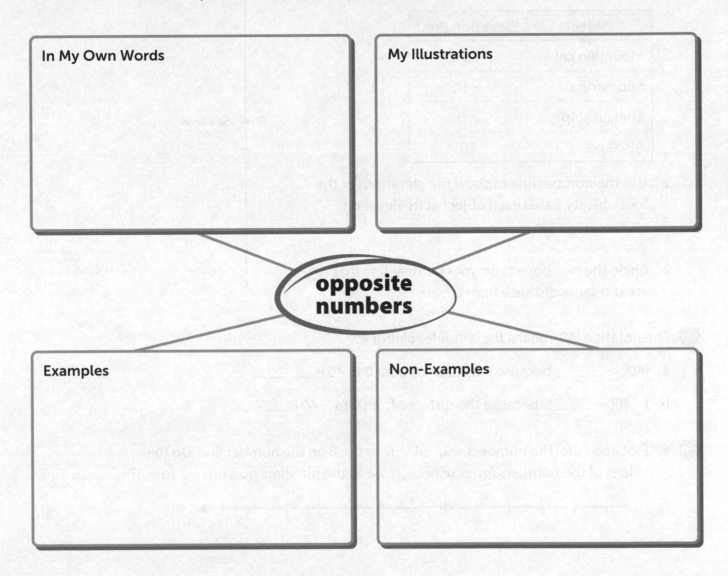

opposite numbers

Examples	Non-Examples

2 Look at the number line. Which pair of points appears to show
   a pair of opposite numbers? Explain your reasoning.

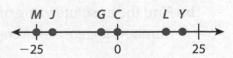

➤ **Complete problems 3–5.**

3 The table shows the elevations of four objects relative to sea level.

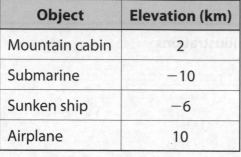

Object	Elevation (km)
Mountain cabin	2
Submarine	−10
Sunken ship	−6
Airplane	10

0 —●— Sea level

a. Use the number line to show the elevations of the four objects. Label each object at its elevation.

b. Circle the two objects on your number line that are the same distance from 0.

4 The notation |40| means *the absolute value of 40*.

a. |40| = _____ because the distance from 0 to 40 is _____.

b. |−40| = _____ because the distance from 0 to −40 is _____.

5 **a.** Plot and label the numbers −2, −4, −6, and −8 on the number line. Do the values of the numbers *increase* or *decrease* as the numbers go from −2 to −8?

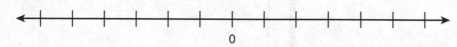

0

b. Find the absolute value of each number. Do the absolute values of the numbers *increase* or *decrease* as the numbers go from −2 to −8?

|−2| = _____ |−4| = _____ |−6| = _____ |−8| = _____

Vocabulary

absolute value
a number's distance from 0 on the number line. Absolute value is never negative.

Develop Understanding of Absolute Value

Model It: Compare Absolute Values

➤ **Try these two problems about comparing absolute values.**

1 Use the number line to help you compare the numbers and compare their absolute values. Write $<$, $>$, or $=$ in each circle to make a true statement. Explain how you know.

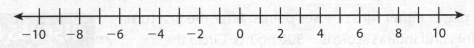

a. -9 ◯ 5 $|-9|$ ◯ $|5|$

b. -1 ◯ 2 $|-1|$ ◯ $|2|$

c. -8 ◯ 8 $|-8|$ ◯ $|8|$

> **DISCUSS IT**
>
> *Ask:* How does a number line help you determine which absolute value is greater?
>
> *Share:* I think that when you compare two numbers and then compare their absolute values, the inequality symbols can be different because . . .

2 Plot and label points for two numbers a and b so that $a < b$ and $|a| > |b|$. Explain your thinking.

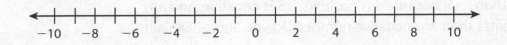

Model It: Interpret Absolute Value

➤ **Try these two problems about interpreting absolute value.**

3 The absolute value of a number may be used to describe the size, or magnitude, of a real-world quantity. Complete each equation and sentence.

a. $|-20| = $ _____ $-\$20$ means you owe $\$$_____ .

b. $|+10| = $ _____   A score of $+10$ points means you win _____ points.

c. $|-10| = $ _____   A score of -10 points means you _____ points.

4 In each turn of a game, a player either wins or loses points. After the first turn, Jacob's score is -250 points and Indira's score is -300 points. Circle the inequality that makes a correct comparison. Then write a sentence to tell what the inequality means in this situation.

a. $-300 > -250$ $-300 < -250$

b. $|-300| > |-250|$ $|-300| < |-250|$

> **DISCUSS IT**
>
> **Ask:** How would you interpret the absolute value of a negative temperature?
>
> **Share:** I think you can use positive numbers to describe negative quantities because . . .

CONNECT IT

➤ **Complete the problems below.**

5 A whale starts at an elevation of -200 ft relative to sea level and then swims to an elevation of -150 ft. Write an inequality using absolute value notation to compare the distances below sea level. Explain your reasoning.

6 Luis says $|4|$ is greater than $|-5|$ because 4 is positive, -5 is negative, and any positive number is greater than any negative number. Do you agree? Explain.

Name:

Practice Comparing Absolute Values

➤ **Study how the Example shows comparing two numbers and their absolute values. Then solve problems 1–5.**

Example

Use the numbers −7 and 6. Which number has the greater value? Which number has the greater absolute value?

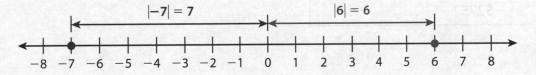

6 is to the right of −7 on the number line, so 6 is greater than −7.

−7 is 7 units from 0.

6 is 6 units from 0.

So, −7 has the greater absolute value.

$-7 < 6$ and $|-7| > |6|$.

---

1 Choose a number less than −2 that is on the number line in the Example. Is your number's absolute value *greater than 2* or *less than 2*? Explain how you know.

2 Use the number line from the Example to help you compare the numbers and compare their absolute values. Write $<$, $>$, or $=$ in each circle to make a true statement. Explain how you know.

a. $-3 \bigcirc 5$ $|-3| \bigcirc |5|$

b. $4 \bigcirc -4$ $|4| \bigcirc |-4|$

> **Vocabulary**
>
> **absolute value**
> a number's distance from 0 on the number line. Absolute value is never negative.

3 Sophia, Malcolm, and Oren are playing a money game. Their bank balances are shown in the table. Complete the table by writing the absolute value of each bank balance to show how much each player owes. Who owes the greatest amount?

Player	Bank Balance	Amount Owed
Sophia	$|-\$150| =$	$\$150$
Malcolm	$|-\$325| =$	$\$325$
Oren	$|-\$275| =$	$\$275$

4 The temperature on Monday is −24°C. The temperature on Tuesday is −21°C. Circle the inequality that makes a correct comparison. Then write a sentence to tell what the inequality means in this situation.

a. $-24 < -21$ $-24 > -21$

b. $|-24| < |-21|$ $|-24| > |-21|$

5 Plot and label points for two numbers c and d so that $c < d$ and $|c| > |d|$. Explain your thinking.

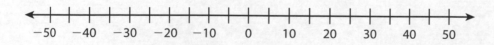

©Curriculum Associates, LLC Copying is not permitted.

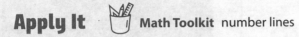

Refine Ideas About Absolute Value

Apply It ✏️ Math Toolkit number lines

➤ Complete problems 1–5.

1 **Deduce** Jia is thinking of a number. She gives three clues about the number: the number is even, the number is less than −12, and the absolute value of the number is between 9 and 15. What is Jia's number? Explain how you know.

2 **Analyze** Ian says that if $x < y$, then $|x| < |y|$. Is Ian's statement *always true*, *sometimes true*, or *never true*? Use a model to help explain your thinking.

3 **Apply** Mrs. Shen writes the expression $|-5| + |3|$ on the board. Show or explain why the sum $|-5| + |3|$ is the distance between −5 and 3 on a number line.

4 A tour group is going sea diving. The ocean floor is at −18 ft relative to sea level. One diver is already at −11 ft. The tour guide is keeping watch on a platform 5 ft above sea level, directly above the diver.

PART A Draw a model of the situation.

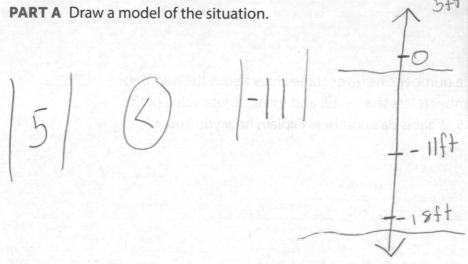

PART B Write an absolute value inequality comparing the distances of the tour guide and the diver to sea level. Who is closer to sea level? Explain how you know.

5 Math Journal Order the numbers 5, −7, −9, and −2 from least to greatest. Then order the absolute values $|5|$, $|-7|$, $|-9|$, and $|-2|$ from least to greatest. Explain how absolute value affects which values are lesser and which values are greater.

✓ End of Lesson Checklist

☐ **INTERACTIVE GLOSSARY** Find the entry for *absolute value*. Explain why the absolute value of −4 is greater than the absolute value of 3.

Dear Family,

This week your student is learning how to write and graph inequalities with a variable. An inequality compares two values using one of these inequality symbols.

<	less than	>	greater than
≤	less than or equal to	≥	greater than or equal to

A **solution of an inequality** is a value that can be substituted for a variable in the inequality to make it true. Solutions can be represented on a number line.

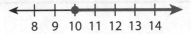
8 9 10 11 12 13 14

This number line shows the solutions of $x \geq 10$.

Any number that is shaded, such as 10, 15, or 12.5, is a solution of $x \leq 10$.

Any number that is not shaded, such as 9.9 or $6\frac{1}{2}$, is not a solution of $x \leq 10$.

Your student will be learning to solve problems like the one below.

> Students in a karate class must be taller than 5 feet. The inequality $x > 5$, where x is a number of feet, represents the heights of students who can attend the class. Which values in the set {4.5, 5, 5.5} are solutions of the inequality $x > 5$?

➤ **ONE WAY** to check solutions of an inequality is with a number line.

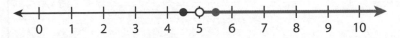
0   1   2   3   4   5   6   7   8   9   10

The number **5.5** is in the shaded part of the number line, but **4.5** and **5** are not.

➤ **ANOTHER WAY** is to substitute each value in the set to check whether the value makes the inequality true.

$$x > 5$$

$x = 4.5$	$4.5 > 5$	← **False**
$x = 5$	$5 > 5$	← **False**
$x = 5.5$	$5.5 > 5$	← **True**

Using either method, 5.5 is the only value in the set {4.5, 5, 5.5} that is a solution of the inequality $x > 5$.

 Use the next page to start a conversation about inequalities.

Activity Thinking About Inequalities Around You

➤ **Do this activity together to investigate inequalities in the real world.**

Have you ever seen weight limit signs on the side of the road? The phrase *Weight Limit 5 Tons* means that only vehicles that weigh 5 tons or less can travel on that road. Roads need to have weight limits because overly heavy vehicles can cause damage.

You can represent a weight limit of 5 tons with the inequality $x \leq 5$, where x is the weight in tons of any vehicle allowed to travel on that road.

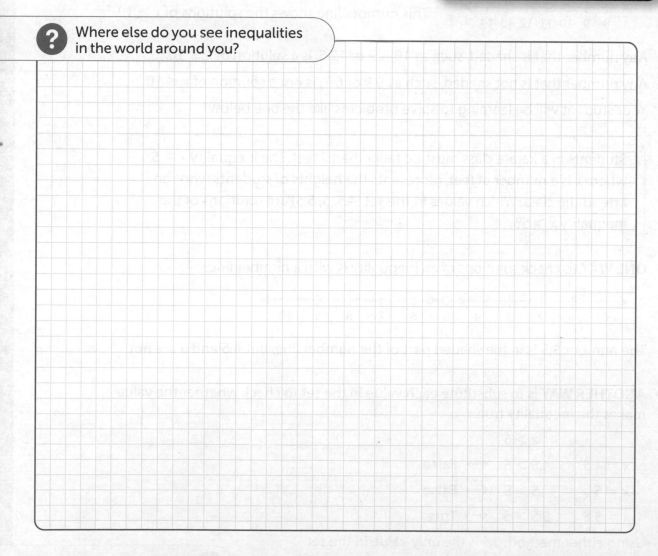

? Where else do you see inequalities in the world around you?

Explore One-Variable Inequalities

Previously, you learned about one-variable equations.
In this lesson, you will learn about one-variable inequalities.

➤ **Use what you know to try to solve the problem below.**

The thermostat in an office is set to turn the heat on any time the temperature drops below 15°C. What are all the temperatures at which the heat is on? Use words, symbols, or pictures to describe all the temperatures.

 TRY IT

 Math Toolkit number lines

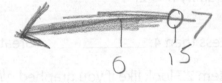

DISCUSS IT

Ask: How can you restate the given information in your own words?

Share: The given information says . . .

Learning Targets SMP 1, SMP 2, SMP 3, SMP 4, SMP 5, SMP 6, SMP 8
• Use substitution to determine whether a given number in a specified set makes an inequality true.
• Write an inequality of the form $x > c$ or $x < c$ to represent a constraint or condition in a real-world or mathematical problem. Recognize that inequalities of the form $x > c$ or $x < c$ have infinitely many solutions; represent solutions of such inequalities on number line diagrams.

LESSON 26 Write and Graph One-Variable Inequalities   **583**

CONNECT IT

1 **Look Back** What are different ways to describe all the temperatures at which the heat is on?

2 **Look Ahead** You can describe a range of values using an inequality with a variable.

all values greater than 10   any value less than 3

$x > 10$ $a < 3$

a. Circle each value of n that makes the inequality $n > 2$ a true statement.

-2 $-1\frac{1}{2}$ 0 2 2.5 5 6 $7\frac{1}{2}$

b. A **solution of an inequality** is a value of a variable that makes the inequality true. Graph the solutions of $n > 2$ that you found in problem 2a.

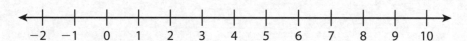

c. Name three more solutions of the inequality $n > 2$.

Between 6 and 7: _____   Less than 4: _____   Greater than 8: _____

d. What would your number line in problem 2b look like if you graphed *all* the solutions of $n > 2$?

3 **Reflect** There is no limit to how many solutions you could list for $n > 2$. There are *infinitely many* solutions. Explain why the equation $t = 15$ has one solution, but the inequality $t < 15$ has infinitely many solutions.

Prepare for Writing and Graphing One-Variable Inequalities

1 Think about what you know about comparing and ordering numbers. Fill in each box. Use words, numbers, and pictures. Show as many ideas as you can.

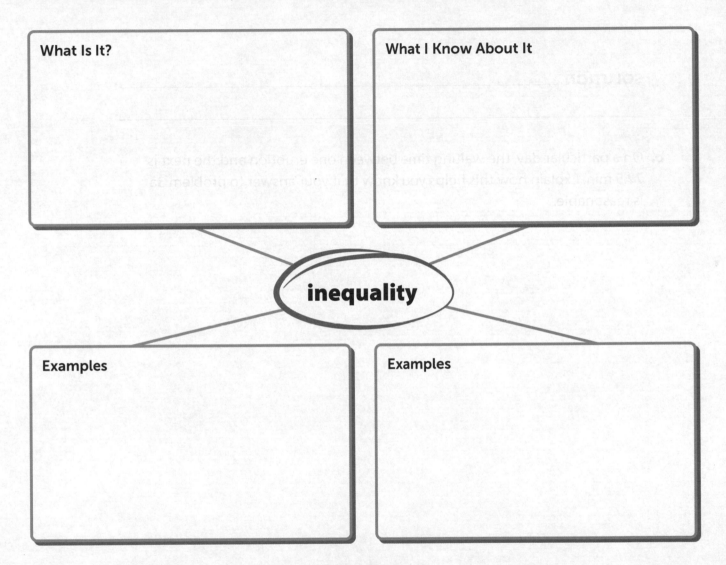

What Is It?

What I Know About It

inequality

Examples

Examples

2 On a horizontal number line, $-\frac{7}{9}$ is to the right of $-\frac{4}{5}$. Write two inequalities, using $<$ and $>$, to compare the values.

3 Many visitors to Yellowstone National Park see the geyser Old Faithful. The waiting time between eruptions is more than 59 min.

a. What are all of the possible waiting times between eruptions? Show your work.

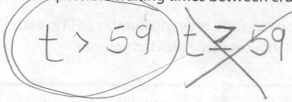

SOLUTION _____

_____

b. On a particular day, the waiting time between one eruption and the next is 72.5 min. Explain how this helps you know that your answer to problem 3a is reasonable.

Develop Representing Inequalities

➤ **Read and try to solve the problem below.**

Andre and his friends are participating in a gumbo cook-off.
The rules for each team are shown below. $q > 20$

Rule 1: Each team must prepare more than 20 qt of gumbo. $w < 10$

Rule 2: The width of each team's booth must be under 10 ft.

Use words, symbols, or pictures to describe all of the values that are possible for each rule.

  Math Toolkit number lines

DISCUSS IT

Ask: What are the advantages and disadvantages in your way of describing the values?

Share: In my way, the advantages are . . . The disadvantages are . . .

➤ **Explore different ways to represent inequality situations.**

Andre and his friends are participating in a gumbo cook-off. The rules are shown below.

Rule 1: Each team must prepare more than 20 qt of gumbo.

Rule 2: The width of each team's booth must be under 10 ft.

Use words, symbols, or pictures to describe all of the values that are possible for each rule.

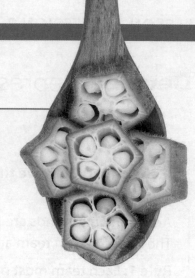

Many gumbo recipes include okra.

Picture It

You can draw a graph to show all values greater than or less than a given value.

Rule 1

Shade all values that are *more than 20.*

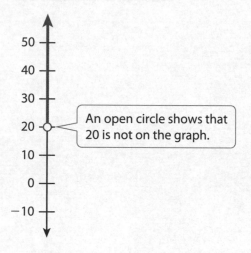

An open circle shows that 20 is not on the graph.

Rule 2

Shade all values that are *under 10.*

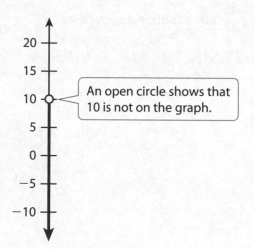

An open circle shows that 10 is not on the graph.

Model It

You can write an inequality with a variable.

Rule 1

Let *g* be a number of quarts of gumbo.

g must be more than 20.

 g **is greater than** 20.

  $g > 20$

Rule 2

Let *w* be the width of a booth in feet.

w must be under 10.

 w **is less than** 10.

  $w < 10$

➤ **Use the problem from the previous page to help you understand how to represent inequality situations.**

1 Look at Rule 1 in **Picture It**. List at least five numbers that are *more than 20*. Why is the number line shaded above 20? Why is the graph shown as an arrow?

2 How do the graph and the inequality for Rule 2 represent the same numbers?

3 The graph for Rule 2 represents all of the solutions of the inequality $w < 10$. Why is 10 not a point on the graph?

4 Cece wrote the inequality for Rule 1 as $20 < g$. Write this inequality in words. Why is $20 < g$ also an inequality that represents all numbers greater than 20?

5 Write the inequality for Rule 2 using the symbol $>$.

6 Think about how graphs and inequalities represent all numbers greater than or less than a given value. What are the advantages of a graph? What are the advantages of an inequality?

7 **Reflect** Think about all the models and strategies you have discussed today. Describe how one of them helped you better understand how to solve the **Try It** problem.

Apply It

➤ **Use what you learned to solve these problems.**

More than 3/4 lb in every basket!

8 At a farm stand, every basket of strawberries weighs more than
$\frac{3}{4}$ lb. Draw a graph and write an inequality to represent the
weight in pounds, *w*, of a basket of strawberries.

9 Which of the following can be represented by the inequality $x < 3$?
Select all that apply.

A The price decreases by $3.

B The temperature is below 3°F.

C The airplane's elevation is higher than 3 mi.

D
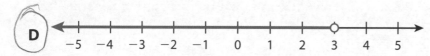

E
```
←──┼──┼──┼──┼──┼──┼──┼──┼──○──┼──┼──→
  −5  −4  −3  −2  −1   0   1   2   3   4   5
```

10 A state park has several campsites. All of the campsites are at an elevation of less
than 6 m. An elevation of 0 m represents sea level. Use an inequality and a graph
to represent the possible elevations of a campsite in the park.

$x < 6$

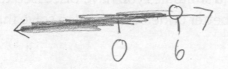

©Curriculum Associates, LLC   Copying is not permitted.

Name:

Practice Representing Inequalities

➤ **Study the Example showing how to represent an inequality.
Then solve problems 1–5.**

Example

An elevation of 0 m represents sea level. At a marine reserve, the elevation of every coral reef is higher than −10 m. Draw a graph and write an inequality to represent the possible elevations of a coral reef.

The elevation in meters can be any value that is greater than −10.

Use a number line to draw a graph.

Shade all values **greater than** −10. These are all values **above** −10.

Use a variable to write an inequality.

Let e = the elevation in meters of a coral reef.

e is greater than −10.

$$e > -10$$

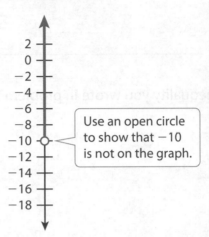

Use an open circle to show that −10 is not on the graph.

---

1. In the Example, suppose all of the coral reefs are below an elevation of −10 m.

   a. Describe how you could change the graph in the Example to show the possible elevations of a coral reef.

   b. Describe how you could change the inequality in the Example to show the possible elevations of a coral reef. Write the inequality.

2. Write an inequality for the graph. Use the variable y.

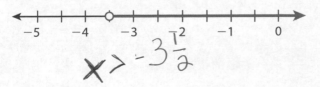

$$x > -3\tfrac{1}{2}$$

SOLUTION _____

Vocabulary

inequality
a mathematical statement that uses an inequality symbol to show the relationship between values of expressions.

An observation deck

3 A skyscraper has an observation deck. There are always 5 employees on the deck. At any time, there must be fewer than 40 people on the deck.

a. Write an inequality that represents the number of visitors, v, who can be on the deck at any time. Show your work.

SOLUTION _____

b. Graph the inequality you wrote in problem 3a.

4 Which of these values would be on a graph of the inequality $45 > n$? Select all that apply.

A 50   B −75

C 0   D 15

E 45   F −5

5 A laboratory has several freezers. The temperature in every freezer is less than $-2\frac{1}{2}$°F. Draw a graph and write an inequality to represent the possible temperatures in a freezer.

Develop Writing and Graphing One-Variable Inequalities

➤ **Read and try to solve the problem below.**

Sea level is at an elevation 0 ft. Some parts of a cave are below sea level. Visitors to the cave can choose from two different tours. The sign shows the elevations visitors explore on each tour. Use words, symbols, or pictures to describe all of the elevations that visitors may explore on each tour.

Mystery Cave TOURS

Standard	Advanced
Elevations: 16 m or less	Elevations: less than −8 m

 TRY IT

 Math Toolkit number lines

DISCUSS IT

Ask: How does your strategy or model describe *all* the possible elevations on each tour?

Share: My strategy or model includes . . .

➤ **Explore different ways to write and graph one-variable inequalities.**

Sea level is at an elevation 0 ft. Some parts of a cave are below sea level. Visitors to the cave can choose from two different tours. The table shows the elevations visitors explore on each tour. Use words, symbols, or pictures to describe all of the elevations that visitors may explore on each tour.

Tour	Elevations
Standard	16 m or less
Advanced	Less than −8 m

Model It

You can use symbols to write an inequality with a variable.

Standard Tour

Let *s* be an elevation in meters on the tour.

Either   *s* is less than 16   or   *s* is equal to 16.

$$s < 16 \quad \text{or} \quad s = 16$$

$$s \leq 16$$

less than or equal to

Advanced Tour

Let *a* be an elevation in meters on the tour.

a is less than −8.

$$a < -8$$

Model It

You can use a number line graph to show the solutions of an inequality.

Standard Tour

$s \leq 16$

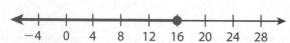

Advanced Tour

$a < -8$

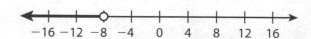

➤ **Use the problem from the previous page to help you understand how to write and graph one-variable inequalities.**

1 Look at the first **Model It**. The inequality for the Standard tour uses a symbol that combines the less than symbol (<) with the equal sign (=). Why do you need to use *equal to*, as well as *less than*, when describing all possible values for *s*?

2 Why does the inequality for the Advanced tour use only the *less than* symbol?

3 Look at the second **Model It**. Why does one graph have a closed circle at the end of the arrow, while the other graph has an open circle?

4 Raúl uses a *greater than or equal to* symbol (≥) to write the inequality $16 \geq s$. Does this inequality also represent the graph for the Standard tour? Explain.

5 When you write an inequality with a variable, how do you decide which inequality symbol to use (<, >, ≤, or ≥)?

6 **Reflect** Think about all the models and strategies you have discussed today. Describe how one of them helped you better understand how to write and graph one-variable inequalities.

Apply It

➤ **Use what you learned to solve these problems.**

7 Leah plans to drive from Memphis to Jackson. She looks up driving routes between the cities. She finds that there is no driving route with a distance under 208 mi. Write an inequality that represents the number of miles, *m*, Leah might drive. Show your work.

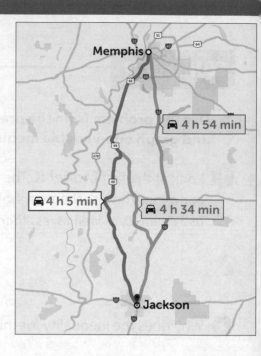

SOLUTION _____

8 Which inequality describes the values shown on the number line?

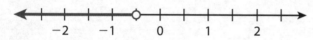

A $\frac{1}{2} > x$

B $-\frac{1}{2} > x$

C $\frac{1}{2} \geq x$

D $-\frac{1}{2} \geq x$

9 At a theme park, visitors must be at least 36 in. tall to ride the roller coaster alone. Write and graph an inequality to show the heights of visitors who may ride the roller coaster alone.

Practice Writing and Graphing One-Variable Inequalities

➤ **Study the Example showing how to write and graph an inequality. Then solve problems 1–5.**

Example

Kazuko's score on a game show is no more than −15. Write and graph an inequality to show Kazuko's possible scores.

Let s be a possible score.

The phrase *no more than* means that s could be −15, but s could not be greater than −15.

So, s must be less than or equal to −15.

$s \leq -15$

Graph the inequality $s \leq -15$. Use a solid circle at −15 because it is included as a solution of the inequality.

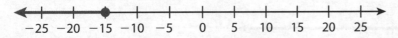

1 **a.** Write the inequality from the Example so that the variable s is on the right side of the inequality.

b. Does writing the inequality with the variable on the right change the values that are solutions of the inequality? Explain.

2 Chase buys 200 yd of thread. He uses some of the thread to make a costume. Write an inequality to show the possible lengths of thread that Chase has left. Show your work.

SOLUTION _____

3 There are at least 12 people on a bus.

   a. Write and graph an inequality to show the number of people who may be on the bus.

   b. Three people get on the bus at the next stop and no one gets off. Write an inequality that represents the number of people who may be on the bus now. Explain your thinking.

4 The possible values for the variable *n* are shown on the number line. Write an inequality for values of *n* so that the variable appears on the right side of the inequality. Show your work.

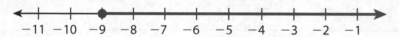

   SOLUTION _____

5 At Central Theatre, the cost of a matinee movie is under $5.50. The cost of a popcorn is exactly $2.25. Write an inequality for the possible total cost, *c*, of a movie and popcorn. Show your work.

   SOLUTION _____

Develop Using Substitution to Identify Solutions of Inequalities

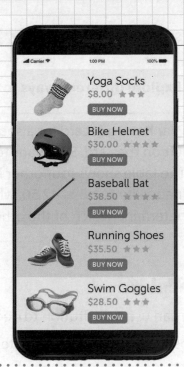

Yoga Socks
$8.00 ★ ★ ★
BUY NOW

Bike Helmet
$30.00 ★ ★ ★ ★

BUY NOW

Baseball Bat
$38.50 ★ ★ ★ ★
BUY NOW

Running Shoes
$35.50 ★ ★ ★
BUY NOW

Swim Goggles
$28.50 ★ ★ ★
BUY NOW

➤ **Read and try to solve the problem below.**

Pilar has a gift card for a sporting goods store. She has $42.50 left on the card. She plans to buy one pair of yoga socks for $8. There are four other items that she is looking at. Use the inequality $x + 8 \leq 42.50$, where x is the price of an item, to determine which of the other four items Pilar can buy.

TRY IT

Math Toolkit number lines

DISCUSS IT

Ask: How did you use the inequality when solving the problem?

Share: I used the inequality by . . .

➤ **Explore different ways to identify solutions of an inequality.**

Pilar has a gift card for a sporting goods store. She has $42.50 left on the card. She plans to buy one pair of yoga socks for $8. The table shows four other items that she is looking at. Use the inequality $x + 8 \leq 42.50$, where x is the price of an item, to determine which of the other four items Pilar can buy.

Item	Price
Bike helmet	$30.00
Baseball bat	$38.50
Running shoes	$35.50
Swim goggles	$28.50

Model It

You can use substitution to decide whether a value is a solution of an inequality.

Substitute the price of each item for x in the inequality $x + 8 \leq 42.50$.

Item	Swim goggles	Bike helmet	Running shoes	Baseball bat
Price	28.50	30.00	35.50	38.50
Inequality	$28.50 + 8 \leq 42.50$ $36.50 \leq 42.50$	$30.00 + 8 \leq 42.50$ $38.00 \leq 42.50$	$35.50 + 8 \leq 42.50$ $43.50 \leq 42.50$	$38.50 + 8 \leq 42.50$ $46.50 \leq 42.50$
True or False?	True	True	False	False

Analyze It

You can use an equation and a graph to identify solutions of an inequality.

Think: For what value of x is $x + 8 = 42.50$?

$$x + 8 = 42.50$$
$$x + 8 - 8 = 42.50 - 8$$
$$x = 34.50$$

If x is a value less than 34.50, $x + 8$ will be less than 42.50.

If x is a value greater than 34.50, $x + 8$ will be greater than 42.50.

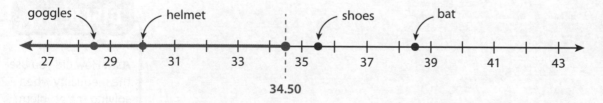

CONNECT IT

➤ **Use the problem from the previous page to help you understand how to identify solutions of an inequality.**

1 Look at **Model It**. How do you know if a value is a solution of an inequality?

2 Which numbers in the set {28.5, 30, 35.5, 38.5} are solutions of the inequality $x + 8 \leq 42.50$? Which of the items at the sporting goods store can Pilar buy?

3 The table shows the items listed in order from least price to greatest price. How does organizing the information this way relate to the graph in **Analyze It**? Where would an item with a price of $34.50 be in the table?

4 How does solving the equation $x + 8 = 42.50$ help you identify solutions of the inequality $x + 8 < 42.50$?

5 Suppose you are given the inequality $10 > 2.5x$ along with a set of 20 values. Describe how you could decide which values are solutions of the inequality.

6 **Reflect** Think about all the models and strategies you have discussed today. Describe how one of them helped you better understand how to identify solutions of an inequality.

Apply It

➤ **Use what you learned to solve these problems.**

7 Aimee works up to 50 hours a month and earns $12 per hour. She wants to save
more than $240 to buy a computer. The inequality $12h > 240$, where h is the
number of hours Aimee works this month, models this situation. Which values
from 0 to 50 are solutions of the inequality? What do the solutions mean in this
situation? Explain your reasoning.

8 Which of the following values of c are solutions of the inequality $c - 2 < 16$?
Select all that apply.

A 2   B 16

C 17.5   D 18

E 20

9 Hiroaki has 23 keychains in his collection. He has a goal of collecting at least 30
keychains. He uses the inequality $30 \leq 23 + x$, where x is a number of keychains,
to represent how he can reach his goal. Which values in the set {6, 7, 8}
are solutions of Hiroaki's inequality? Show your work.

SOLUTION _____

Practice Using Substitution to Identify Solutions of Inequalities

➤ **Study the Example showing how to use substitution to identify solutions of an inequality. Then solve problems 1–5.**

Example

Fadil's car travels 26 mi per gallon of gas used. He plans to drive less than 400 mi this week. The inequality $26g < 400$, where g is a number of gallons of gas models this situation. Which values in the set {12, 15, 18} are solutions of the inequality? What do the solutions mean in this situation?

Substitute the given values for g. Determine whether each value makes a true or false statement.

$$26 \cdot g \ < 400$$

$g = 12$	$26 \cdot 12 < 400$	$312 < 400$	← True
$g = 15$	$26 \cdot 15 < 400$	$390 < 400$	← True
$g = 18$	$26 \cdot 18 < 400$	$468 < 400$	← False

The values 12 and 15 are solutions of the inequality $26g < 400$.

Fadil can use 12 gal or 15 gal of gas and still drive less than 400 mi.

---

1. Show that 20 is not a solution of the inequality in the Example. Explain what this means about Fadil's driving this week.

2. Is 4.5 a solution of the inequality $13 < 3x$? Show your work.

> **Vocabulary**
>
> **solution of an inequality**
> a value that can be substituted for a variable to make an inequality true.

SOLUTION _____

3 Ellie needs more than 10 packs of thread to make friendship bracelets for her classmates. She already has 6 packs of thread. She models this situation with the inequality $6 + p > 10$, where p is a number of packs of thread. Which values in the set {4, 5, 6, 7} are solutions of Ellie's inequality? Show your work.

SOLUTION _____

4 Noah writes the inequality $y + 3 > -2$. He says that every positive value of y is a solution of the inequality. Is he correct? Explain.

5 A shower uses 2.5 gal of water each minute. Yolanda wants to be sure each shower she takes uses no more than 15 gal of water. She writes the inequality $2.5m \leq 15$, where m is a number of minutes. Which values from 0 to 100 are solutions of the inequality? What do the solutions tell you? Explain your reasoning.

2.5 gallons per minute

Refine Writing and Graphing One-Variable Inequalities

➤ **Complete the Example below. Then solve problems 1–9.**

Example

A city bus tour only runs if there are more than 15 passengers. The bus can hold a total of 65 passengers. Write two inequalities to describe the number of passengers, *p,* on a bus tour.

Look at how you could use a graph to show the possible numbers of passengers.

p must be greater than 15.

p must also be less than or equal to 65.

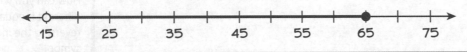

SOLUTION _____

CONSIDER THIS . . .
The graph shows all values of *p* that make both inequalities true.

PAIR/SHARE
What is an example of a value for *p* that is a solution of one of the inequalities but not both inequalities?

Apply It

1 Which values in the set {1, 1.5, 2, 2.5} are solutions of the inequality $8 + 12h \le 35$? Show your work.

CONSIDER THIS . . .
Think about the order of operations when testing if each value from the set is a solution.

PAIR/SHARE
How would your answer be different if you replaced 35 with 30 in the inequality?

SOLUTION _____

2 Each week, Patrick buys more than 2 pounds of apples. Apples cost $1.37 per pound. Draw a graph that represents the possible amounts of money, m, that Patrick spends on apples in a week. Then write an inequality that represents your graph. Show your work.

CONSIDER THIS...
Since Patrick buys more than 2 pounds of apples, he must spend more than the cost of 2 pounds of apples.

PAIR/SHARE
How can you write a different inequality by reversing the inequality symbol?

SOLUTION _____

3 Tiana cannot read traffic signs that are more than 50 m away. Which inequality represents the distances, d, at which Tiana *can* read traffic signs?

A $d > 50$

B $d \geq 50$

C $d < 50$

D $d \leq 50$

Erik chose A as the correct answer. How might he have gotten that answer?

CONSIDER THIS...
You can use a number line to represent the distances at which Tiana can read traffic signs.

PAIR/SHARE
How can you check that you chose the correct inequality?

4 Every Sunday, Sarah makes trail mix for the week. She always makes more than $3\frac{1}{2}$ cups of the mix. Then she divides it equally into 7 bags. Write an inequality for the number of cups of trail mix, x, in each bag. Show your work.

SOLUTION _____

5 Which values are solutions of the inequality $|y| < 3$? Select all that apply.

A -4 **B** -3

C -1.5 **D** 2

E 2.4   **F** 3

6 Every student at Ria's school lives no more than $4\frac{1}{2}$ mi from the school.

Tell whether each inequality represents this situation. Choose *Yes* or *No*.

	Yes	No
a. $4\frac{1}{2} > x$	○	○
b. $4\frac{1}{2} \geq x$	○	○
c. $x \leq 4\frac{1}{2}$	○	○
d. $x > 4\frac{1}{2}$	○	○

7. Pedro wants to make a square pen for his goats. He plans that the pen will have a perimeter of at most 60 ft and that a side of the pen will be at least 10 ft long. He has enough money to buy fencing for a pen as large as 40 ft on a side.

   a. The inequality $4n \leq 60$ models the amount of fence Pedro will use for a pen with side length n ft. Which values from 10 to 40 are solutions of the inequality? Write your answer using two inequalities.

   SOLUTION _____

   b. What do the solutions mean about the amount of fence Pedro will buy?

8. A student says that the inequality $0 \leq |z|$ is true for all values of z. Is the student correct? Explain.

9. **Math Journal** Write an inequality with a variable on one side, a negative integer on the other side, and one of the inequality symbols ($<$, $>$, $\leq$, or $\geq$) in between. Give a value that is a solution of the inequality and a value that is not a solution of the inequality. Then show how to graph the inequality.

✓ End of Lesson Checklist

☐ **INTERACTIVE GLOSSARY** Find the entry for *solution of an inequality*. Tell how solutions of inequalities and solutions of equations are alike.

☐ **SELF CHECK** Go back to the Unit 6 Opener and see what you can check off.

Dear Family,

This week your student is exploring the four-quadrant coordinate plane.

Previously, your student plotted points (x, y) in the upper right **quadrant** of the coordinate plane, where all x-coordinates and y-coordinates are positive. The four-quadrant coordinate plane extends the x-axis and y-axis to include points with negative coordinates.

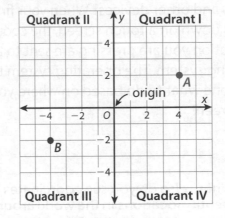

To plot point A at (4, 2), move **4 units right** and **2 units up** from the origin. To plot point B at (−4, −2), move **4 units left** and **2 units down** from the origin.

Your student will be describing the location of points like the one below.

Point S and T are shown in the coordinate plane. Describe the location of point S.

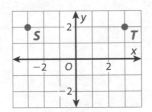

➤ **ONE WAY** to describe the location of a point is with coordinates.

Point S is 3 units left of the origin, which means the x-coordinate is −3. Point S is 2 units up from the origin, which means the y-coordinate is 2. The coordinates of point S are (−3, 2).

➤ **ANOTHER WAY** is to describe how the given point is related to another point.

Point T is 3 units to the right of the y-axis. Point S is 3 units to the left of the y-axis and on the same horizontal line as point T. This means point S is a **reflection** of point T across the y-axis.

Both ways of describing the location of point S help you understand the four-quadrant coordinate plane.

 Use the next page to start a conversation about the coordinate plane.

Activity Thinking About Coordinate Planes Around You

➤ **Do this activity together to investigate coordinate planes in the real world.**

Did you know that technology companies use coordinates to develop touch screens on cell phones and other devices? When your finger presses down on a touch screen, the coordinates of the location you are pressing are sent to the phone's operating system. The operating system then tells the phone what to do based on where you touched your screen!

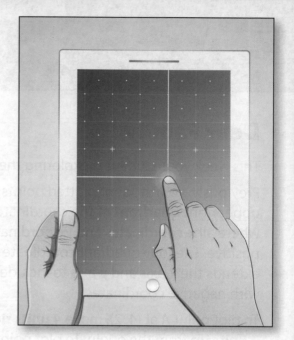

? Where else do you see coordinates being used to identify locations in the world around you?

Explore The Four-Quadrant Coordinate Plane

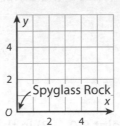

Model It

➤ **Complete the problems about the coordinate plane.**

1 A treasure map is drawn in the coordinate plane with Spyglass Rock at the origin. The *x*-axis points east and the *y*-axis points north.

a. The map states that a diamond is located at (1, 3). Plot a point to show the location of the diamond. Label the point with its coordinates.

b. The map says a diamond can be found 4 units east and 2 units north of Spyglass Rock. Plot a point to show the location of the diamond and label the point with its coordinates.

2 To show locations west and south of Spyglass Rock, the axes in the coordinate plane can be extended to show negative numbers. The axes intersect at the origin and divide the coordinate plane into four regions, or **quadrants**.

a. To plot the point for a ruby at (−3, 1),

move 3 units _____ and

1 unit _____ from the origin.

b. The map says a black pearl can be found 2 units west and 4 units south of Spyglass Rock. Plot a point to show the location of the black pearl and label the point with its coordinates.

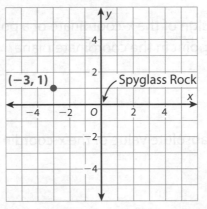

DISCUSS IT

Ask: Why does it make sense that the *x*-coordinate of a point to the left of the origin is negative?

Share: I think that a negative *y*-coordinate means that . . .

◎ Learning Targets SMP 2, SMP 3, SMP 7
• Understand signs of numbers in ordered pairs as indicating locations in quadrants of the coordinate plane; recognize that when two ordered pairs differ only by signs, the locations of the points are related by reflections across one or both axes.
• Find and position pairs of integers and other rational numbers on a coordinate plane.

Model It

➤ **Complete the problems about ordered pairs with negative coordinates.**

3 The coordinate plane shows point A.

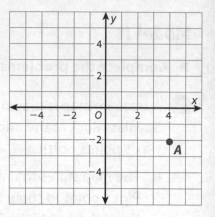

    a. Describe how to move along grid lines from the origin to point A in two steps.

    b. How can you use your answer to problem 3a to write the ordered pair for point A? What is the ordered pair for point A?

    c. Plot and label point $B(0, -3)$ in the coordinate plane. How do you know where to plot point B?

4 **a.** What does the sign of the x-coordinate of a point tell you about the location of the point in the coordinate plane?

    b. What does the absolute value of the x-coordinate tell you?

> **DISCUSS IT**
>
> **Ask:** What do all points that are to the right of the origin have in common?
>
> **Share:** I can tell from coordinates if a point is above or below the origin by . . .

5 **Reflect** What does it mean when the x-coordinate of an ordered pair is negative? What does it mean when the y-coordinate is negative?

Prepare for Understanding the Four-Quadrant Coordinate Plane

1 Think about what you know about the coordinate plane. Fill in each box. Use words, numbers, and pictures. Show as many ideas as you can.

Word	In My Own Words	Example
x-axis		
y-axis		
origin		
x-coordinate		
y-coordinate		

2 The ordered pair for point *A* is (4, 0). Avery says that point *A* is on the *x*-axis. Is Avery correct? Explain.

➤ **Complete problems 3–5.**

3 A map is shown in the coordinate plane, with City Hall at the origin.

a. To plot the point for a library at (2, −3), move 2 units _____

and 3 units _____ from the origin.

b. A movie theater is located 4 units left and 4 units up from City Hall. Plot a point to show the location of the movie theater and label the point with its coordinates.

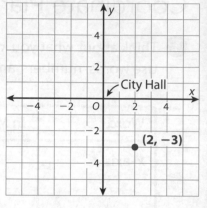

4 The coordinate plane shows point J.

a. Describe how to move from the origin to point J.

b. How can you use your answer to problem 4a to write the ordered pair for point J? What is the ordered pair for point J?

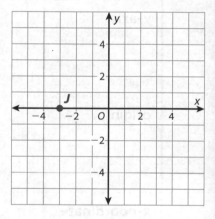

c. Plot and label point K(−4, −5) in the coordinate plane. How do you know where to plot point K?

5 **a.** What does the sign of the y-coordinate of a point tell you about the location of the point in the coordinate plane?

b. What does the absolute value of the y-coordinate tell you?

Develop Understanding of the Four-Quadrant Coordinate Plane

Model It: Quadrants

➤ **Try these two problems about points in the four-quadrant coordinate plane.**

1   The quadrants in the coordinate plane are numbered 1 to 4 using the Roman numerals I, II, III, and IV. Depending on the quadrant, coordinates can be positive or negative.

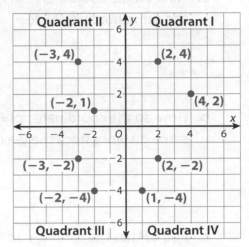

a. Look at the points in Quadrant III. What do you notice about the signs of the coordinates of these points?

b. What is the same about the signs of the coordinates of points in Quadrants II and IV? What is different about the signs of the coordinates of points in these two quadrants?

2   The coordinate plane shows point A(3, 2).

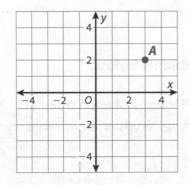

a. Plot and label point B(−3, 2). What is the same about points A and B? What is different?

b. Plot and label point C(3, −2). What is the same about points A and C? What is different?

Model It: Reflections

➤ **Try this problem about points with opposite coordinates.**

3 Points *F* and *G* are on the same horizontal line. They are the same distance from the *y*-axis and on opposite sides of it. This means they are **reflections** of each other across the *y*-axis.

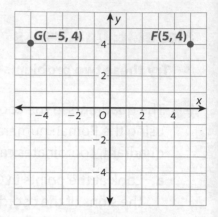

a. How do the coordinates of *F* and *G* show that these points are on the same horizontal line?

b. How do the coordinates of *F* and *G* show that these points are the same distance from the *y*-axis but on opposite sides?

c. Point *H* has the same *x*-coordinate as point *F* but the opposite *y*-coordinate. Plot point *H*, and label it with its coordinates.

d. Explain why *F* and *H* are reflections of each other across the *x*-axis.

DISCUSS IT

Ask: How is point *G* related to point *H*?

Share: I think you could call point *G* the *mirror image* of point *F* because . . .

CONNECT IT

➤ **Complete the problems below.**

4 Two points are reflections of each other across the *y*-axis. The *y*-coordinate of each point is positive. In which quadrants are the points? Explain how you know.

5 Point *P* has coordinates (−2.5, 3). Point *Q* is a reflection of point *P* across the *x*-axis. What are the coordinates of point *Q*? Which quadrant is it in? Draw a graph to show how you know.

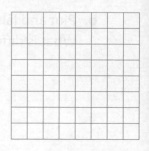

Practice Locating Points in the Four-Quadrant Coordinate Plane

➤ **Study how the Example shows using points in the four-quadrant coordinate plane. Then solve problems 1–4.**

Example

Point A is at (4, 3). The x-coordinate of point B is the opposite of the x-coordinate of point A. The y-coordinates of the two points are the same. Points A and B are related by a reflection across which axis?

Use the coordinates of point A to find the coordinates of point B.

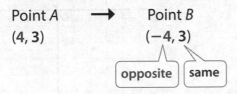

Point A   →   Point B

(4, 3)   (−4, 3)

opposite   same

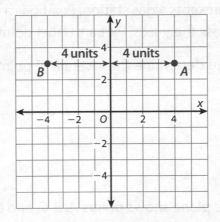

Points A and B are the same distance from the y-axis, but on opposite sides. They are also on the same horizontal line.

Points A and B are related by a reflection across the y-axis.

1   The x-coordinate of point C is the same as the x-coordinate of point B in the Example. The y-coordinate of point C is the opposite of the y-coordinate of point B.

   a. Plot point C on the coordinate plane in the Example.

   b. Points B and C are related by a reflection across which axis? Explain.

2   In which quadrant of the coordinate plane is point J(1, −2)? Explain how you know. Draw a graph to show the location of point J.

Vocabulary

quadrants
the four regions of the coordinate plane that are formed when the x-axis and y-axis intersect at the origin.

reflection
when a figure is flipped (reflected) across a line to form a mirror image.

    LESSON 27 Understand the Four-Quadrant Coordinate Plane   **617**

3 The table shows the coordinates of several locations.

Location	Coordinates
Middle school	$M(-2, -3)$
High school	$H(1, -2)$
Post office	$P(0, -4)$
Restaurant	$R(-5, 4)$

a. In which quadrant is the middle school located? How can you tell by looking at the signs of the coordinates?

b. Plot a point for each location in the table. Label the point with its letter name.

c. Point G represents a gas station. Point G is a reflection of point R across the y-axis. Plot and label point G.

d. How did you determine the location of point G?

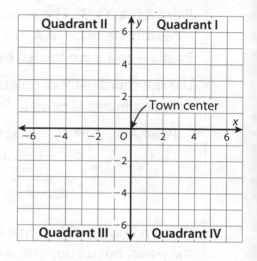

4 The coordinate plane shows points A, B, C, and D.

a. Label each point with its coordinates.

b. What is the same about the four points? What is different?

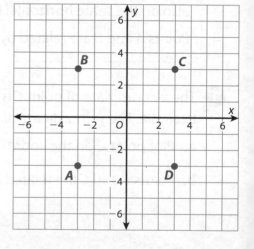

c. Describe how to use two reflections across an axis to move from point A to point C.

Refine Ideas About the Four-Quadrant Coordinate Plane

Apply It Math Toolkit graph paper

➤ **Complete problems 1–5.**

1 Analyze Enrique thinks of a point in the coordinate plane. The *y*-coordinate of the point is the opposite of its *x*-coordinate. In which quadrant or quadrants of the coordinate plane could this point be located? Explain how you know.

2 Evaluate Seth plots point *B* by reflecting point *A*(3.5, 4) across the *x*-axis and then reflecting the result across the *y*-axis. Seth says that point *B* has coordinates $(-4, -3.5)$. Use words and a graph to show why Seth is incorrect.

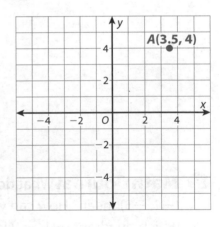

3 Relate Point *P* with coordinates (*a*, *b*) is in Quadrant I of the coordinate plane. Point *Q* has coordinates $(-a, b)$. In which quadrant is point *Q*? How are the locations of points *P* and *Q* related? Use words and draw a graph to explain.

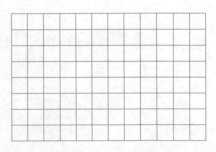

4 Zhen draws triangle *ABC* in the coordinate plane. She wants to draw a mirror image of the triangle by reflecting it across an axis. She begins by reflecting vertex *A* across the *x*-axis to point *R*.

PART A Reflect vertices *B* and *C* across the *x*-axis to points *S* and *T*. Then draw triangle *RST*.

PART B Write the ordered pair for each point.

Point *A* _____   Point *R* _____

Point *B* _____   Point *S* _____

Point *C* _____   Point *T* _____

PART C Look at the coordinates of points *A* and *R*, points *B* and *S*, and points *C* and *T*. How does reflecting a point across the *x*-axis change the point's coordinates? Why?

5 **Math Journal** What do the negative coordinates in the ordered pair (−1, −3) mean? How can you use the signs of the coordinates to determine which quadrant (−1, −3) is in? Include a graph in your response.

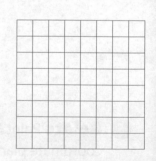

✓ End of Lesson Checklist

☐ **INTERACTIVE GLOSSARY** Find the entry for *reflection*. Add two important things you learned about the reflection of a point across the *x*- or *y*-axis in this lesson.

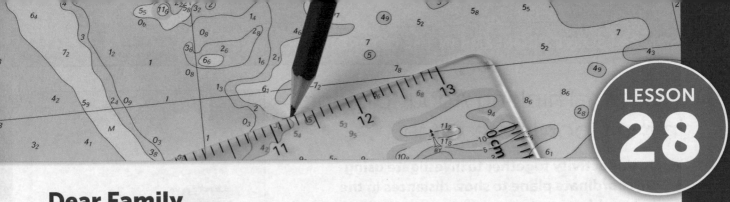

Dear Family,

This week your student is learning how to find the distance between points on the same horizontal or vertical line in the coordinate plane.

Point *A* and point *B* are in **different quadrants**. So, **add the absolute values** of the coordinates that are different to find the distance between *A* and *B*.

$$|-3| + |2| = 3 + 2 = 5$$

Point *D* and point *C* are in the **same quadrant**. So, **subtract the absolute values** of the coordinates that are different to find the distance between *D* and *C*.

$$|-4| - |-2| = 4 - 2 = 2$$

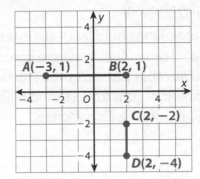

Your student will be learning to solve problems like the one below.

A rectangle has vertices at $A(-2, -1)$, $B(2, -1)$, $C(2, -3)$ and $D(-2, -3)$. What is the perimeter of the rectangle?

➤ **ONE WAY** to find the lengths of the sides is to use absolute value.

$AB = |-2| + |2| = 4$
$BC = |-3| - |-1| = 2$
$CD = |-2| + |2| = 4$
$AD = |-3| - |-1| = 2$
$4 + 2 + 4 + 2 = 12$

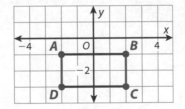

➤ **ANOTHER WAY** to is to use properties of polygons.

Opposite sides of rectangles have the same length.

$\ell = DC = |-2| + |2| = 4$
$w = DA = |-3| - |-1| = 2$
$2(4) + 2(2) = 12$

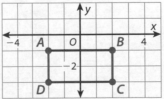

Using either method, the perimeter of the rectangle is 12 units.

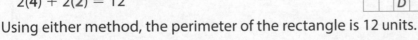

▶ Use the next page to start a conversation about coordinate planes.

Activity Thinking About Distance in the Coordinate Plane

➤ **Do this activity together to investigate using the coordinate plane to show distances in the real world.**

A land surveyor is someone who measures land to mark property boundaries, especially for construction of new buildings or houses.

Coordinate planes help land surveyors make precise maps that clearly identify where one person's property ends and another person's property begins. It would be a big problem if someone started building a new house right in someone else's backyard!

? How else can a coordinate plane be used when planning the construction of a new building or house?

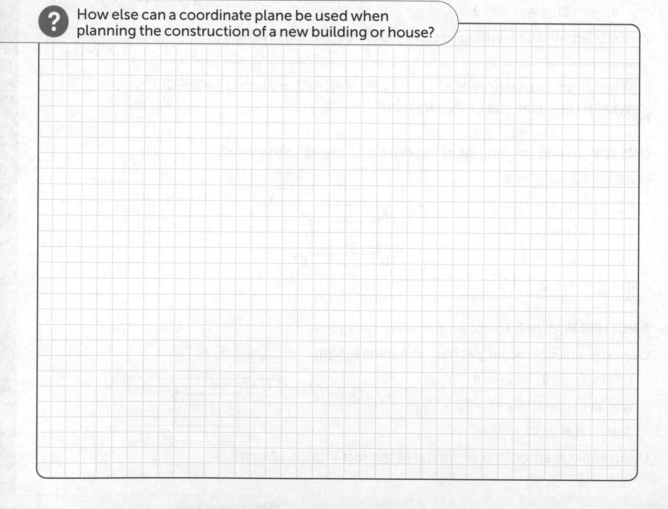

Explore Problems in the Coordinate Plane

Meek's Lake	3.5 mi	↑
Lookout Point	1.5 mi	→
Pilar's Rock	2.0 mi	↑
Sandy Creek	2.0 mi	←

Previously, you learned about the four-quadrant coordinate plane. In this lesson, you will learn about solving problems in the coordinate plane.

➤ **Use what you know to try to solve the problem below.**

A sign at an intersection of two snowshoe trails shows the distance along the trails to four locations. When traveling along the trails, how much farther is it from Sandy Creek to Lookout Point than it is from Pilar's Rock to Meek's Lake?

 TRY IT **Math Toolkit** graph paper

DISCUSS IT

Ask: How did you get started?

Share: I got started by thinking about . . .

Learning Targets SMP 1, SMP 2, SMP 3, SMP 4, SMP 5, SMP 6, SMP 7
- Solve problems by graphing points in all four quadrants of the coordinate plane. Use coordinates and absolute value to find distances between points with the same first coordinate or the same second coordinate.
- Draw polygons in the coordinate plane given coordinates for the vertices; use coordinates to find the length of a side joining points with the same first coordinate or the same second coordinate.

CONNECT IT

1 Look Back How much farther is it from Sandy Creek to Lookout Point than it is from Pilar's Rock to Meek's Lake? Explain how you know.

2 Look Ahead One way to find the distances between the locations on the snowshoe trails is to model the problem on the axes in a coordinate plane. You can find the distance between two points on an axis by using the distances of the points from the origin.

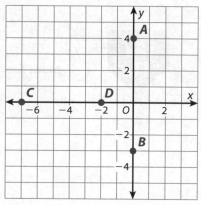

a. Points *A* and *B* are on the *y*-axis and on opposite sides of the origin. How many units is each of these points from the origin?

A: 4 units
B: 3 units

b. To find the distance between points *A* and *B*, do you add their distances from the origin or subtract them? Why?

A: (0,4)   C: (-7,0)   You add them because it will be a positive number that makes sense.
B: (0,-3)   D: (-2,0)

c. Points *C* and *D* are on the *x*-axis and on the same side of the origin. How many units is each of these points from the origin?

C: 7 units
D: 2 units

d. To find the distance between points *C* and *D*, do you add their distances from the origin or subtract them? Why?

You have to subtract them because it's on the x axis.

3 Reflect How can you determine the distance between any two points on an axis by using their distances from the origin?

Name:

Prepare for Solving Problems in the Coordinate Plane

1 Think about what you know about absolute value. Fill in each box. Use words, numbers, and pictures. Show as many ideas as you can.

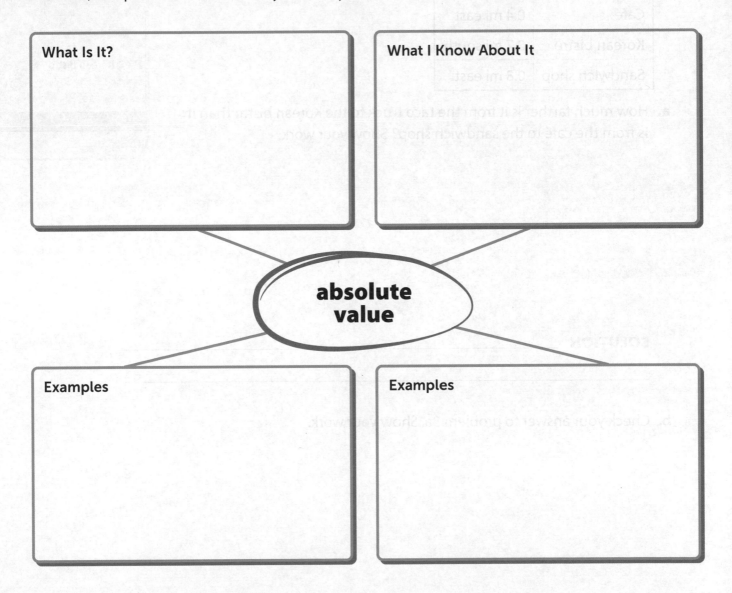

What Is It?

What I Know About It

absolute value

Examples

Examples

2 Morgan says that the absolute value of −8 is greater than the absolute value of 7. Do you agree with Morgan? Explain.

3 A map on Rodrigo's phone shows the distances from his apartment building to the nearest restaurants.

Restaurant	Distance
Taco truck	0.3 mi north
Café	0.4 mi east
Korean bistro	0.7 mi south
Sandwich shop	0.8 mi east

a. How much farther is it from the taco truck to the Korean bistro than it is from the café to the sandwich shop? Show your work.

SOLUTION _____

_____

b. Check your answer to problem 3a. Show your work.

Develop Finding Distance Between Points on a Horizontal or Vertical Line

➤ **Read and try to solve the problem below.**

Madison competes in a robotics challenge. For one task, she programs her robot to move to locations on a grid. The robot picks up a ball at point $A(-6, 3)$ and moves it first to point $B(-6, -4)$ and then to point $C(-2, -4)$ along straight paths. Each unit on the grid represents 1 ft. What is the total distance Madison's robot moves with the ball?

Robotics Challenge

1. Pick up ball at point $A(-6, 3)$.
2. Then, travel to point $B(-6, -4)$ along straight paths.
3. Then, travel to point $C(-2, -4)$ along straight paths.

  TRY IT **Math Toolkit** graph paper

DISCUSS IT

Ask: How does your model show distance?

Share: My model shows distance . . .

LESSON 28 Solve Problems in the Coordinate Plane   **627**

➤ **Explore different ways to find distance between points on a horizontal or vertical line.**

Madison competes in a robotics challenge. For one task, she programs her robot to move to locations on a grid. The robot picks up a ball at point $A(-6, 3)$ and moves it first to point $B(-6, -4)$ and then to point $C(-2, -4)$ along straight paths. Each unit on the grid represents 1 ft. What is the total distance Madison's robot moves with the ball?

Model It

You can use a graph to understand how to find the distance between points on a horizontal or vertical line.

Points $A(-6, 3)$ and $B(-6, -4)$ are on the same vertical line and opposite sides of the x-axis.

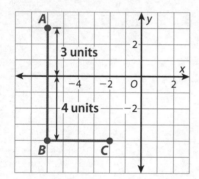

Use the distance of each point from the x-axis to find the distance between them.

Distance from A to $B = 3 + 4$

Points $B(-6, -4)$ and $C(-2, -4)$ are on the same horizontal line and the same side of the y-axis.

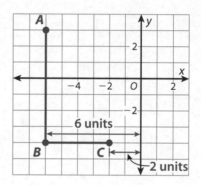

Use the distance of each point from the y-axis to find the distance between them.

Distance from B to $C = 6 - 2$

Analyze It

You can use absolute value to find the distance between points with the same first coordinate or the same second coordinate.

Points A and B have the same x-coordinate. Their y-coordinates have opposite signs.

$A(-6, \mathbf{3})$
$B(-6, \mathbf{-4})$ Distance from A to $B = |\mathbf{3}| + |\mathbf{-4}|$

Points C and D have the same y-coordinate. Their x-coordinates have the same sign.

$B(\mathbf{-6}, -4)$
$C(\mathbf{-2}, -4)$ Distance from B to $C = |\mathbf{-6}| - |\mathbf{-2}|$

➤ **Use the problem from the previous page to help you understand how to find the distance between points on a horizontal or vertical line.**

1 Look at **Model It**. Do you use *x*-coordinates or *y*-coordinates to find the distance between points *A* and *B*? Explain.

2 Look at the expression $|-6| + |-2|$ in **Analyze It**. What distances do $|-6|$ and $|-2|$ represent in the coordinate plane in **Model It**?

3 Why do you add to find the distance between points *A* and *B*?

4 Why do you subtract to find the distance between points *B* and *C*?

5 What is the total distance Madison's robot moves with the ball? How do you know?

6 How is finding the distance between two points on a horizontal line affected by whether the points are on the same side of the *y*-axis or on different sides?

7 **Reflect** Think about all the models and strategies you have discussed today. Describe how one of them helped you better understand how to solve the **Try It** problem.

Apply It

➤ **Use what you learned to solve these problems.**

8 **a.** Reflect point *B* across the *x*-axis and label the point *C*. What is the distance between points *B* and *C*? Show your work.

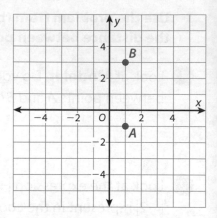

SOLUTION _____

b. Why do you always add the absolute values when finding the distance between a point and its reflection across an axis?

9 What is the distance between point *J*(−8.5, 6) and point *K*(5.5, 6)?

A 3 units

B 4 units

C 12 units

D 14 units

10 A map of an airport is laid out in a coordinate plane. Distances on the map are in miles. An airplane starts at a gate at (0, 0.1). To reach a runway, the plane travels west to (−0.4, 0.1), then south to (−0.4, −0.8), and then west to (−0.8, −0.8). What is the total distance the plane travels? Show your work.

SOLUTION _____

Practice Finding Distance Between Points on a Horizontal or Vertical Line

➤ **Study the Example showing how to find distance between points on a horizontal or vertical line. Then solve problems 1–5.**

Example

What is the distance between point J(−3, −4) and point K(4, −4) in the coordinate plane?

You can use coordinates and absolute value to find the distance between points on a horizontal or vertical line.

Points J and K are on the same horizontal line. Because the points are in different quadrants, you can add their distances to the y-axis to find the distance between them.

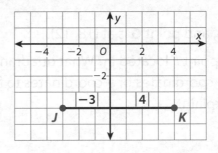

$$|-3| + |4| = 3 + 4$$
$$= 7$$

The distance between points J and K is 7 units.

1. Point L is located at (4, −1). Plot point L. Explain how to use absolute value to find the distance between point L and point K.

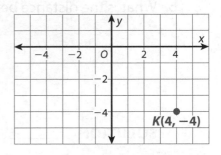

2. A map in the coordinate plane shows the distance between two cities in miles. The x-axis runs east/west, and the y-axis runs north/south. The town of Elgin is located at (−3, 2). The town of McDade is 8 mi east and 4.5 mi south of Elgin. Plot and label the locations of both towns in the coordinate plane.

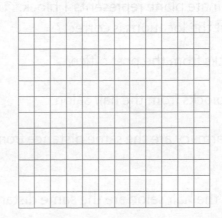

Vocabulary

quadrants
the four regions of the coordinate plane that are formed when the x-axis and y-axis intersect at the origin.

3 Jasmine walks east from her house to a tennis court. She plays for 1.5 hours and then walks home. Her walking speed is 3 miles per hour. Distances on the map are in miles. For how many hours is Jasmine away from home? Show your work.

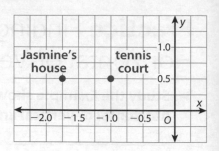

SOLUTION _____

4 Point *F* is at (−10, 12), and point *G* is at (18, 12).

a. What quadrant is point *F* located in? What quadrant is point *G* located in? Can you use the *x*-coordinates or *y*-coordinates to find the distance between points *F* and *G*? Explain.

b. What is the distance between points *F* and *G*? Show your work.

SOLUTION _____

5 The coordinate plane shows several locations in a neighborhood. Each unit on the coordinate plane represents 1 block. Which statement about the locations is correct?

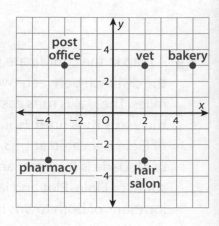

A The bakery is 6 blocks from the post office.

B The pharmacy is 5 blocks from the hair salon.

C The vet and the pharmacy are the same distance from the hair salon.

D The post office and the hair salon are the same distance from the vet.

Develop Solving Problems About Polygons in the Coordinate Plane

➤ **Read and try to solve the problem below.**

Archaeologists are studying a shipwreck on the ocean floor. The wreck site is roughly shaped like a parallelogram. The archaeologists make a map of the site in the coordinate plane. Each unit on the map represents 1 m. According to the map, what is the area of the wreck site?

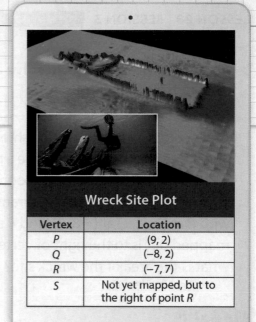

Wreck Site Plot

Vertex	Location
P	(9, 2)
Q	(−8, 2)
R	(−7, 7)
S	Not yet mapped, but to the right of point R

TRY IT

Math Toolkit graph paper, rulers

➤ **Explore different ways to solve a problem about a polygon in the coordinate plane.**

Archaeologists are studying a shipwreck on the ocean floor. The wreck site is roughly shaped like a parallelogram. The archaeologists make a map of the site in the coordinate plane. Each unit on the map represents 1 m. Parallelogram *PQRS* represents the wreck site, with *P* at (9, 2), *Q* at (−8, 2), and *R* at (−7, 7). Vertex *S* is not yet mapped but is to the right of vertex *R*. According to the map, what is the area of the wreck site?

Model It

You can use properties of polygons to draw the parallelogram in the coordinate plane.

Opposite sides of a parallelogram are parallel and have the same length. $\overline{QP}$ is horizontal, so $\overline{RS}$ must also be horizontal and have the same length.

$QP = |-8| + |9|$

$\quad = 8 + 9$

$\quad = 17$

$\overline{QP}$ has a length of 17 m, so $\overline{RS}$ also has a length of 17 m.

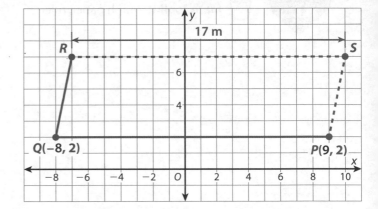

Model It

You can find the height of the parallelogram and use an area formula.

Use $\overline{QP}$ as the base of the parallelogram. Then a vertical segment joining $\overline{QP}$ to $\overline{RS}$ is the height.

$b = QP = 17$

$h = |7| - |2|$

$\quad = 7 - 2$

$\quad = 5$

Use the formula for the area of a parallelogram.

$A = b \cdot h$

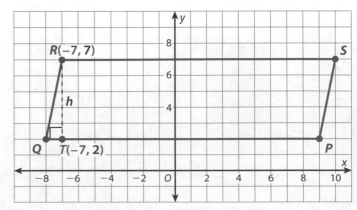

➤ **Use the problem from the previous page to help you understand how to solve problems about polygons in the coordinate plane.**

1 Look at the first **Model It**. What are the coordinates of point S? How does finding the length of $\overline{QP}$ help you locate point S?

2 How can you use points R and S to check that the length of $\overline{RS}$ is 17 m?

3 Look at the second **Model It**. The point where the height intersects the base is labeled T. Explain why the coordinates of T are $(-7, 2)$.

4 What is the area of the wreck site? Explain how you know.

5 How can you find the area or perimeter of a polygon in the coordinate plane when you know only the coordinates of its vertices?

6 **Reflect** Think about all the models and strategies you have discussed today. Describe how one of them helped you better understand how to solve the **Try It** problem.

Apply It

➤ **Use what you learned to solve these problems.**

7 Central Park in New York City is shaped like a rectangle. On a map of the park in the coordinate plane, three of the vertices are located at $(-1.25, -0.25)$, $(-1.25, 0.25)$, and $(1.25, 0.25)$. Distances on the map are in miles. What is the perimeter of Central Park? Show your work.

SOLUTION _____

8 Explain why the expression $\frac{1}{2} \cdot (|-5| + |5|)(|-4|)$ represents the area of triangle *RST*.

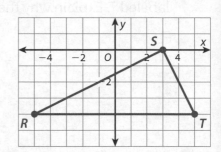

9 Trapezoid *FGHJ* has vertices at $F(2, -3)$, $G(2, 4)$, $H(6, 4)$, and $J(9, -3)$. What is the area of the trapezoid? Show your work.

SOLUTION _____

Practice Solving Problems About Polygons in the Coordinate Plane

➤ Study the Example showing how to solve problems about polygons in the coordinate plane. Then solve problems 1–5.

Example

A triangle has vertices at $A(-3, 2)$, $B(4, 6)$, and $C(4, 1)$ in the coordinate plane. What is the area of the triangle?

Use coordinates to find the base and height.

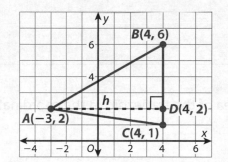

$b = BC$

$\quad = |6| - |1|$

$\quad = 6 - 1$

$\quad = 5$

$h = AD$

$\quad = |-3| + |4|$

$\quad = 3 + 4$

$\quad = 7$

$A = \frac{1}{2}bh$

$\quad = \frac{1}{2}(5)(7)$

$\quad = 17.5$

The area of the triangle is 17.5 square units.

1. How is the height of the triangle in the Example found once $\overline{BC}$ is selected as the base?

2. A rhombus is a four-sided figure with all sides the same length. Points $F(-2, -2)$, $G(-2, 3)$, and $H(2, 6)$ are three vertices of rhombus $FGHJ$. Vertex J is directly below vertex H.

   a. Graph rhombus $FGHJ$. Label J with its coordinates.

   b. What is the perimeter of the rhombus? Show your work.

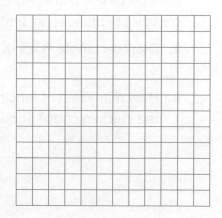

SOLUTION _____

3 A plan for a baseball diamond is drawn in a coordinate plane. The baseball diamond is in the shape of a square with vertices at approximately (0, 64), (64, 0), (0, −64), and (−64, 0). One unit in the coordinate plane represents 1 ft. What is the approximate area of the baseball diamond? Show your work.

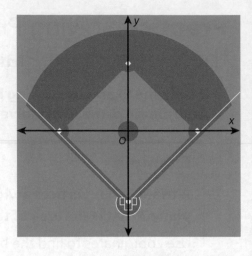

SOLUTION _____

4 What is the area of the trapezoid in the coordinate plane? Show your work.

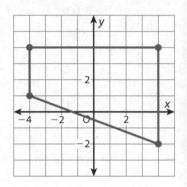

SOLUTION _____

5 Christopher is designing a rectangular fence to go around his school's chicken coop. The length should be 2 ft longer than the width. Christopher marks two vertices of the rectangle at *P* and *Q* in the coordinate plane. $\overline{PQ}$ is one of the shorter sides. Each unit in the coordinate plane represents 1 ft.

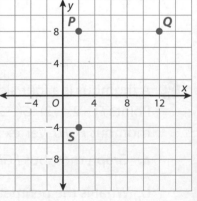

a. Draw rectangle *PQRS* in the coordinate plane to model the fence.

b. How many feet of fencing does Christopher need to go around the chicken coop? Show your work.

SOLUTION _____

Refine Solving Problems in the Coordinate Plane

➤ **Complete the Example below. Then solve problems 1–9.**

Example

The graph shows the coordinates of points *A*, *B*, and *C*. The distance between points *A* and *B* is the same as the distance between points *B* and *C*. What is the value of *n*?

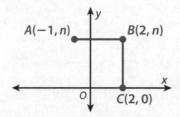

Look at how you could use coordinates to solve the problem.

Points *A* and *B* have the same *y*-coordinate and are in different quadrants. The distance *AB* is $|-1| + |2| = 3$.

Points *B* and *C* have the same *x*-coordinate and *C* is on the *x*-axis. Because *n* is positive, the distance $BC = n$.

The problem states that the distances *AB* and *BC* are equal.

SOLUTION _____

Apply It

1 Dario walks from his house to a comic book store along the route shown. Distances in the coordinate plane are in units of miles. How many miles does Dario walk to reach the comic book store? Show your work.

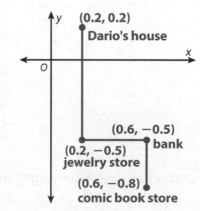

SOLUTION _____

2 The tile on the floor of a kitchen is being replaced. The new tile costs $1.79 per square foot. The kitchen floor is shaped like a polygon. In a coordinate plane, the vertices of the polygon, in counterclockwise order, are at (0, 0), (0, 4), (−9, 4), (−9, −4), (−5, −4), and (−5, 0). Units in the coordinate plane are in feet. What is the total cost of the new tile for the kitchen? Show your work.

SOLUTION _____

3 Which expression represents the distance from point *P* to point *Q*?

A $|-6| - |-2|$

B $|-6| - |-4|$

C $|-2| + |-4|$

D $|-2| + |-6|$

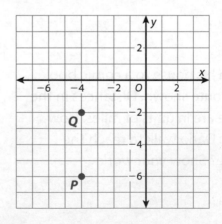

Alita chose D as the correct answer. How might she have gotten that answer?

4 The coordinate plane shows several locations of stations in a city's subway system. Distances are in miles. Tell whether each statement is *True* or *False*.

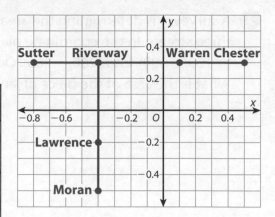

	True	False
a. The distance between Lawrence and Riverway is 0.5 mi.	○	○
b. The distance in miles from Moran to Lawrence is $|-0.5| + |-0.2|$.	○	○
c. The distance between Sutter and Warren is the same as the distance between Riverway and Chester.	○	○

5 One side of a rectangle in the coordinate plane has vertices at $(-5, 1)$ and $(4, 1)$. The perimeter of the rectangle is 26 units. What are all the possible coordinates of the other two vertices of the rectangle? Show your work.

SOLUTION _____

6 Triangle *JKL* has vertices $J(-2, -3)$, $K(-2, 3)$, and $L(6, -3)$. The perimeter of triangle *JKL* is 24 units. What is the length, in units, of $\overline{KL}$?

7 A surveyor is determining the area of a triangular piece of land bordered by three streets. In the coordinate plane, the vertices of the triangle are at (0, 0), (−100, −300), and (200, −200). One unit in the coordinate plane represents 1 m. What is the area of the piece of land? Show your work.

SOLUTION _____

8 Points R(−6, −5), S(−2, −5), and T(−2, n) are plotted in the coordinate plane. The distance between points R and S is half the distance between points S and T.

The value of n could be _____ or _____ .

9 **Math Journal** Choose a point in Quadrant III and a point in Quadrant IV on the same horizontal line. Explain how to use absolute value to find the distance between the two points.

✓ **End of Lesson Checklist**

☐ **INTERACTIVE GLOSSARY** Find the entry for *quadrants*. Tell how to find the distance between two points that are in different quadrants and on the same vertical line.

☐ **SELF CHECK** Go back to the Unit 6 Opener and see what you can check off.

Study an Example Problem and Solution

SMP 1 Make sense of problems and persevere in solving them.

➤ **Read this problem involving negative numbers and the coordinate plane. Then look at one student's solution to this problem on the following pages.**

Mapping Maya Ruins

Teams of archaeologists are studying the Maya ruins in several locations in Central America. Agustin is one of the archaeologists. Read the notes he takes about the structures his team is examining.

Choose one of the structures Agustin has not already mapped, and draw its base using his coordinate system. What is the area of the structure's base? How does it compare to the area of the base of Structure 1?

FIELD NOTES

JUNE 10

Structure 1 is a pyramid. The map at the right shows the base of Structure 1. One unit on the map represents 1 meter.

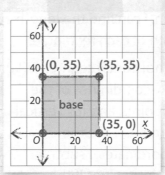

We also surveyed three other structures today. Here are the map coordinates of the vertices of their bases.

- **Structure 13:**
  (−85, 30), (−70, 30), (−70, −15), (−100, −15), (−100, 0), (−85, 0)

- **Structure 14:**
  (−90, −40), (−55, −40), (−55, −60), (−70, −60), (−70, −50), (−90, −50)

- **Structure 15:**
  (−60, −80), (−50, −80), (−50, −155), (−70, −155), (−70, −95), (−60, −95)

Many Maya pyramids are stepped pyramids. Stepped pyramids are formed from a series of flat platforms, or steps.

One Student's Solution

> **First, I have to choose one of the structures.**
>
> I choose Structure 13. Agustin's notes give me the coordinates of the base of this structure.

> **I can map the base of the structure by drawing it in the coordinate plane.**
>
> I plot a point for each vertex, and then connect the points to form a polygon.

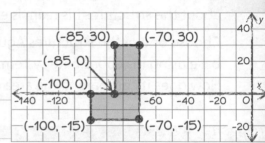

NOTICE THAT...
All of the vertices have a negative x-coordinate, which tells you that all of the vertices are to the left of the origin.

> **I can decompose the figure into two rectangles to make it easier to find the area.**
>
> Then, I can find the length and width of each rectangle.
>
> For horizontal segments, I use the x-coordinates of the endpoints, and for vertical segments, I use the y-coordinates. I subtract absolute values if the endpoints are in the same quadrant and add absolute values if they are in different quadrants.

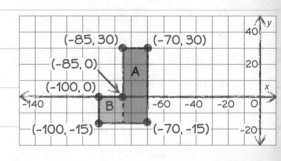

NOTICE THAT...
There is more than one way the structure could be decomposed into rectangles.

Rectangle A:

Length: $|-85| - |-70| = 85 - 70 = $ **15**

Width: $|30| + |-15| = 30 + 15 = $ **45**

Rectangle B:

Length: $|-100| - |-85| = 100 - 85 = $ **15**

Width: $|-15| - |0| = 15 - 0 = $ **15**

✓ **Problem-Solving Checklist**

☐ Tell what is known.

☐ Tell what the problem is asking.

☐ Show all your work.

☐ Show that the solution works.

Now, I can calculate the area of the base of Structure 13.

Rectangle A:

$A = \ell w$

$= (15)(45)$

$= 675$

Rectangle B:

$A = \ell w$

$= (15)(15)$

$= 225$

Total area: $675 + 225 = 900$

The base of Structure 13 has an area of 900 m².

Then, I can find the area of the base of Structure 1.

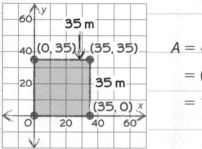

$A = \ell w$

$= (35)(35)$

$= 1,225$

The base of Structure 1 has an area of 1,225 m².

Finally, I can compare the areas of the bases of the two structures.

The area of the base of Structure 13 is 900 m², and the area of the base of Structure 1 is 1,225 m².

$1,225 - 900 = 325$

The area of the base of Structure 1 is 325 m² greater than the area of the base of Structure 13.

In 2018, laser technology helped archaeologists discover more than 60,000 previously unknown ancient Maya structures in Guatemala.

Try Another Approach

➤ **There are many ways to solve problems. Think about how you might solve the Mapping Maya Ruins problem in a different way.**

Mapping Maya Ruins

Teams of archaeologists are studying the Maya ruins in several locations in Central America. Agustin is one of the archaeologists. Read the notes he takes about the structures his team is examining.

Choose one of the structures Agustin has not already mapped, and draw its base using his coordinate system. What is the area of the structure's base? How does it compare to the area of the base of Structure 1?

FIELD NOTES

JUNE 10

Structure 1 is a pyramid. The map at the right shows the base of Structure 1. One unit on the map represents 1 meter.

We also surveyed three other structures today. Here are the map coordinates of the vertices of their bases.

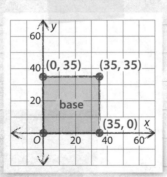

- **Structure 13:**
  (−85, 30), (−70, 30), (−70, −15), (−100, −15), (−100, 0), (−85, 0)

- **Structure 14:**
  (−90, −40), (−55, −40), (−55, −60), (−70, −60), (−70, −50), (−90, −50)

- **Structure 15:**
  (−60, −80), (−50, −80), (−50, −155), (−70, −155), (−70, −95), (−60, −95)

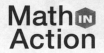
Plan It

➤ **Answer these questions to help you start thinking about a plan.**

a. Which structure will you choose to map?

b. What scale will you use on the axes of your coordinate plane?

Solve It

➤ **Find a different solution for the Mapping Maya Ruins problem. Show all your work on a separate sheet of paper. You may want to use the Problem-Solving Tips to get started.**

PROBLEM-SOLVING TIPS

 Math Toolkit graph paper, ruler

Key Terms

absolute value	integers	negative numbers
ordered pair	positive numbers	quadrant
vertex	*x*-coordinate	*y*-coordinate

Questions

• How can you decompose the base of the structure you chose into familiar shapes?

• How do you know which vertices are on the same horizontal line? How do you know which vertices are on the same vertical line?

Reflect

Use Mathematical Practices As you work through the problem, discuss these questions with a partner.

• **Reason Mathematically** Is the structure you picked located in one quadrant or in more than one quadrant? How can you tell based on the coordinates of the vertices?

• **Make Sense of Problems** Do you need to find the length of each side of the base of the structure you picked to find its area? Explain.

Discuss Models and Strategies

➤ **Read the problem. Write a solution on a separate sheet of paper. Remember, there can be lots of ways to solve a problem.**

Analyzing Special Finds

Laqueta is studying Maya ruins at a different location than Agustin. Read her notes about the special finds she and her team uncovered from dig sites at two locations in a plaza. A special find is an artifact that is rare at a particular dig site.

Choose one of the dig sites, and model it with a vertical number line that shows the ground surface with an elevation of 0 m. Mark the elevation of each special find. Which level of the dig site has the greatest number of special finds? Are there any levels without special finds? If so, which ones?

Dig Site Elevation (in meters)

```
  0
        Level 1
-0.2
        Level 2
-0.4
        Level 3

        Level 4

        Level 5

        Level 6

        Level 7

        Level 8

        Level 9
```

FIELD NOTES

JUNE 10

Special finds recovered from the plaza:

EASTERN Dig Site

Special Find	Depth (m)
Arrow point	0.22
Blade fragment	1.52
Figurine body	1.24
Figurine head	1.18
Jade bead fragment	1.37
Stone drill	0.54

NORTHERN Dig Site

Special Find	Depth (m)
Carved animal bone	1.08
Chocolate pot spout	0.45
Inkpot	1.62
Mask fragment	0.12
Round stone	1.18
Shell bead	0.70

At each dig site, elevation is compared to the ground surface. Level 1 goes from an elevation of 0 m to an elevation of −0.2 m. Level 2 goes from an elevation of −0.2 m to an elevation of −0.4 m.

This pattern continues down to Level 9, with each level going 0.2 m deeper than the previous level.

Plan It and Solve It

➤ **Find a solution to the Analyzing Special Finds problem.**

Write a detailed plan and support your answer. Be sure to include:

- a vertical number line that models the dig site you chose.
- labeled elevations of each special find from the dig site.
- the number of the dig level with the greatest number of special finds.
- the numbers of the dig levels with no special finds, if any.

PROBLEM-SOLVING TIPS

Math Toolkit graph paper, number lines

Key Terms

| absolute value | inequality | negative numbers |
| opposite numbers | positive numbers | rational numbers |

Sentence Starters

- I know the . . . has a greater elevation than the . . . because . . .
- I know the . . . is in Level . . . because . . .

Reflect

Use Mathematical Practices As you work through the problem, discuss these questions with a partner.

- **Repeated Reasoning** How is the depth of an artifact related to its elevation?
- **Reason Mathematically** What is the deepest level with artifacts at the dig site you chose? How do you know?

These bird figurines were used as whistles.

Persevere On Your Own

➤ **Read the problem. Write a solution on a separate sheet of paper.**

Estimating Ages of Artifacts

Daria is an archaeologist in the same group as Agustin and Laqueta. She is working at a Maya ruin at a third location.

Daria's team wants to estimate the ages of ceramic pottery found in different parts of the ruin. Ceramic pottery is usually made from clay that has been heated to a high temperature to harden it. Read this email from Daria to her assistant Jordan, and help Jordan respond to Daria.

| Delete | Archive | | Reply | Reply All | Forward |

To: Jordan
Subject: Estimated ages

Hi Jordan,

The lab sent results back on our ceramic samples, so we now have age estimates for each one.

Archaeology Lab RESULTS			
Ceramic Sample	Ceramic Type	Estimated Age in Years	
		Least	Greatest
A	Xate	1,784	1,929
B	Junco	1,483	1,614
C	Tepejilote	1,255	1,363
D	Bayal	1,033	1,242

WHAT YOU CAN DO:

• Choose one of the ceramic samples. Write and graph an inequality to represent the possible ages of the sample based on the least age given in the table.

• Write and graph a second inequality to represent the possible ages of the sample based on the greatest age given in the table.

• List three possible years in which the ceramic could have been made (an early estimate, a middle estimate, and a late estimate).

Thanks!

Daria

Solve It

➤ **Find a solution to the Estimating Ages of Artifacts problem.**

- Choose a sample. Write an inequality to represent the possible ages of the sample based on the least age given in the table. Then graph the inequality.

- Write an inequality to represent the possible ages of the sample based on the greatest age given in the table. Then graph the inequality.

- List three possible years in which the ceramic could have been made. Give an early estimate, a middle estimate, and a late estimate.

Reflect

Use Mathematical Practices After you complete the problem, choose one of these questions to discuss with a partner.

- **Be Precise** How did you know whether to use an open circle or a solid circle when graphing your inequalities?

- **Use a Model** How could you show the possible estimated ages of the ceramic sample using a single number line?

The ceramic vessels above were used by the Maya to drink a popular chocolate beverage. The spicy, sugarless drink was made with cocoa beans, water, and chili peppers.

In this unit you learned to . . .

Skill	Lesson
Plot integers and rational numbers on number lines to represent real-world contexts.	**23, 24**
Compare and order positive and negative numbers.	**24**
Determine whether a number is a solution of an inequality.	**26**
Write and graph inequalities to represent real-world contexts.	**26**
Plot ordered pairs in all four quadrants of the coordinate plane.	**27, 28**
Use absolute value to find the distance between points on a horizontal or vertical line.	**28**
Solve problems about polygons in the coordinate plane.	**28**
Listen carefully during discussion in order to understand and explain another person's ideas.	**23–28**

Think about what you have learned.

➤ **Use words, numbers, and drawings.**

1 The most important math I learned was _____ because . . .

2 Something I know well is . . .

3 One thing I still need to work on is . . .

➤ **Review the unit vocabulary. Put a check mark by items you can use in speaking and writing. Look up the meaning of any terms you do not know.**

Math Vocabulary		Academic Vocabulary
☐ absolute value	☐ quadrants (I, II, III, IV)	☐ at least
☐ integers	☐ rational numbers	☐ at most
☐ negative numbers	☐ reflection	☐ decrease
☐ opposite numbers	☐ solution of an inequality	☐ increase
☐ positive numbers		☐ no more than

➤ **Use the unit vocabulary to complete the problems.**

1 Label the coordinate plane with at least five math vocabulary terms.

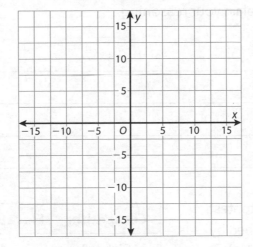

2 How are rational numbers and integers alike? How are they different?

3 Synonyms are words and phrases whose meanings are the same or almost the same. Antonyms have opposite meanings. Write one pair of synonyms and one pair of antonyms from the academic vocabulary. Tell what each term means.

➤ **Use what you have learned to complete these problems.**

1 Jenna plans a vacation that is less than 100 mi away. Which inequality represents the distances, x, that Jenna may plan?

A $x > 100$ **B** $x \geq 100$

C $x < 100$ **D** $x \leq 100$

2 Plot and label the opposites of $\frac{1}{2}$, $-\frac{3}{4}$, and $\frac{7}{8}$ on the number line.

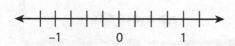

3 Scientists conduct experiments on samples of a compound. Dr. Fielden has a sample at 2.8°C, and Dr. Pierre has a sample at -4.6°C. Write an absolute value inequality comparing the temperatures of each sample to 0°C. Whose sample has a temperature closer to 0°C? Explain your reasoning.

SOLUTION _____

_____

_____

_____

4 A shovel company holds a digging contest. The table shows the elevations reached by this year's competitors. Last year's winner reached an elevation of -12.9 ft. Which of this year's competitors reached a lower elevation than last year's champion? Explain your reasoning.

Competitor	Elevation (ft)
Richard	-12.7
Alizee	-13.2
Daniel	-12.4
Simone	-13.0

SOLUTION _____

_____

5 A playground is shaped like a rectangle. A map of the playground is shown in the coordinate plane. The vertices are located at $(-50, -10)$, $(-50, 10)$, $(50, 10)$, and $(50, -10)$. Distances on the map are in meters. What is the perimeter of the playground? Show your work.

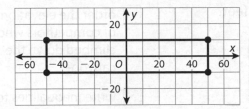

SOLUTION _____

6 In which quadrant of the coordinate plane is point $G(-12, -15)$? Explain your reasoning.

SOLUTION _____

_____

_____

7 A triangle has vertices at $B(-2, 4)$, $C(3, -2)$, and $D(-4, -2)$ in the coordinate plane. What is the area of triangle BCD, in square units? Record your answer on the grid. Then fill in the bubbles.

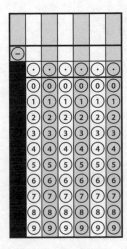

Performance Task

➤ **Answer the questions and show all your work on separate paper.**

A rock-climbing group competes at a mountain and a canyon. The base of the mountain and the top of the canyon each begin at sea level. Each competitor climbs up the mountain or down the canyon for one hour. Their final elevations are shown in the table, in feet.

Lamar	Bella	Alex	Jackson	Maria
225.6	−220.8	−223.7	215.8	222.9

Hwan	Pascal	Ina	George	Jennifer
−227.0	220.5	−212.9		

Trophies will be awarded in three categories: the two highest elevations climbing up the mountain, the two lowest elevations climbing down the canyon, and the two greatest distances.

George and Jennifer have not yet completed their climbs. Help them analyze the results so that they can understand what they must do to win trophies.

• Write elevations from lowest to highest for competitors who climbed up the mountain. George is climbing up the mountain. Write an inequality that shows what his final elevation must be to receive one of the two trophies for highest elevation.

• Write elevations from highest to lowest for competitors who climbed down the canyon. Jennifer is climbing down the canyon. Write an inequality that shows what her final elevation must be to receive one of the two trophies for lowest elevation.

• Write an inequality that shows how George or Jennifer could win at least one of the trophies for greatest distance climbed.

Reflect

Use Mathematical Practices
After you complete the task, choose one of the following questions to answer.

• **Make Sense of the Problem** How can you use the final elevations in the table to tell who climbed up the mountain and who climbed down the canyon?

• **Be Precise** How does determining the two greatest distances differ from determining the two highest elevations?

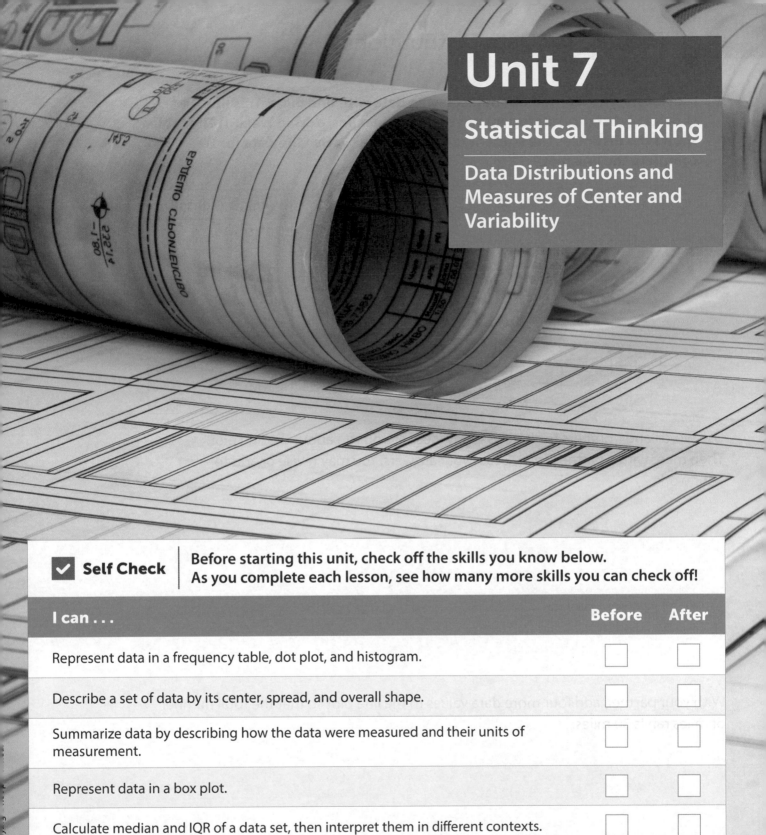

Unit 7

Statistical Thinking

Data Distributions and Measures of Center and Variability

✓ **Self Check** | Before starting this unit, check off the skills you know below.
As you complete each lesson, see how many more skills you can check off!

I can . . .	Before	After
Represent data in a frequency table, dot plot, and histogram.	☐	☐
Describe a set of data by its center, spread, and overall shape.	☐	☐
Summarize data by describing how the data were measured and their units of measurement.	☐	☐
Represent data in a box plot.	☐	☐
Calculate median and IQR of a data set, then interpret them in different contexts.	☐	☐
Calculate the mean and MAD of a data set, then interpret them in different contexts.	☐	☐
Compare measures of center and variability, then choose measures of center and variability to summarize the data set.	☐	☐
Use math vocabulary and precise language to describe sets of data.	☐	☐

➤ **Previously, you learned about displaying data with line plots. This line plot shows the distances a student ran each day, in miles, during Week 1. The table shows the distances the student ran during Week 2. Use the data for Week 2 to complete the line plot.**

Week 2: Miles Run	
2	$2\frac{1}{2}$
$\frac{1}{2}$	$1\frac{1}{2}$
2	$\frac{1}{4}$
$2\frac{1}{4}$	

Running Distances

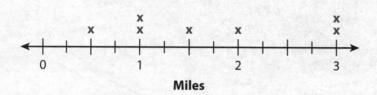

Miles

Use words and numbers to share as many ideas as you can about the line plot. Then meet with a partner and discuss your answers. You may revise or add to your work.

With your partner, add four more data values to the line plot so that the total number of miles ran is 30 miles.

Dear Family,

This week your student is exploring how to display and describe data collected to answer **statistical questions**. The data collected to answer a statistical question are expected to vary, or show **variability**.

You can collect data to answer this statistical question.

How old are the students in the swim class?

You can use a table to show the **frequency** of each data value, or the number of times each value occurs. A frequency table displays the **distribution** of the data.

Your student will be displaying and describing distributions of data sets like the one below.

Age	Frequency
9				
10						
11			

This list shows the number of pets owned by each of 11 students.

1, 0, 0, 1, 0, 1, 1, 3, 1, 1, 0

➤ **ONE WAY** to display the data distribution is in a frequency table.

Number of Pets	Frequency
0					
1						
2	
3		

You can describe the data as being spread out from 0 pets to 3 pets.

The data show that most people have 0 pets or 1 pet.

➤ **ANOTHER WAY** is to use a **dot plot**.

Each dot represents one data value.

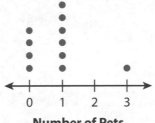

Number of Pets

The shape of the data distribution shows one large group of data points at 0 and 1, with a single point at 3.

Both displays show the data values in order from least to greatest and can help you describe the distribution of the data.

 Use the next page to start a conversation about statistical questions.

Activity Thinking About Statistical Questions Around You

➤ **Do this activity together to investigate statistical questions in the real world.**

Did you know that scientists collect data to study earthquake patterns? They do this by using special equipment to measure the magnitude, or strength, of an earthquake each time one occurs.

Scientists use the data they collect to help predict when the next earthquakes may happen. Scientists ask and answer statistical questions such as *What magnitudes of earthquakes occur in this region?* and *How often do earthquakes of these magnitudes occur?*

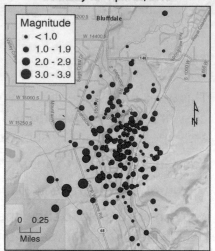

Earthquakes near Bluffdale, Utah
February 13 - April 20, 2019

University of Utah Seismograph Stations

 Where else do you see statistical questions being used in the world around you?

Explore Statistical Questions and Data Distributions

Model It

➤ **Complete the problems about data and statistical questions.**

1 Keiko is on her school's track team. She collects data to answer this question.

How high did members of the track team jump in yesterday's high jump event?

Complete the **dot plot** to show Keiko's data.

High Jump Heights (in.)				
$53\frac{1}{4}$	$52\frac{1}{2}$	$51\frac{3}{4}$	$53\frac{3}{4}$	52
$52\frac{1}{4}$	$53\frac{1}{4}$	$52\frac{1}{2}$	$50\frac{1}{2}$	52

High Jump Heights

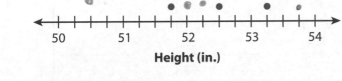

Height (in.)

2 A **statistical question** is a question that can be answered by collecting data that are expected to vary.

a. In problem 1, why is Keiko's question a statistical question?

because the heights ones reciving, vary.

b. Keiko's teammate Lillie asks *How high did the track team's captain jump in yesterday's high jump event?* Is Lillie's question a statistical question? Why or why not?

No because it's only one piece of info.

◎ **Learning Targets**   SMP 2, SMP 3, SMP 7
• Recognize a statistical question as one that anticipates variability in the data related to the question.
• Understand that a set of data collected to answer a statistical question has a distribution which can be described by its center, spread, and overall shape.
• Summarize numerical data sets in relation to their context by reporting the number of observations.

Model It

➤ **Complete the problems about statistical questions.**

3 Keiko and Lillie ask more questions about their track team. Complete the table.

	Keiko's and Lillie's Question	What data do Keiko and Lillie need to collect?	Are the data likely to vary?
a.	What is a typical time for a member of the track team to run the 100-meter dash? ●	several 100-meter dash times for each team member	yes
b.	How many team members ran in yesterday's track meet?	the number of members who ran in the meet	No
c.	How much faster did Lillie run the 100-meter dash than Keiko in yesterday's track meet?	Lillie's and keiko's times from yesterday's meet	No
d.	How much faster does Lillie usually run the 100-m dash than Keiko?	Lillie's and keiko's times from several meets	yes
e.	Is the high jump or the 100-meter dash more popular among spectators at track meets?		yes

4 Which questions from the table in problem 3 are statistical questions?

5 Write another statistical question that Keiko and Lillie could ask about their track team.

6 **Reflect** Does a question need to have more than one answer to be a statistical question? Explain.

DISCUSS IT

Ask: Which question in problem 3 does not require numerical data to answer?

Share: I think I could draw a dot plot for data collected to answer my question because . . .

Name:

Prepare for Understanding Statistical Questions and Data Distributions

1 Think about what you know about data. Fill in each box. Use words, numbers, and pictures. Show as many ideas as you can.

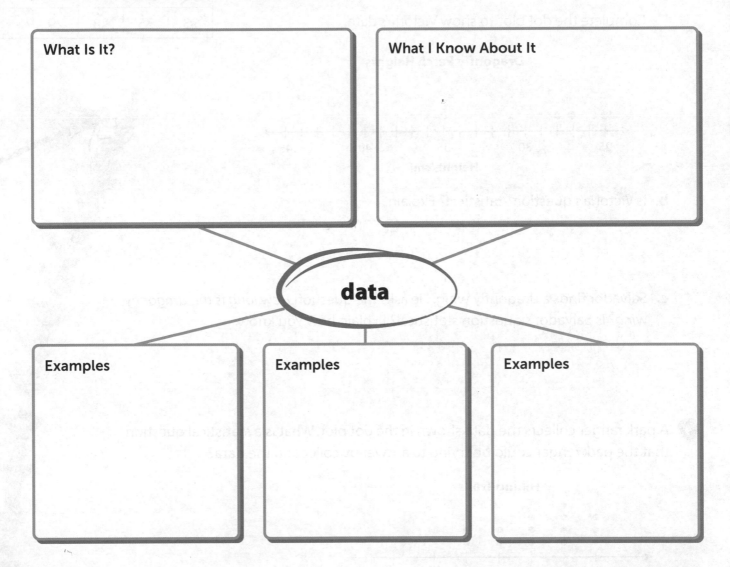

What Is It?

What I Know About It

data

Examples

Examples

Examples

2 Adsila says that she can display the set of data shown in the table by making a dot plot. Do you agree with Adsila? Explain.

Items for Sale	
Type	**Number**
Mugs	6
Stickers	5
T-shirts	12

➤ **Complete problems 3–4.**

3 A science class is studying the dragonflies at a small pond.

a. Victoria collects data to answer this question.

At what height do dragonflies typically perch when they land?

Complete the dot plot to show Victoria's data.

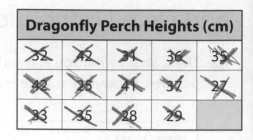

Dragonfly Perch Heights (cm)				
~~32~~	~~42~~	~~34~~	~~36~~	~~35~~
~~42~~	~~26~~	~~41~~	~~37~~	~~27~~
~~33~~	~~35~~	~~28~~	~~29~~	

Dragonfly Perch Heights

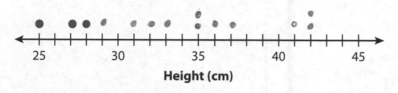

Height (cm)

b. Is Victoria's question statistical? Explain.

yes because the data varys

c. Salvador finds a dragonfly wing. He asks the question *How long is this dragonfly wing?* Is Salvador's question statistical? Explain how you know.

No because the data does not vary.

4 A park ranger collects the data shown in the dot plot. What is a statistical question that the park ranger could be trying to answer by collecting the data?

Hiking Trails

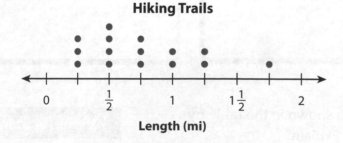

Length (mi)

Vocabulary

statistical question

a question that can be answered by collecting data that are expected to vary.

Develop Understanding of Statistical Questions and Data Distributions

Model It: Data Displays

➤ **Try these two problems about displaying and describing data.**

1. The **frequency** of a data value is the number of times it occurs in a data set. For example, the frequency of the value 3 in the set {3, 5, 3, 4, 9, 1} is 2.

   a. The frequency table below uses tally marks to show how long it took the students in Ms. Gordon's class to complete a math puzzle. Use the frequency table to complete the dot plot.

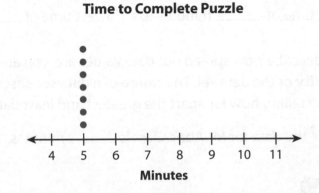

Minutes	Frequency
5	ⅢⅢ ‖
6	ⅢⅢ
7	ⅢⅢ
8	‖‖
9	‖

Time to Complete Puzzle

Minutes

   b. How many students completed the puzzle? How do you know?

2. A **distribution** displays the values in a data set and shows how often the values occur.

   a. How do the dot plot and the frequency table in problem 1 help you see the distribution of the times?

   b. Describe the shape of the distribution in the dot plot.

DISCUSS IT

Ask: What is a statistical question that the dot plot could be used to answer?

Share: A frequency table is similar to a dot plot because . . .

Model It: Data Descriptions

➤ **Try these two problems about describing data distributions.**

3 **a.** Mr. Aba's students do a math puzzle. Use the dot plot to complete the frequency table.

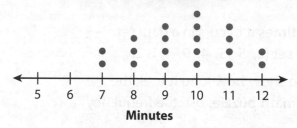

Time to Complete Puzzle

Minutes

Minutes	Frequency
	2
8	
9	
	5
12	

b. The data for Mr. Aba's class is spread from

a fastest time of _____ minutes to a slowest time of _____ minutes.

4 When you describe how spread out data values are, you are describing the **variability** of the data set. The **range** of a data set describes the variability by telling how far apart the greatest and least data values are.

The range of the data for Mr Aba's Class is _____ minutes.

DISCUSS IT

Ask: How would you describe the shape of the distribution for Mr. Aba's students?

Share: I think you can find the range of a data set by . . .

CONNECT IT

➤ **Complete the problems below.**

5 How are a frequency table and a dot plot similar in the way they show the range of a data set? How are they different?

6 Describe the shape and variability of the distribution of the data shown in the dot plot.

African Weaver Ants

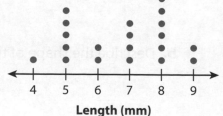

Length (mm)

Practice Statistical Questions and Data Distributions

➤ **Study how the Example shows describing a data distribution. Then solve problems 1–3.**

Example

Students in Mr. Lincoln's class measure the distance they walk with one step. Describe the shape and variability of the distribution of their data set.

You can display the data in a dot plot.

Step Lengths (in.)					
21	24	28	26	25	25
25	25	25	24	22	23
23	24	26	22	23	24

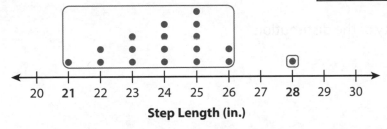

Step Length (in.)

Shape: There is **one large group** of data points with its **highest point** at 25 in. There is a **single point** at 28 in. to the right of the large group.

Variability: The distribution is spread from **21 in.** to **28 in.** Since 28 − 21 = 7, the range is **7 in.**

---

1 a. How many students measured their step length in the Example? Use the dot plot to explain how you know.

b. What statistical question do you think the students in Mr. Lincoln's class are trying to answer?

c. How do you know that the question you wrote is statistical?

Vocabulary

distribution
a representation that shows how often values in a data set occur.

statistical question
a question that can be answered by collecting data that are expected to vary.

variability
how spread out or close together values in a data set are.

2 Customers who buy an adventure game sold by an app store can give the game a rating from 1 star to 5 stars. The frequency table shows the number of 1-star, 2-star, 3-star, 4-star, and 5-star ratings.

Number of Stars	Frequency
1	HHT II
2	HHT
3	I
4	III
5	HHT II

a. The game has a total of _____ ratings.

b. Make a dot plot of the data set shown in the frequency table.

c. Describe the shape and variability of the distribution.

d. How would the shape and variability of the distribution change if the game receives 20 more ratings of 5 stars?

3 The dot plot shows the data Gavin collects to answer the question *What is a typical number of seconds that I can stay in a handstand?*

a. Why is Gavin's question a statistical question?

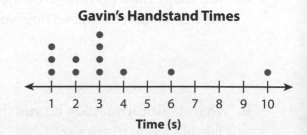

Gavin's Handstand Times

Time (s)

b. Describe the shape and variability of the distribution of Gavin's data set.

Refine Ideas About Statistical Questions and Data Distributions

Apply It **Math Toolkit** graph paper, number lines

➤ **Complete problems 1–5.**

1 **Evaluate** Rafael says that the question below is a statistical question because there is more than one possible answer. Explain why Rafael is incorrect and tell how you could modify the question so that it is a statistical question.

Does my math teacher prefer reading history books or graphic novels?

2 **Compare** Which question would likely result in more variability if you asked each student in your school? Explain.

About how many hours per week do you play sports?

What grade are you in?

3 **Predict** The dot plot shows the cost per ounce of different brands of peanut butter sold at a store. The store plans to add a new brand of peanut butter. The new brand has a 16-oz jar that sells for $3.84. Based on its cost per ounce, do you think the new brand is a good deal compared to the other brands? Use the distribution shown in the dot plot to support your answer.

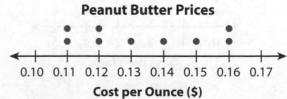

Peanut Butter Prices

Cost per Ounce ($)

4 The data show the flight times, in minutes, of 21 toy drones.

PART A Use a model to represent the distribution of the flight times.

Drone Flight Times (min)						
3	7	7	4.5	5	5	5
10	9	9	10	7	6.5	6.5
5	3	4.5	3.5	6.5	5.5	5

PART B About how long does a drone typically fly? Explain your reasoning.

5 **Math Journal** Agustin collects the data set shown in the dot plot to answer the question *How many days each week do students in my class eat a cafeteria lunch?* Why is Agustin's question statistical? Describe the distribution of the data collected to answer this statistical question.

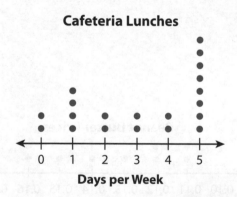

Cafeteria Lunches

Days per Week

✓ End of Lesson Checklist

☐ **INTERACTIVE GLOSSARY** Find the entry for *statistical question*. Write two important things you learned about statistical questions in this lesson.

Dear Family,

This week your student is learning how to use dot plots and histograms to describe data distributions.

A **histogram** displays the frequency of data in equal-size intervals of the number line. This histogram shows 4 players whose heights are from 50 in. up to, but not including, 52 in. A player whose height is 52 in. would instead be counted in the next interval.

Your student will be learning how to solve problems like the one below.

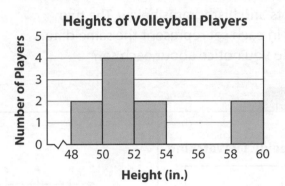

Heights of Volleyball Players

The list shows the heights, in inches, of 13 soccer players. Display and describe the distribution of the data.

65, 63, 64, 59, 66, 65, 64, 66, 66, 64, 63, 65, 66

➤ **ONE WAY** to display a data distribution is with a frequency table.

Height (in.)	Frequency
59–60	I
61–62	
63–64	IIII
65–66	IIIII II

No player is 61 in. or 62 in. tall. This is a **gap** in the data. Most of the data are in a **cluster** near the higher values. There is a **peak** at 65 in. to 66 in.

Both displays can be used to describe the shape of the data distribution.

➤ **ANOTHER WAY** is to use a histogram.

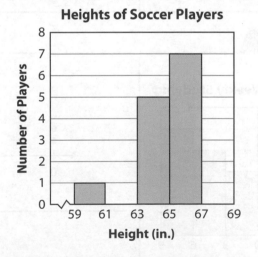

Heights of Soccer Players

When data are clustered near higher values, the distribution is **skewed left**.

 Use the next page to start a conversation about data displays.

Activity Exploring Dot Plots and Histograms

➤ **Do this activity together to look for relationships between dot plots and histograms.**

Dot plots and histograms can be used to display numerical data. There are two sets of dot plots and histograms below. The two graphs in each set represent the same data. What do you notice about each set?

SET 1

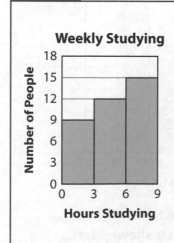

Weekly TV Watching

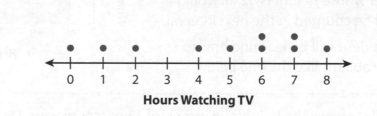

Hours Watching TV

SET 2

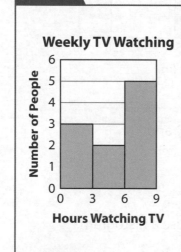

Weekly Studying

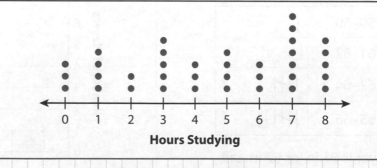

Hours Studying

> **?** How can you use each dot plot to make a histogram with a larger or smaller interval?

Explore Dot Plots and Histograms

Previously, you learned about statistical questions and data distributions. In this lesson, you will learn about displaying and describing data distributions with dot plots and histograms.

➤ **Use what you know to try to solve the problem below.**

The parks department can add one new program to its summer camp. The data show the ages of children who have signed up. Based on **Data Set: Ages in Years,** which age group should get the new program?

Ages in Years				
10	6	8	8	14
10	9	7	11	10

See page DS1 for the complete data set.

PARKS DEPARTMENT

SUMMER CAMP
Programs for all ages

Join us for a summer packed with fun and exciting activities!

— AGE GROUPS —

3–5   6–8
9–11
12–14   15–17

TRY IT

 Math Toolkit connecting cubes, counters, graph paper, sticky notes, unit tiles

DISCUSS IT

Ask: How does your model show the age groups?

Share: In my model, I showed the age groups by . . .

 Learning Targets   SMP 1, SMP 2, SMP 3, SMP 4, SMP 5, SMP 6, SMP 7
- Understand that a distribution can be described by its center, spread, and overall shape.
- Display numerical data in plots on a number line, including dot plots, histograms, and box plots.
- Summarize numerical data sets in relation to their context by describing the nature of the attribute under investigation, including how it was measured and its units of measurement.

CONNECT IT

1 **Look Back** Which age group of children should get the new program from the parks department? Explain how you know.

2 **Look Ahead** When working with large data sets, it is sometimes helpful to show the frequencies of groups of data values instead of individual values. A **histogram** organizes data values into equal-size intervals of the number line. A bar is used to show how many data values are in each interval.

a. This histogram shows the distribution of ages of visitors at a science museum at noon on one day. The first bar represents visitors in the age group 0–9, the second bar represents visitors in the age group 10–19, and so on. How many visitors are in the age group 0–9? How do you know?

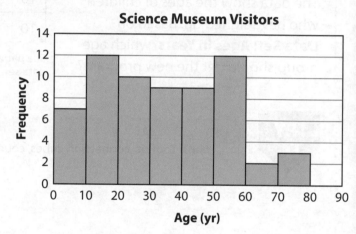

Science Museum Visitors

b. Two visitors at the museum are 70 years old. Which bar includes these visitors?

c. Can you use the histogram to tell how many visitors are 13 years old? Explain.

d. The size of the age interval for each bar is the number of years included in the interval. What is the size of the age intervals in the histogram?

3 **Reflect** Suppose you make the interval size in the histogram twice as large. How would this change affect the histogram?

Prepare for Using Dot Plots and Histograms to Describe Data Distributions

1   Think about what you know about data distributions. Fill in each box. Use words, numbers, and pictures. Show as many ideas as you can.

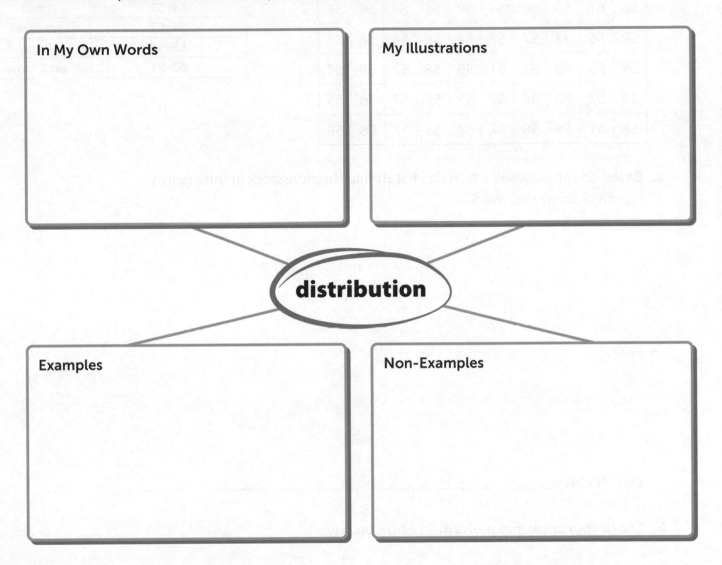

In My Own Words

My Illustrations

distribution

Examples

Non-Examples

2   How does the dot plot show the distribution of sunflower heights?

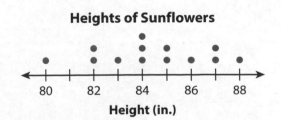

Heights of Sunflowers

Height (in.)

3 A person's hat size is based on the distance around the person's head. The data show this distance, in centimeters, of the last 50 customers who bought hats in a hat store.

Distance Around (cm)									
58	61	55	60	54	59	55	57	56	56
58	56	57	57	57	54	58	54	58	55
59	55	58	54	61	56	58	57	59	54
59	57	60	55	59	55	57	57	56	55
58	61	58	58	57	59	55	57	58	58

Distance Around (cm)	Hat Size
54–55	small
56–57	medium
58–59	large
60–61	extra large

a. Based on this data set, which size hat should the store stock in the greatest number? Show your work.

SOLUTION _____

b. Check your answer to problem 3a. Show your work.

Develop Displaying Data with a Histogram

➤ **Read and try to solve the problem below.**

Elizabeth records the number of points her favorite basketball team scores in each game. She predicts that the team will score about 120 points in its next game. Is Elizabeth's prediction reasonable? Display **Data Set: Points Scored** in a way that supports your answer.

Points Scored

Date	Points
Oct. 16	81
Oct. 19	88
Oct. 21	91
Oct. 24	102

See page DS2 for the complete data set.

TRY IT

Math Toolkit graph paper, number lines, sticky notes

LESSON 30 Use Dot Plots and Histograms to Describe Data Distributions **677**

➤ **Explore different ways to represent a data distribution.**

Elizabeth records the number of points her favorite basketball team scores in each game. She predicts that the team will score about 120 points in its next game. Is Elizabeth's prediction reasonable? Display **Data Set: Points Scored** in a way that supports your answer.

Points Scored	
Date	**Points**
Oct. 16	81
Oct. 19	88

See page DS2 for the complete data set.

Model It

You can use a frequency table to organize the data values into equal-size intervals.

The least value in the data set is 81 points and the greatest value is 141 points. The intervals need to include values from **81** to **141**.

You can group the data into 10-point intervals starting from **80**. The last interval ends at **149**.

The tally marks show how many data values are in each interval.

Points Scored	Frequency
80–89	||
90–99	||||
100–109	ⅢⅢ ⅢⅢ
110–119	ⅢⅢ ⅢⅢ |
120–129	ⅢⅢ ⅢⅢ ⅢⅢ ||
130–139	|||
140–149	|||

Model It

You can use a histogram to display the data distribution.

The histogram shows the frequency of the data values using an interval size of 10.

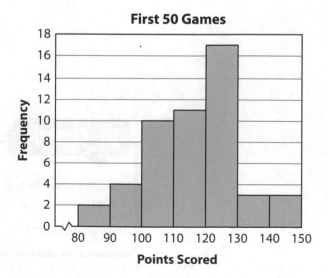

First 50 Games

➤ **Use the problem from the previous page to help you understand how to display data with a histogram.**

1 Look at the first **Model It**. What do the 4 tally marks for interval 90–99 mean?

2 Look at the second **Model It**. How is interval 90–99 shown in the histogram? How does this show the same information as the frequency table?

3 What challenges might Elizabeth face if she tries to display the data in a dot plot?

4 How is a histogram similar to a dot plot? How is it different?

5 Is Elizabeth's prediction reasonable? Explain how the histogram can help you analyze Elizabeth's prediction.

6 When is it helpful to use a histogram to organize and display data?

7 **Reflect** Think about all the models and strategies you have discussed today. Describe how one of them helped you better understand how to solve the **Try It** problem.

Apply It

➤ **Use what you learned to solve these problems.**

8 Oliver wonders how much his teachers use text messages to communicate. He asks each teacher at his school how many text messages they sent yesterday. The histogram shows his data.

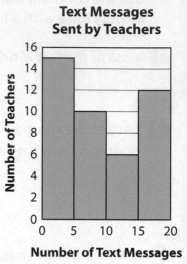

Text Messages Sent by Teachers

a. What could have been the least number of text messages sent?

b. Explain why it is helpful to see this distribution in a histogram.

c. When Oliver collects his data, he has the teachers count each sent text message as 1 text. He notices that some teachers send several short text messages, while other teachers send one long text message. What change could Oliver make to the way he collects the data to address this issue?

9 Eldora records the low temperature in her town each day for 6 weeks. Make a histogram to display Eldora's data.

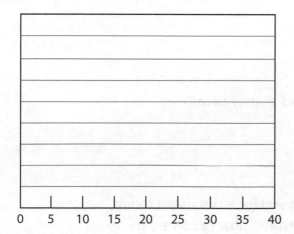

Low Temperatures (°F)						
22	23	24	10	18	26	26
27	26	29	7	15	20	27
29	30	30	22	23	31	32
28	23	36	33	32	31	30
36	33	33	30	32	37	34
32	30	37	34	38	35	31

Name:

Practice Displaying Data with a Histogram

➤ **Study the Example showing how to display data with a histogram. Then solve problems 1–3.**

Example

The frequency table shows data on the number of guitars a music shop repairs in a week. Display the data in a histogram.

Use the frequency of each interval as the height of the corresponding bar.

Number of Repairs	Frequency
0–4	
5–9	‖
10–14	‖‖
15–19	卌	
20–24	‖|

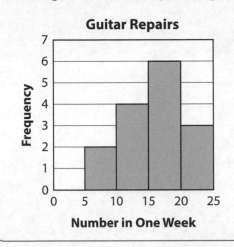

Guitar Repairs

1 **a.** How many weeks did the shop in the Example repair at least 15 guitars?

b. What information would a dot plot show that the histogram and frequency table do not show?

2 Shanika uses the data from the Example to make a histogram with an interval size of 10. How will this change the shape of the histogram?

3 Alyssa completes a science project about using Calories to measure the energy found in food. She collects data on the number of Calories per serving for each of the items in her refrigerator.

Calories per Serving				
15	56	102	43	223
166	124	72	7	344
105	65	203	104	50
259	112	79	358	48
132	31	14	227	188

a. Complete the frequency table for Alyssa's data.

Calories per Serving	Frequency
0–99	
100–199	
200–299	
300–399	

b. Make a histogram to represent Alyssa's data.

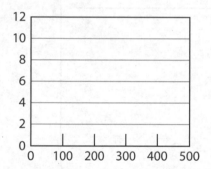

c. Describe the shape of the data distribution and what it means in terms of numbers of Calories.

d. How do the frequency table and histogram show the number of items in Alyssa's refrigerator?

e. Alyssa decides to collect the same information for the school cafeteria refrigerator. There are 250 items in the cafeteria refrigerator. Should Alyssa use a histogram or a dot plot to represent her data? Explain your choice.

Develop Using Dot Plots and Histograms to Describe Data Distributions

➤ **Read and try to solve the problem below.**

Francisca organizes her capoeira club's annual show where club members perform different routines to music. She times each song using a stopwatch, rounds the lengths of the songs to the nearest 0.5 min, and makes a dot plot of the results. Describe the distribution of the data and what it means in terms of song lengths.

Song Lengths

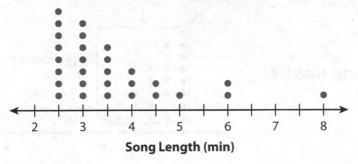

Song Length (min)

TRY IT

DISCUSS IT

Ask: What did you notice about the shape of the distribution?

Share: I noticed . . .

LESSON 30 Use Dot Plots and Histograms to Describe Data Distributions   **683**

➤ **Explore different ways to describe a data distribution.**

Francisca organizes her capoeira club's annual show where club members perform different routines to music. She times each song using a stopwatch, rounds the lengths of the songs to the nearest 0.5 min, and makes a dot plot of the results. Describe the distribution of the data and what it means in terms of song lengths.

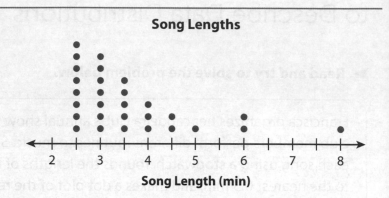

Analyze It

You can describe patterns or features of a data distribution.

Clusters of data points are separated by **gaps**.

Each cluster may have a **peak**, or high point.

Outliers are data values much less or much greater than the other data values.

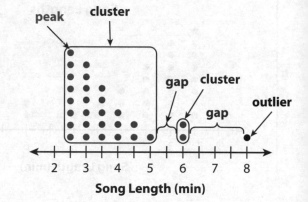

Analyze It

You can describe the general shape of a data distribution.

When most of the data points are near lower values, the distribution is **skewed right**.
When most of the data points are near higher values, the distribution is **skewed left**.
If the middle of the distribution splits the data into two matching halves, the distribution is **symmetric**.

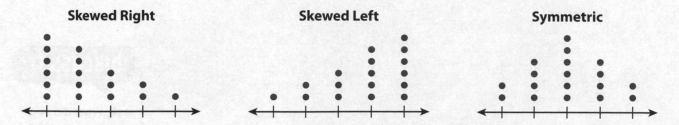

➤ **Use the problem from the previous page to help you understand how to describe data distributions.**

1 What is another way Francisca can collect and record each song length?

2 Look at the first **Analyze It**. Describe the distribution of the song lengths using the terms *cluster*, *gap*, *peak*, and *outlier*. What do these features tell you about the song lengths?

3 What effect does an outlier have on the range of a data distribution?

4 Look at the second **Analyze It**. Is the distribution of Francisca's song lengths *skewed right, skewed left,* or *symmetric?* What does this tell you about the data?

5 Why can it be helpful to describe features such as peaks, gaps, and skew of a distribution?

6 **Reflect** Think about all the models and strategies you have discussed today. Describe how one of them helped you better understand how to describe data distributions.

Apply It

➤ **Use what you learned to solve these problems.**

7 Each histogram shows the numbers of daily customers at a kayak shop.

a. Describe the distributions using the terms *clusters*, *gaps*, *peaks*, and *outliers*. What do these values tell you about the data?

b. Describe the skew of the histograms. What can you conclude about the number of customers in April compared to May?

8 Tara collects data about how many photos her classmates took yesterday and displays the data in a histogram. Describe the shape of the distribution shown in the histogram.

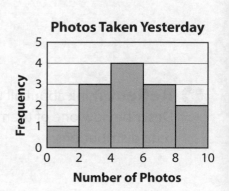

Photos Taken Yesterday

Practice Using Dot Plots and Histograms to Describe Data Distributions

➤ **Study the Example showing how to describe a data distribution using a histogram. Then solve problems 1–2.**

Example

The histogram shows the top speeds of some of the fastest roller coasters in the world. Use the shape of the data distribution to make a conclusion about the top speed of a typical fast roller coaster.

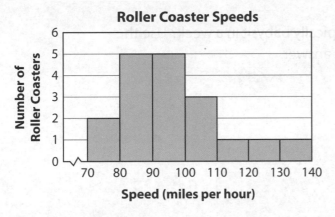

Roller Coaster Speeds

The histogram is skewed right because most of the data points are clustered near lower values. There is a peak from 80 to 99 miles per hour.

A typical fast roller coaster could reach 80 to 99 miles per hour.

---

1 Badru makes a histogram of the data he collects about the number of pages in 21 science fiction books. Describe the shape of the data distribution.

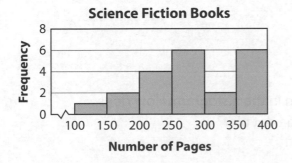

Science Fiction Books

2 Wyatt is thinking about starting to babysit. He wonders how many hours he might expect to be able to babysit. He asks 20 babysitters: *How many hours did you babysit last week?*

Hours Spent Babysitting				
7	0	5	8	3
9	4	1	5	6
6	11	6	0	7
2	8	4	11	6

a. Draw a dot plot of the data.

b. About how many hours does a person typically babysit in a week? Use the shape of the distribution to support your answer.

c. Draw a histogram with the same data.

d. Describe the shape of the data distribution shown in the histogram. How does this compare to how the data are distributed in the dot plot?

Refine Using Dot Plots and Histograms to Describe Data Distributions

➤ **Complete the Example below. Then solve problems 1–9.**

Example

An aquarium technician records the number of inches a painted turtle grows each month for a year. Describe the distribution of the data.

Monthly Turtle Growth (in.)										
$\frac{1}{16}$	$\frac{1}{4}$	$\frac{1}{8}$	$\frac{3}{16}$	$\frac{1}{8}$	$\frac{1}{4}$	$\frac{3}{16}$	$\frac{1}{8}$	$\frac{1}{8}$	$\frac{1}{2}$	$\frac{1}{16}$

Look at how you could display this data with a dot plot in order to describe the distribution.

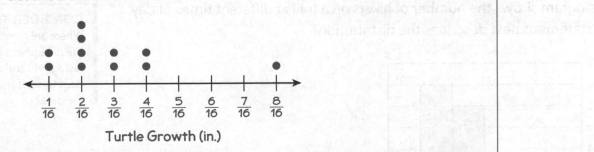

Turtle Growth (in.)

SOLUTION _____

_____

CONSIDER THIS ...
The scale on the number line is based on a common denominator of the fractions.

PAIR/SHARE
About how much does the turtle grow each month? Justify your reasoning.

Apply It

1 Is the data distribution symmetric? Use a data display to show your work.

13, 5, 6, 1, 7, 5, 6, 12, 4, 2, 4, 3, 2, 3, 3, 4, 4, 12, 13

SOLUTION _____

CONSIDER THIS ...
In a symmetric graph, the left and right sides are matching.

PAIR/SHARE
Would a histogram and a dot plot show the same pattern? Explain.

2 The dot plot shows the weights of green beans that people buy at a market. The owner wants to sell green beans in pre-packaged bags all with the same weight. What weight should the owner choose for her pre-packaged green beans? Use the dot plot to support your answer.

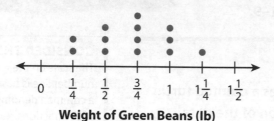

Weight of Green Beans (lb)

CONSIDER THIS...
How would you describe the distribution of the data?

PAIR/SHARE
If someone buys 2 lb of green beans, how would that affect the distribution?

3 The histogram shows the number of hikers on a trail at different times of day. Which statement best describes the distribution?

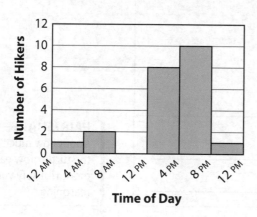

CONSIDER THIS...
Where are most of the data points in the histogram, and what does this tell you about the data?

A The distribution is skewed right.

B The distribution is skewed left.

C The distribution is symmetric.

D The distribution contains an outlier.

Caleb chose D as the correct answer. How might he have gotten that answer?

PAIR/SHARE
What statistical question could be answered using this histogram?

4 The histogram and dot plot show how many siblings Xavier's classmates have. Why could you argue that the dot plot is a better representation of the data?

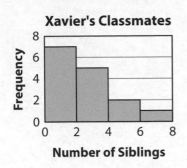

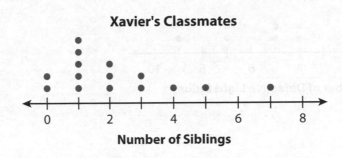

5 Is it always possible to find the range of a data set from a dot plot? Is it always possible to find the range from a histogram? Explain.

6 Which statements must be true based on the histogram? Select all that apply.

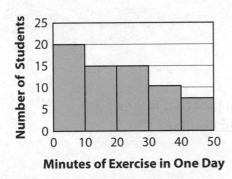

A The range of the data set is 50 min.

B The distribution has gaps in it.

C The most common amount of exercise is 0 to 9 min.

D Five students exercised for 40 min.

E The distribution is skewed right.

7 A factory manager records the number of defective light bulbs per case in a dot plot. Describe the shape of the distributions and explain what the patterns mean in terms of the data.

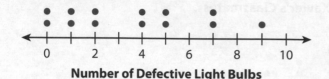

Number of Defective Light Bulbs

8 Display the data from problem 7 in a histogram. Which display, the *dot plot* or the *histogram,* do you think the factory manager would choose to use to show the data? Explain your reasoning.

9 **Math Journal** Make your own data set to display on a dot plot that is skewed left and has an outlier, a peak, and a gap. Describe the data distribution.

✓ End of Lesson Checklist

☐ **INTERACTIVE GLOSSARY** Find the entry for *histogram*. Add two important things you learned about histograms in this lesson.

☐ **SELF CHECK** Go back to the Unit 7 Opener and see what you can check off.

Dear Family,

This week your student is learning how to summarize a data set using a measure of center and a measure of variability. A **measure of center** is a single number that represents a typical value. A **measure of variability** describes how spread out the values in a data set are.

Your student will be learning to solve problems like the one below.

> The ages, in years, of 11 new members of a family fitness center are listed. How can you summarize the ages of the new members?
>
> 11, 5, 32, 7, 10, 41, 40, 15, 28, 80, 10

➤ **ONE WAY** to summarize a data set is with a measure of center.

The **median** of a data set is the middle number when the data values are listed from least to greatest.

5, 7, 10, 10, 11, (15,) 28, 32, 40, 41, 80
median

➤ **ANOTHER WAY** to summarize a data set is with a measure of variability.

The **median** separates the data into two halves. The median of the lower half is the **lower quartile** and the median of the upper half is the **upper quartile**. You can display the data on a **box plot** to see how the data in each quarter are spread out. The box in the middle shows the **interquartile range (IQR)**.

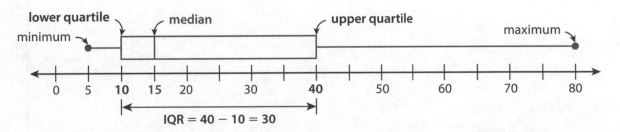

You can use the median and IQR together to describe the distribution of the data. The median age of a new member is 15 years and 50% (or half) the ages are within the 30-year range of 10 years to 40 years.

 Use the next page to start a conversation about medians.

Activity Thinking About Medians Around You

➤ **Do this activity together to investigate medians in the real world.**

Online videos are a popular form of entertainment. Sometimes videos with a lot of views can earn money from showing advertisements. There are videos that have as many as one billion views!

Did you know that the median number of views for all videos uploaded in 2016 was only 89? This means half of these videos were viewed fewer than 89 times. That view count is much too low to earn any money!

? Describe a situation where you might want to know the median of a data set.

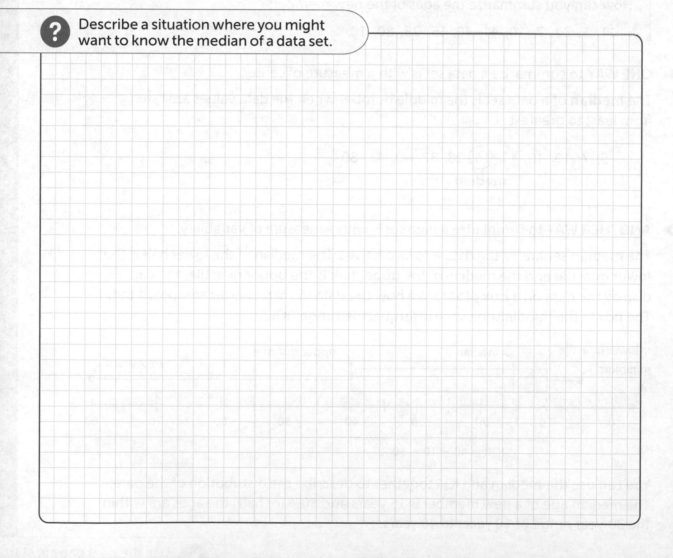

Explore The Median of a Data Set

Previously, you learned about displaying data distributions with dot plots and histograms. In this lesson, you will learn about displaying data distributions with box plots.

➤ **Use what you know to try to solve the problem below.**

The data show the number of grams of sugar in one serving of different types of yogurt. Suppose you are given a serving of yogurt. About how many grams of sugar would you expect it to have?

Grams of Sugar

Serving Size: 5 ounces
Servings per Container: about 6

7	9	15	10	9
5	13	9	8	15

 TRY IT

 Math Toolkit graph paper, number lines, sticky notes

DISCUSS IT

Ask: How is your strategy similar to mine? How is it different?

Share: My strategy shows . . .

◎ **Learning Targets** SMP 1, SMP 2, SMP 3, SMP 4, SMP 5, SMP 6
• Recognize that a measure of center for a numerical data set summarizes all of its values with a single number, while a measure of variation describes how its values vary with a single number.
• Display numerical data in plots on a number line, including dot plots, histograms, and box plots.
• Summarize numerical data sets in relation to their context by giving quantitative measures of center and variability.

CONNECT IT

1 **Look Back** About how many grams of sugar would you expect there to be in one serving of yogurt? Explain how you can answer this question.

2 **Look Ahead** In the **Try It** problem, you chose one number to represent a typical amount of sugar in a serving of yogurt. When you use a single value to summarize a data set, you are using a **measure of center**. One measure of center is the **median**, or middle value when the data values are listed in order.

a. The table shows the number of grams of sugar in one serving of different drinks. List the values in order from least to greatest. What is the middle value of the data set? Describe how you found it.

Grams of Sugar				
14	15	5	30	13
6	8	9	12	7
12	8	13	16	8
24	5			

b. What is the median number of grams of sugar in a drink? How do you know?

c. The median splits the data into two halves. Complete the statements.

About half of the drinks have less than _____ grams of sugar per serving.

About 50% of the drinks have more than _____ grams of sugar per serving.

d. When a data set has an even number of values, there are two middle values. The number halfway between these two values is the median. What is the median of the data set shown below?

4, 4, 5, ⟨5, 7⟩ 8, 10, 11

3 **Reflect** Explain why the median could be a good value to use to summarize all the values of a data set, or to represent a typical value.

Prepare for Interpreting Median and Interquartile Range in Box Plots

1 Think about what you know about data distributions. Fill in each box. Use words, numbers, and pictures. Show as many ideas as you can.

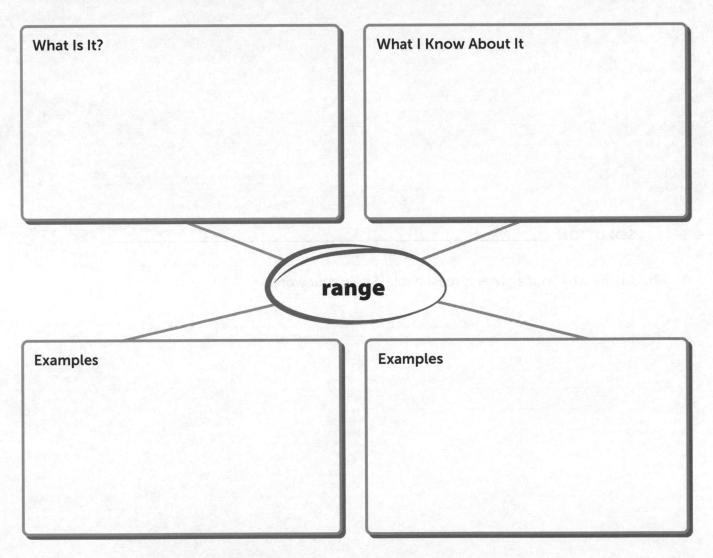

What Is It?	What I Know About It

range

Examples	Examples

2 Explain why the data in Dot Plot A have a greater range than the data in Dot Plot B.

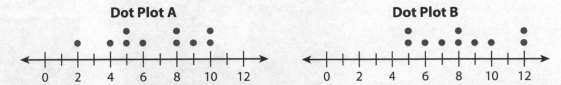

Dot Plot A

0 2 4 6 8 10 12

Dot Plot B

0 2 4 6 8 10 12

3 The list shows how many grams of protein there are in one serving of different brands of yogurt.

8, 10, 6, 12, 14, 6, 10, 12, 13, 6

a. About how many grams of protein would you expect a typical serving of yogurt to have? Show your work.

SOLUTION _____

b. Justify why your answer is reasonable. Show your work.

Develop Finding the Median and Quartiles

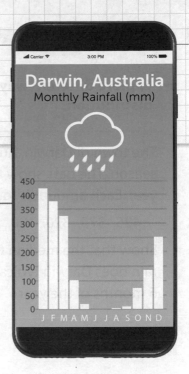

Darwin, Australia
Monthly Rainfall (mm)

➤ **Read and try to solve the problem below.**

The town of Darwin, Australia, has a rainy season and a dry season.
The data show the monthly amount of rainfall in one year. Each amount
is rounded to the nearest 5 millimeters.

425, 375, 320, 100, 20, 0, 0, 5, 15, 70, 140, 250

Show that the median rainfall per month is 85 mm. How much rain does
Darwin typically get per month during the drier 6 months of the year?

TRY IT

 Math Toolkit graph paper, number lines, sticky notes

DISCUSS IT

Ask: How did you use
your model to find a
typical value?

Share: In my
model, . . .

➤ **Explore different ways to use medians to describe a data distribution.**

The town of Darwin, Australia, has a rainy season and a dry season. The data show the monthly amount of rainfall in one year. Each amount is rounded to the nearest 5 millimeters.

425, 375, 320, 100, 20, 0, 0, 5, 15, 70, 140, 250

Show that the median rainfall per month is 85 mm. How much rain does Darwin typically get per month during the drier 6 months of the year?

Model It

You can use the median to describe the center of a data distribution.

To find the median, first list the values in order from least to greatest. Then find the middle value, or the two middle values.

0, 0, 5, 15, 20, (70, 100,) 140, 250, 320, 375, 425

The median is halfway between the **6th** and **7th** values.

You can use a number line to find the halfway point between 70 and 100.

The distance from **70** to **100** is **30** and half of this distance is **15**.

Add half of the distance from 70 to 100 to 70.

The median is **85**.

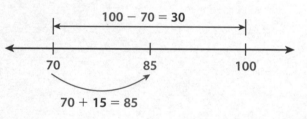

$100 - 70 = 30$

$70 + 15 = 85$

Analyze It

You can find the median of each half of a data distribution.

The median, 85, separates the rainfall data into two halves. The median of the lower half of the data is the **lower quartile (Q1)**. The median of the upper half of the data is the **upper quartile (Q3)**. The median of the whole data set is Q2.

drier 6 months   wetter 6 months

0,   0,   5, ↑15,   20,   70, ↑100,   140,   250, ↑320,   375,   425

lower quartile   median   upper quartile

Q1 = ?   Q2 = 85   Q3 = ?

CONNECT IT

➤ **Use the problem from the previous page to help you understand how to use medians to describe a data distribution.**

1 Look at **Model It.** What does the median, 85, tell you about the amount of rainfall during the year in Darwin, Australia?

2 Look at **Analyze It.** What is the value of the lower quartile (Q1) for the monthly rainfall data? Use Q1 to describe a typical amount of rainfall per month during the drier 6 months of the year.

3 What is the value of the upper quartile (Q3) for the monthly rainfall data? What does this value tell you about rainfall in Darwin, Australia?

4 You can use a median or quartile to help you identify groups of data values.

a. What fraction of the monthly rainfall data is greater than 85 mm?

b. What percent of the data is less than 285 mm?

c. Which data values are in the middle 50% of the monthly rainfall data set?

5 Why are the median, lower quartile, and upper quartile useful for describing data distributions?

6 **Reflect** Think about all the models and strategies you have discussed today. Describe how one of them helped you better understand how to use medians to describe data distributions.

Apply It

➤ **Use what you learned to solve these problems.**

7 A gym has rowing machines with digital screens that display time, distance, and speed. The data show the numbers of miles that members row on Tuesday.

Miles Rowed

2.4	6.8	1.4	3.5	1.8
2.3	0.1	2.2	10.0	0.9
2.0	4.3	3.9	1.0	2.4

3:40/500m   30 MPH
SWEEPER 2

a. Find the median, the lower quartile, and the upper quartile of the data set. (*Note:* When the number of data values is odd, do not include the median in either half of the data as you find Q1 and Q3.) Show your work.

SOLUTION _____

b. What does the median tell you about the number of miles rowed?

8 Students sell coupon books for a fundraiser and report the number sold. The median number of coupon books sold is 2 and the lower and upper quartiles for the data are Q1 = 1 and Q3 = 3.5. Which statement is true?

A   About half of the students sold 2 or more coupon books.

B   About 75% of the students sold more than 3 coupon books.

C   About one fourth of the students sold more than 1 coupon book.

D   About 50% of the students sold either 1 or 2 coupon books.

9 The dot plot shows the number of books in some large libraries in the U.S. What is the median and the lower quartile of the data set? Show your work.

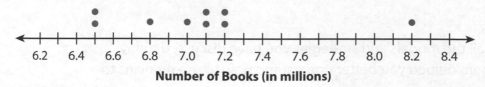

Number of Books (in millions)

SOLUTION _____

Practice Finding the Median and Quartiles

➤ **Study the Example showing how to summarize a data set with a single number. Then solve problems 1–5.**

Example

Noe recorded the price of his favorite granola bar at 9 different stores. What is the median cost of the granola bar at these stores?

$0.85, $0.99, $1.15, $1.27, $1.28, $1.30, $1.30, $1.84, $1.89

Order the values from least to greatest. Find the middle value.

0.85, 0.99, 1.15, 1.27, (1.28,) 1.30, 1.30, 1.84, 1.89

The median cost for the granola bar is $1.28.

1 **a.** Look at the Example. What is the lower quartile (Q1) and upper quartile (Q3) of the granola bar prices? Show your work.

SOLUTION _____

b. What do these values tell you about the cost of the granola bars?

2 Noe sees his favorite granola bar from the Example in a vending machine at an airport. The cost is $2.75. What are the new values of the median, lower quartile, and upper quartile? Show your work.

SOLUTION _____

Vocabulary

median
the middle number, or halfway point between the two middle numbers, in an ordered set of numbers.

lower quartile
the middle number between the minimum and the median in an ordered set of numbers.

upper quartile
the middle number between the median and the maximum in an ordered set of numbers.

3 The table shows the lengths of various musicals in hours.

Musical Lengths (hours)								
2.8	2.8	2.5	2.5	2.3	2.9	2.5	2.6	2.3
2.5	2.5	2.5	2.3	2.6	2.3	5.3	2.5	

a. What are the lower quartile and upper quartile? Show your work.

SOLUTION _____

b. What do the lower and upper quartiles tell you about the middle 50% of the data?

c. Suppose Elias removes the outlier of 5.3 hours. How do the median, Q1, and Q3 change?

4 The data show the number of hours a part-time waiter works each week.

7, 11, 8, 10, 11, 8, 13, 9, 10, 9, 9

Tell whether each statement about the data is *True* or *False*.

	True	False
a. He works more than 9 hours about 50% of the time.	○	○
b. He works 8 or fewer hours about 25% of the time.	○	○
c. He works 10 or more hours about 75% of the time.	○	○

5 Each day for 9 days, a school principal records the number of 6th graders who are absent. Hai says the upper quartile for the data below is 5. Is Hai correct? Explain.

0, 1, 0, 2, 4, 3, 5, 12, 9

Develop Using Box Plots and IQR to Describe Variability

➤ **Read and try to solve the problem below.**

Ziplife company claims that its external battery pack typically adds 9 hours of battery life to a smartphone. Researchers tested a group of the battery packs and recorded the number of extra hours of battery life. Their data are shown in the table. Do you agree with the company's claim? Use data to support your reasoning.

Extra Hours of Battery Life

9.5	3.5	5.5	6.5	6.0
12.5	11.5	13.5	7.5	8.0
8.5	9.5	10.0	10.5	9.0

 TRY IT

 Math Toolkit graph paper, number lines, sticky notes

DISCUSS IT

Ask: How did you get started?

Share: I started by . . .

➤ **Explore different ways to describe the variability of a data set.**

ZipLife company claims that its external battery pack typically adds 9 hours of battery life to a smartphone. Researchers tested a group of the battery packs and recorded the number of extra hours of battery life. Their data are shown in the table. Do you agree with the company's claim? Use data to support your reasoning.

Extra Hours of Battery Life				
9.5	3.5	5.5	6.5	6.0
12.5	11.5	13.5	7.5	8.0
8.5	9.5	10.0	10.5	9.0

Model It

You can use a dot plot to show the variability of a data set.

The minimum (min) and maximum (max) data values determine the range of the data. Locate the median, the lower quartile (Q1), and the upper quartile (Q3).

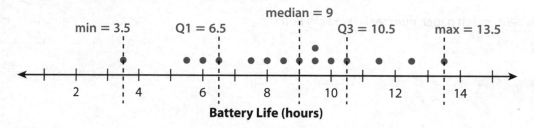

Together, these values are called the *five-number summary* of the data. They can be used to construct a data display called a **box plot**.

Model It

You can use a box plot to analyze the variability of a data set.

A box plot shows how the data in each quarter of the data set are spread out.

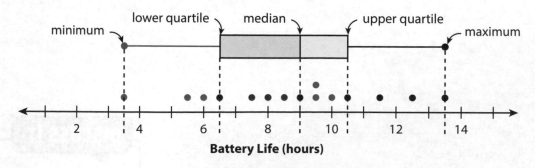

The range and the **interquartile range (IQR)** are both **measures of variability** of a data set.

Range = max − min   Interquartile range = Q3 − Q1

➤ **Use the problem from the previous page to help you understand how to describe the variability of a data set.**

1 Look at the second **Model It**. What are the range and the IQR for the Ziplife battery data? How is the IQR represented in the box plot?

2 Why is the left side of the box wider than the right side of the box?

3 Could Ziplife use the box plot to support its claim? Explain.

4 The researchers test a similar external battery made by the company Novabolt. The double box plot shows the distribution of the data for each company. What can you tell about the center and variability of the two distributions?

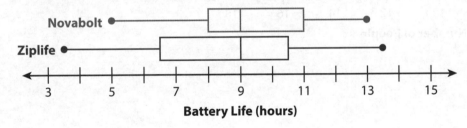

5 How do box plots, range, and IQR help you to analyze variability?

6 **Reflect** Think about all the models and strategies you have discussed today. Describe how one of them helped you better understand how to describe the variability of a data set.

Apply It

➤ **Use what you learned to solve these problems.**

7 Two food truck owners record the number of people who visit
their trucks each day for one week. Which data set has more
variability? Explain.

Food Truck 1
32, 16, 60, 15, 36, 45, 50

Food Truck 2
15, 22, 25, 16, 72, 26, 65

8 A yoga teacher leads a beginner class and an advanced class. He records the
number of people who attend each class for several months. The box plots show
the data. Compare the measures of center and variability.

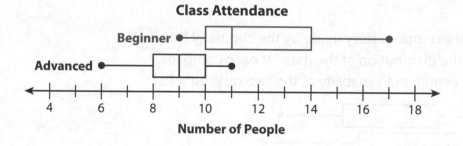

9 Ignacio researched the average
number of students per math class in
different countries. The table shows
the data. Display the data in a box plot.

Number of Students								
21.0	21.5	25.0	21.5	22.0	27.0	22.5	22.0	23.0
23.5	24.0	25.0	25.0	25.0	26.0	26.0	27.0	

Practice Using Box Plots and IQR to Describe Variability

➤ Study the Example showing how to find measures of variability of a data set. Then solve problems 1–4.

Example

Julio earns money as a dog walker. He charges $10 per dog. He records how much money he earns each day in a dot plot. Find the range and IQR of his data.

Daily Dog Walking Earnings

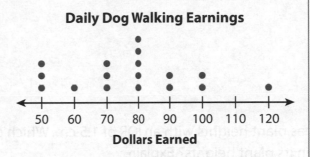

Dollars Earned

Identify the maximum and minimum data values, the median, and the upper and lower quartiles.

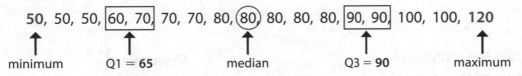

50, 50, 50, 60, 70, 70, 70, 80, 80, 80, 80, 80, 90, 90, 100, 100, 120

minimum   Q1 = 65   median   Q3 = 90   maximum

Range: maximum − minimum = 120 − 50 = 70

IQR: Q3 − Q1 = 90 − 65 = 25

1 a. Use a box plot to display the data from the Example.

b. What does the range tell you about the data?

c. What does the IQR tell you about the data?

Vocabulary

box plot
a visual display of a data set that shows the minimum, the lower quartile, the median, the upper quartile, and the maximum.

interquartile range (IQR)
the difference between the upper quartile and the lower quartile.

2 Students measure the heights, in centimeters, of the plants in two different gardens.

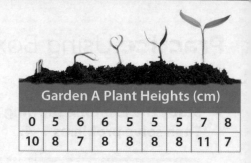

a. The table shows the data for Garden A. Display the data in a box plot.

Garden A Plant Heights (cm)							
0	5	6	6	5	5	5	7	8
10	8	7	8	8	8	8	11	7

b. Garden B has plant heights with an IQR of 1.5 cm. Which garden has less variability in its plant heights? Explain.

3 The box plot shows the number of floors of some skyscrapers in the U.S. Which statements about the box plot are true?

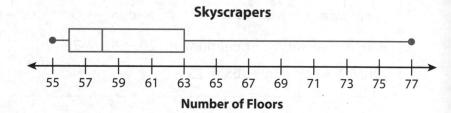

Skyscrapers

55 57 59 61 63 65 67 69 71 73 75 77

Number of Floors

A The range of the data is 22.

B The median number of floors is 58.

C The greatest number of floors is 63.

D About half of the buildings have 56 to 63 floors.

E There are 15 buildings in the data set.

4 Two airlines report their number of delayed flights each month for one year. Airline A has an IQR of 83.5 and Airline B has an IQR of 22. Which airline is the most consistent in not having delays? Explain.

Refine Interpreting Median and Interquartile Range in Box Plots

➤ **Complete the Example below. Then solve problems 1–9.**

Example

A track team needs another runner. The team analyzes the times for the 60-m dash for Runner A and Runner B. What information can you learn from the box plots?

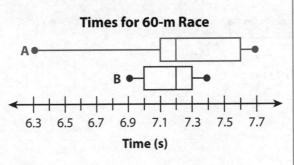

Times for 60-m Race

Time (s)

Look how you could analyze the distributions.

A: median = 7.2; IQR = 7.6 − 7.1 = 0.5; range = 7.7 − 6.3 = 1.4

B: median = 7.2; IQR = 7.3 − 7.0 = 0.3; range = 7.4 − 6.9 = 0.5

SOLUTION _____

_____

_____

Apply It

1 Two types of commercials during awards shows are tracked over a 25-year period. Which type of commercial was more consistently aired? Explain.

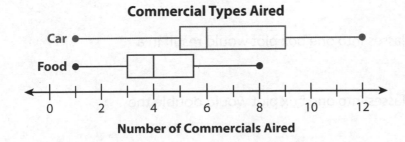

Commercial Types Aired

Number of Commercials Aired

2 Acid rain damages a town's trees. During each rainfall, a scientist collects data on the rain's pH (a measure of acidity). The dot plot shows her data. Draw a box plot above the dot plot to display the distribution. About what percent of the data does the box represent? Explain how the box plot shows this.

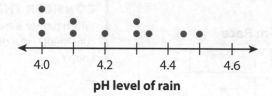

pH level of rain

3 Which statement about the box plots is true?

Average Time Spent on Homework

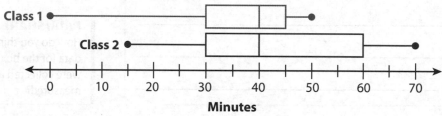

Minutes

A Moving the students from the top 25% of Class 1 into Class 2 would increase the Class 2 median.

B Removing the data for students in Class 1 who did not homework would increase the Class 1 IQR.

C Combining the data from both classes into one box plot would result in a box plot with a range of 105.

D Combining the data from both classes into one box plot would double the current median for Class 1.

Noor chose B as the correct answer. How might she have gotten that answer?

4 Two concert venues record the number of tickets they sell at each show for a year. The box plots show the distribution of the data. Compare the measures of center and variability and explain what they mean in terms of the problem.

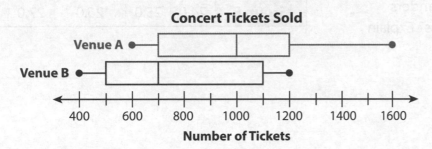

Concert Tickets Sold

5 A farm has 14 spotted pigs. Each spotted pig has at least 1 spot. The median number of spots is 5. The difference between the maximum number of spots and the minimum number of spots is 14.

Which statements are true? Select all that apply.

A There must be at least 1 pig with 5 spots.

B One of the pigs could have 3 spots.

C A pig could have more than 20 spots.

D All pigs must have 15 or fewer spots.

E At least 1 pig has fewer than 5 spots.

6 Researchers test the miles per gallon for two cars. Which car has the greater median? Explain what this means in terms of the situation.

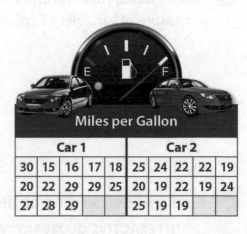

Miles per Gallon

Car 1					Car 2				
30	15	16	17	18	25	24	22	22	19
20	22	29	29	25	20	19	22	19	24
27	28	29			25	19	19		

7 A scientist reports the the information shown about the masses, in grams, of two groups of salamanders. Construct a box plot for each data set. Which group of salamanders shows greater variability in mass? Explain how you know.

	Min	Q1	Median	Q3	Max
Group A	14.5	17.0	20.0	22.0	30.0
Group B	24.0	25.0	26.0	27.0	28.0

8 Hockey Team A records its final score for every game in a season. The minimum is 0, Q1 is 1, the median is 2, Q3 is 3, and the maximum is 5. Hockey Team B's final scores for the season have an IQR of 6. Which team is more consistent in its number of points scored per game? Explain your reasoning.

9 **Math Journal** Construct a data set that has 10 as a measure of center and 7 as a measure of variability. Explain what these measures mean in terms of the data.

✔ End of Lesson Checklist

☐ **INTERACTIVE GLOSSARY** Write a new entry for *interquartile range (IQR)*. Tell how the interquartile range (IQR) of a data set varies with the situation.

☐ **SELF CHECK** Go back to the Unit 7 Opener and see what you can check off.

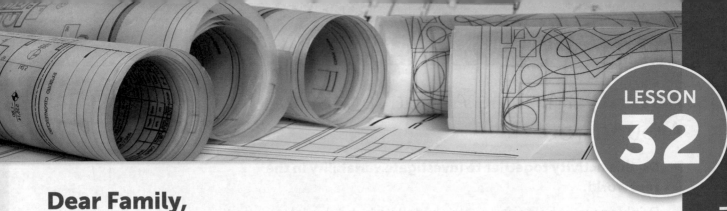

Dear Family,

This week your student is learning how to find the mean and mean absolute deviation of a data set.

The **mean** of a data set is a measure of center that represents the average of the data values. The **mean absolute deviation (MAD)** is a measure of variability that represents the average distance of a data point from the mean. The MAD describes how spread out the values are from the mean value.

Your student will be learning to solve problems like the one below.

> The ages, in years, of 5 new members of a school architecture club are listed. How can you describe the ages of the new members?
>
> 12, 12, 16, 15, 15

➤ **ONE WAY** to describe, or summarize, a data set is with a measure of center.

To find the mean of a data set, divide the **sum of the data values** by the **number of data values**.

$$\frac{12 + 12 + 16 + 15 + 15}{5} = \frac{70}{5} = 14$$

➤ **ANOTHER WAY** to summarize a data set is with a measure of variability.

To find the average distance of a data value from the mean, you must first find each data value's distance from the **mean**, 14.

Data Value	12	12	16	15	15
Distance from 14	2	2	2	1	1

Now look at the data set in the second row of the table. Find the mean of this data set. Divide the **sum of the distances from the mean** by the **number of distances**. The result is the **mean absolute deviation (MAD)** of the *original* data set.

$$\frac{2 + 2 + 2 + 1 + 1}{5} = \frac{8}{5} = \textbf{1.6}$$

You can use the mean and MAD together to describe the distribution of the data. The mean age of a new member is 14 years. On average, a new member's age is within 1.6 years of 14 years.

 Use the next page to start a conversation about measures of variability.

Activity Thinking About Variability Around You

➤ **Do this activity together to investigate variability in the real world.**

Drinking water helps you to stay hydrated, but did you know that drinking enough water has other benefits? Water also helps to bring nutrients and oxygen to all the cells in your body. Drinking water even helps you digest your food!

Look at the two dot plots. One dot plot shows how many cups of water 20 children drank in one day. The other dot plot shows how many cups of water 20 adults drank in one day. There is a lot more variability in the number of cups of water children drink than there is in the number of cups of water adults drink.

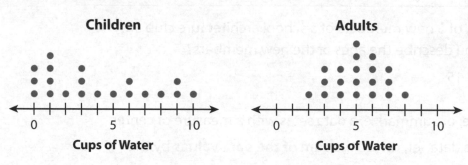

Children

Cups of Water

Adults

Cups of Water

? Why do you think there might be more variability in the amount of water children drink than adults drink?

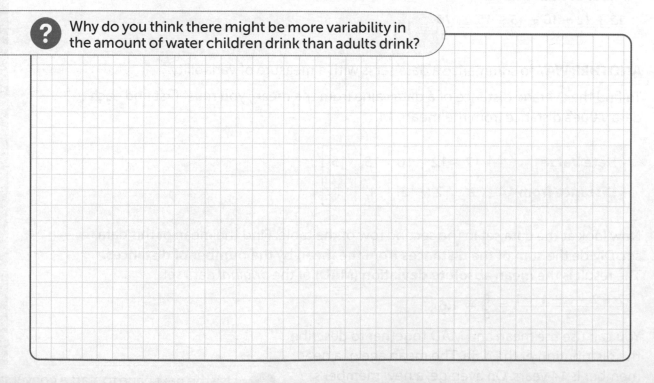

Explore The Mean of a Data Set

Previously, you learned to use the median and interquartile range (IQR) to describe the center and variability of a data set. In this lesson, you will learn about another measure of center, the mean, and another measure of variability, the mean absolute deviation.

➤ **Use what you know to try to solve the problem below.**

A city has a bike-sharing program. A manager of the program wants to know whether there are enough bikes at the bike stations in the neighborhood of Benton Hills. The data show the number of bikes currently at the neighborhood's 25 bike stations. Based on the data set, what is a typical number of bikes at a station?

Benton Hills

Number of Bikes

8	10	3	11	8
21	23	22	8	8
25	12	3	5	12
10	15	5	15	5
0	1	10	4	6

TRY IT

Math Toolkit counters, graph paper, number lines, sticky notes

DISCUSS IT

Ask: What did you do first to identify a typical value for the data set? Why did you do this step?

Share: First, I . . . because . . .

Learning Targets SMP 1, SMP 2, SMP 3, SMP 4, SMP 5, SMP 6
- Recognize that a measure of center for a numerical data set summarizes all of its values with a single number, while a measure of variation describes how its values vary with a single number.
- Summarize numerical data sets in relation to their context by giving quantitative measures of center and variability, as well as describing any overall pattern and any striking deviations from the overall pattern.

CONNECT IT

1 **Look Back** Based on the data set, what is a typical number of bikes at a bike station in the Benton Hills neighborhood? Explain.

2 **Look Ahead** The median is not the only way to use a single number to summarize a data set. Use the data set shown in the bar graph to explore another measure of center.

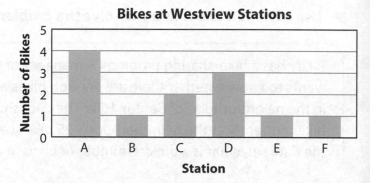

a. The first bar graph shows the number of bikes currently at bike stations A–F in the neighborhood of Westview. Complete the second bar graph to show how many bikes would be at stations A–F if all the bikes are distributed equally among the stations.

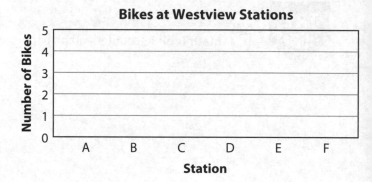

b. How does the number of bikes at each station change when the bikes are distributed equally among the stations?

c. When the bikes are distributed equally, the number of bikes at a station is the **mean**, or average, of the original data set. Like the median of a data set, the mean is a measure of center. What is the mean number of bikes at a station?

3 **Reflect** Why do you think the mean of a data set is sometimes described as a *fair share* of the data set?

Prepare for Interpreting Mean and Mean Absolute Deviation

1 Think about what you know about data and variability. Fill in each box. Use words, numbers, and pictures. Show as many ideas as you can.

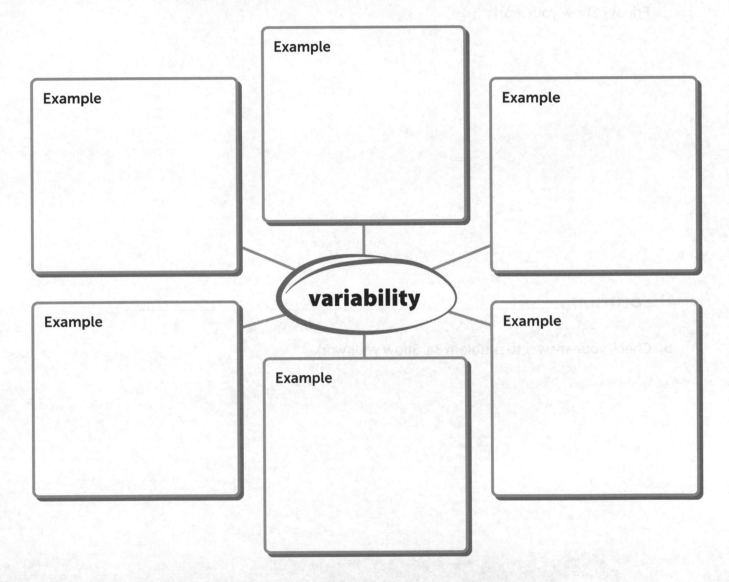

Example

Example

Example

variability

Example

Example

Example

2 Which data set would you expect to have more variability: the ages of the 6th grade students at a school or the ages of the 6th grade teachers at the school? Explain.

LESSON 32 Interpret Mean and Mean Absolute Deviation   **719**

3 Visitors to a state capitol building can take a free tour. The manager in charge of the tours wants to know a typical number of visitors in a tour group. The list shows the number of visitors in the 17 tour groups on Friday.

38, 23, 40, 35, 36, 28, 40, 26, 40, 37, 22, 32, 18, 28, 29, 26, 29

a. Based on the data set, what is a typical number of visitors in a tour group on Friday? Show your work.

SOLUTION _____

b. Check your answer to problem 3a. Show your work.

Develop Finding the Mean

➤ **Read and try to solve the problem below.**

For Earth Day, volunteers are cleaning up the shore of a lake. A team of 9 students is collecting trash. Their goal is to collect 5 lb of trash per person. The list shows the weight, in pounds, of trash each student collects.

Pounds of Trash
7, 2, 4, 4, 6, 3, 7, 9, 3

What is a typical amount of trash that a student on the team collects? How does this amount compare to the team's goal?

TRY IT   **Math Toolkit** connecting cubes, counters, graph paper, number lines

➤ **Explore different ways to find the mean of a data set.**

For Earth Day, volunteers are cleaning up the shore of a lake. A team of 9 students is collecting trash. Their goal is to collect 5 lb of trash per person. The list shows the weight, in pounds, of trash each student collects.

7, 2, 4, 4, 6, 3, 7, 9, 3

What is a typical amount of trash that a student on the team collects? How does this amount compare to the team's goal?

Picture It

You can think of the mean of a data set as the balance point of the data.

To find the balance point, move the left-most and right-most points 1 unit each toward the middle. Repeat this step until all data points stack above a single value.

Step 1

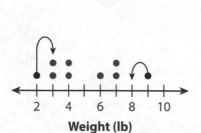

Weight (lb)

Step 2

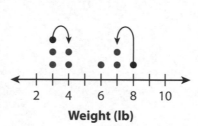

Weight (lb)

Final Step

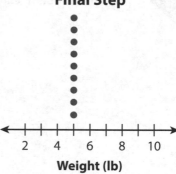

Weight (lb)

Analyze It

You can calculate the mean by finding the average of the data.

The average of a data set is the sum of the data values divided by the number of data values.

Sum of data values: $7 + 2 + 4 + 4 + 6 + 3 + 7 + 9 + 3 = 45$

Sum ÷ number of data values: $\frac{45}{9}$

Mean = ?

➤ **Use the problem from the previous page to help you understand how to find the mean of a data set.**

1 Look at **Picture It**. What does moving a pair of points represent about the pounds of trash two students collect? Does the total amount the team collects change?

2 How does the final dot plot show that the team met its goal?

3 Look at **Analyze It**. What is the mean weight of trash a student on the team collects? Why could you call this a typical amount of trash collected by a student?

4 The dot plots represent three different data sets. Why do the three data sets have the same mean?

5 Why is the mean considered a measure of center of a data set? How is the mean different from the median?

6 **Reflect** Think about all the models and strategies you have discussed today. Describe how one of them helped you better understand how to find the mean of a data set.

Apply It

➤ **Use what you learned to solve these problems.**

7 Lola is in an archery club. She shoots 6 arrows and earns the scores shown in the list.

Lola's Archery Scores
10, 7, 9, 10, 9, 0

   a. How does the mean and median change if the outlier of 0 is left out of the data set? Show your work.

SOLUTION _____

   b. Why does the outlier have a greater effect on the mean than on the median?

8 There are several rare insects on display at the insect exhibit at a science museum. The dot plot shows the lengths of the insects to the nearest $\frac{1}{8}$ in. What is the mean length of the insects? Show your work.

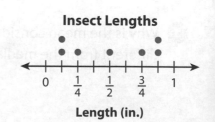

Insect Lengths

Length (in.)

SOLUTION _____

Practice Finding the Mean

➤ **Study the Example showing how to find the mean of a data set. Then solve problems 1–4.**

Example

Students in Fiona's class each listen to a different radio station for 20 min one night and count the number of commercials. The list shows their data.

6, 3, 4, 2, 3, 1, 3, 3, 7, 1, 0, 0, 0, 2, 4

What is the mean number of commercials in 20 min?

You can find the mean by adding the data values and then dividing the sum by the number of values. You can use multiplication to group the values that are the same before adding.

$$\text{Mean} = \frac{(3 \cdot 0) + (2 \cdot 1) + (2 \cdot 2) + (3 \cdot 4) + (2 \cdot 4) + 6 + 7}{15}$$

$$= \frac{39}{15} = 2.6$$

The mean is 2.6, so the mean number of commercials in 20 min is 2.6.

---

1 Lian is absent from class the day the students in the Example combine their data. He counted 13 commercials when he listened for 20 min.

a. How does the mean change when Lian includes his data in the class data set? Show your work.

SOLUTION _____

b. Does Lian's value also change the median of the data set? Why or why not?

2 The dot plot shows the amounts of Michael's last 5 paychecks. What is the mean of the amounts? Show your work.

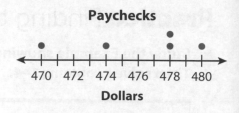

Paychecks

470 472 474 476 478 480

Dollars

SOLUTION _____

3 The lists show the numbers of students in each math class at two different schools.

East Middle School: 24, 26, 28, 27, 24, 24, 22, 26, 27, 22

Grove Middle School: 18, 25, 25, 29, 28, 26, 28, 28, 27, 26

a. Which school has the greater mean number of students per math class? Show your work.

SOLUTION _____

b. What do the means of the data sets represent in this situation?

4 The table shows the number of players on each team in a softball league. Suppose two people on the team with the most players move to the team with the fewest players. How would the mean number of players per team change? Explain how you know.

Number of Players				
12	11	12	12	11
9	13	15	13	12

Develop Finding and Interpreting Mean Absolute Deviation

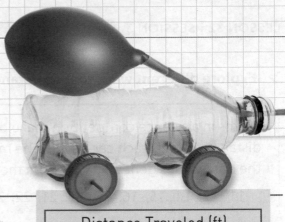

➤ **Read and try to solve the problem below.**

Teams in a science competition make balloon-powered cars. The list shows the distance, in feet, each car travels. The mean distance traveled is 19 ft. How much do the data values generally vary from the mean distance?

Distance Traveled (ft)					
11	12	14	15	16	17
18	21	22	23	28	31

  Math Toolkit graph paper, number lines, sticky notes

➤ **Explore different ways to understand variability in a data set.**

Teams in a science competition make balloon-powered cars. The list shows the distance, in feet, each car travels. The mean distance traveled is 19 ft. How much do the data values generally vary from the mean distance?

11, 12, 14, 15, 16, 17, 18, 21, 22, 23, 28, 31

Model It

You can use a number line to show how far each data value is from the mean.

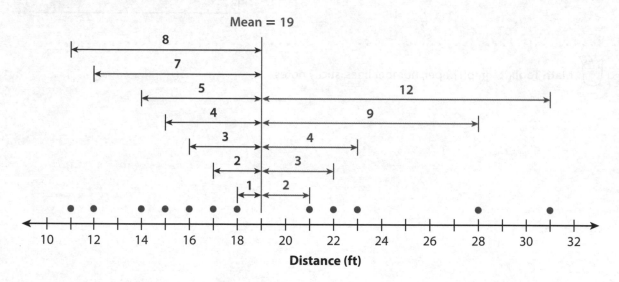

Analyze It

You can use the average distance of data values from the mean as a measure of variability. This average distance is called the **mean absolute deviation (MAD)**.

Data Value	Distance from Mean	Data Value	Distance from Mean
11	19 − 11 = **8**	21	21 − 19 = **2**
12	19 − 12 = **7**	22	22 − 19 = **3**
14	19 − 14 = **5**	23	23 − 19 = **4**
15	19 − 15 = **4**	28	28 − 19 = **9**
16	19 − 16 = **3**	31	31 − 19 = **12**
17	19 − 17 = **2**		
18	19 − 18 = **1**		

MAD

$$= \frac{\text{sum of distances from mean}}{\text{number of data values}}$$

$$= \frac{8 + 7 + 5 + 4 + 3 + 2 + 1 + 2 + 3 + 4 + 9 + 12}{12}$$

$$= \frac{60}{12}$$

$$= 5$$

CONNECT IT

> **Use the problem from the previous page to help you understand variability in a data set.**

1. Look at **Model It**. Find the point for the car that traveled 28 ft. How much farther than the mean distance did this car travel? How is this shown in the model?

2. Describe what the distance labeled **5** tells you about one of the cars.

3. Look at **Analyze It**. What do the data values in the left table have in common? What do the data values in the right table have in common? How are the subtraction equations in the tables related to the number line model?

4. Look at the fractions used to find the MAD. How is the process of finding a MAD like the process of finding a mean? What data set are you finding the mean of?

5. The MAD of the distances the cars traveled is 5. What does a MAD of 5 tell you in this situation?

6. How many cars traveled distances that are within 5 ft of the mean? How does this help you understand MAD as a measure of variability in a data set?

7. **Reflect** Think about all the models and strategies you have discussed today. Describe how one of them helped you better understand variability in a data set.

Apply It

➤ **Use what you learned to solve these problems.**

8 Imani asks 10 students about the number of hours they slept last night. She finds that the mean sleeping time is 9 h. Find the MAD of Imani's data set and describe what it means in this situation. Show your work.

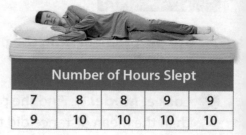

Number of Hours Slept				
7	8	8	9	9
9	10	10	10	10

SOLUTION _____

_____

9 At a doctor's office, the mean amount of time patients spend in the waiting room is 18 min. The MAD of the wait times is 7 min. Based on this information, would it be unusual for a patient to wait for 25 min in the doctor's waiting room? Explain.

10 Students in Naomi's class record the number of hours they spend volunteering in May. The dot plot shows their data. The mean time is 3 hours. Find the MAD of the data set. Show your work.

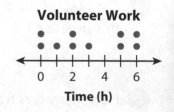

Volunteer Work

Time (h)

SOLUTION _____

Practice Finding and Interpreting Mean Absolute Deviation

➤ **Study the Example showing how to find the mean absolute deviation of a data set. Then solve problems 1–4.**

Example

The list shows the heights, in inches, of the five starting players on a men's college basketball team.

74, 74, 76, 80, 81

The mean height is 77 in. What is the MAD of the heights?

You can find the MAD (mean absolute deviation) of the data by finding the **distance** between each data value and the **mean**. Then find the average of the distances from the mean.

$$\text{MAD} = \frac{\text{sum of distances from mean}}{\text{number of data values}}$$

$$= \frac{3 + 3 + 1 + 3 + 4}{5}$$

$$= \frac{14}{5} = 2.8$$

Data Value	Distance from Mean
74	$77 - 74 = 3$
74	$77 - 74 = 3$
76	$77 - 76 = 1$
80	$80 - 77 = 3$
81	$81 - 77 = 4$

The MAD of the heights is 2.8 in.

1 **a.** What does the MAD of the heights in the Example tell you?

b. The heights of the starting players on a different team have a mean of 78 in. and a MAD of 3.6 in. How do the heights of the players on the two teams compare?

Vocabulary

mean absolute deviation (MAD)
the sum of the distances of each data point from the mean of the data set divided by the number of data points.

Bobcat Weights (lb)
17, 20, 18, 14, 26,
13, 23, 22, 27

2 The list shows the weights of the bobcats at a nature reserve.
What are the mean and MAD of the weights? Show your work.

SOLUTION _____

3 The dot plots show the number of photos Ravi
and Inés took each day for 10 days. How can
you tell, without calculating, which data set has
a greater MAD?

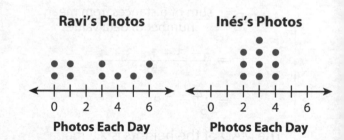

4 Paulo counts the number of cherry fruit snacks in 7 bags of mixed fruit snacks.
The list shows his data. The mean is 23 cherry snacks per bag.

14, 23, 29, 31, 15, 19, 30

Based on the data, would it be unusual to get a bag with 17 cherry snacks?
Use the MAD of the data to support your answer.

Refine Interpreting Mean and Mean Absolute Deviation

➤ **Complete the Example below. Then solve problems 1–8.**

Example

On Fridays, the mean amount a smoothie shop makes in sales is $2,287, with a MAD of $314. On Saturdays, the mean amount the shop makes in sales is $1,934, with a MAD of $152. On which of the two days does the shop typically make more money? On which day are the sales generally more consistent?

Look at how you could interpret the means and MADs.

The mean is a measure of center, so it can represent a typical value in a data set. The mean sales for Fridays are greater than the mean sales for Saturdays.

The MAD is a measure of variability. The less variability a data set has, the more consistent the data values are. The MAD for Saturdays is less than the MAD for Fridays.

SOLUTION _____

_____

PAIR/SHARE
Would it be unusual for the shop to make $2,500 in sales on a Friday? Explain.

Apply It

1 Roberto sells lemonade to raise money for charity. He collects data on the cost of lemonade at other lemonade stands. He uses the mean of his data as the price of lemonade at his stand. How much does lemonade cost at Roberto's stand? Show your work.

Cost of Lemonade ($)		
2.00	1.00	1.25
1.50	0.50	1.25
1.00	0.50	3.00
1.00	1.25	1.50
1.25	1.25	1.25

CONSIDER THIS . . .
You can find the mean of a set of decimals the same way you find the mean of a set of whole numbers.

PAIR/SHARE
How does the cost of lemonade at Roberto's stand compare to the median cost of lemonade at the other stands?

SOLUTION _____

2 The list shows the lengths, in seconds, of the routines in a dance competition.

162, 140, 160, 159, 141, 163, 159, 164

Zara wants to know how much the times for the dance routines vary. What is the MAD of the dance times? Show your work.

CONSIDER THIS . . .
To find the MAD of a data set, you first need to know the mean of the data set.

PAIR/SHARE
How do you know that your answer is reasonable?

SOLUTION _____

3 The table shows the number of books on the shelves in the science fiction section of a library. A librarian adds 32 more books to the shelf with only 6 books. How does this change affect the mean and median number of books per shelf?

Books on a Shelf			
62	56	63	52
56	48	57	6

CONSIDER THIS . . .
How do outliers affect measures of center?

A It increases both the mean and the median.

B It increases the mean, but not the median.

C It increases the median, but not the mean.

D It does not increase the mean or the median.

Uma chose A as the correct answer. How might she have gotten that answer?

PAIR/SHARE
How would the mean and median be affected if the librarian added 32 more books to the shelf with 63 books, instead of the shelf with 6 books?

4 Elijah tracks the number of steps he takes each day for 7 days.

Number of Steps						
10,740	12,168	13,760	12,468	11,541	12,847	11,904

a. What is Elijah's mean number of steps per day? Show your work.

SOLUTION _____

b. On Day 8, Elijah walks 9,924 steps. He says the expression $\frac{85,428 + 9,924}{8}$

represents the mean with the value for Day 8 included. Is Elijah correct? Explain.

5 During a 2-week time period, Denver has a mean high temperature of 72°F with a MAD of 5.66°F. During the same 2-week period, San Diego has a mean high temperature of 70°F with a MAD of 1.65°F. Compare the means and MADs and tell what they indicate about the high temperatures of the two cities.

6 Which of the following could be used to calculate the MAD of a data distribution? Select all that apply.

A Dot plot

B Frequency table

C Box plot

D List of data values

E Histogram

7 Brianna's speed-skating coach times her as she skates laps during practice. The table shows her times, to the nearest tenth of a second, for 8 laps.

a. Brianna's mean lap time is 27.4 seconds. What is the MAD of her lap times? Show your work.

Lap Times (seconds)			
26.6	26.5	25.1	29.3
28.5	27.0	28.5	27.7

SOLUTION _____

b. During the same practice, Layla's mean time for skating a lap is 26.6 seconds with a MAD of 2.1 seconds. Which skater, Brianna or Layla, had more consistent times during practice? Explain how you know.

8 **Math Journal** Make up a data set of five values with a mean of 10 and a median of 12. None of the values in your data set can be repeated. Explain how you determined the values in your set.

✓ **End of Lesson Checklist**

☐ **INTERACTIVE GLOSSARY** Find the entry for *mean*. Tell how the mean and median of a data set are alike.

☐ **SELF CHECK** Go back to the Unit 7 Opener and see what you can check off.

Dear Family,

This week your student is learning about choosing measures of center and variability to summarize and compare data sets.

Your student will be learning to solve problems like the one below.

Alberto and Hannah are practicing throwing fastballs for a baseball game. The lists show the two pitchers' practice speeds in miles per hour.

Alberto: 63, 65, 71, 62, 60, 62, 71, 65, 69, 67, 64

Hannah: 57, 66, 73, 62, 56, 73, 71, 74, 55, 70, 68

How can you compare Alberto's and Hannah's fastball pitching speeds?

➤ **ONE WAY** to compare the two data sets is to compare medians and IQRs.

Use the **median** to represent a typical fastball speed. Use the **lower** and **upper quartiles** to find the **interquartile range (IQR)**.

Alberto

60, 62, **62**, 63, 64, **65**, 65, 67, **69**, 71, 71   IQR = **69** − **62** = 7

Hannah

55, 56, **57**, 62, 66, **68**, 70, 71, **73**, 73, 74   IQR = **73** − **57** = 16

➤ **ANOTHER WAY** is to compare the means and MADs of the data sets.

Use the **mean**, or average, to represent a typical fastball speed. Use the distances of the speeds from the mean to find the average distance from the mean, or the **mean absolute deviation (MAD)**.

Alberto

Mean = $\frac{719}{11}$, or about **65.4**   MAD = $\frac{33.2}{11}$, or about **3**

Hannah

Mean = $\frac{725}{11}$, or about **65.9**   MAD = $\frac{67.3}{11}$, or about **6**

Using either pair of measures of center and variability, you can see that Hannah's typical fastball is faster than Alberto's and Alberto's fastball speeds show less variability. Hannah may often pitch faster than Alberto, but Alberto is the more consistent pitcher.

 Use the next page to start a conversation about measures of center.

Activity Choosing Measures of Center

➤ **Do this activity together to examine choices between measures of center.**

The shape of a distribution can help you choose either the mean, the median, or both as a measure of center that summarizes the data. For the data sets below, the circled measures of center are good choices for a typical value of the data set.

What do you notice about how the choice of measure of center relates to the shape of the distribution?

DATA SET 1

This dot plot shows how many points each player on a basketball team scored during the season.

Median = 3   Mean = 5.65

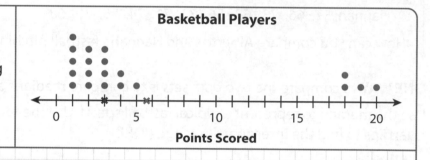

Basketball Players

Points Scored

DATA SET 2

This dot plot shows how many extra credit points math students earned in one month.

Median = 30   Mean = 29$\frac{2}{3}$

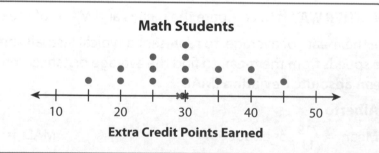

Math Students

Extra Credit Points Earned

? How would you describe the variability of the two data sets?

Explore Choosing a Measure of Center

Previously, you learned about measures of center and variability. In this lesson, you will learn about choosing appropriate measures to describe data.

➤ **Use what you know to try to solve the problem below.**

Mr. Shen wants to know how long it typically takes a student in his class to get to school. Which measure of center do you think he should choose to represent the typical time?

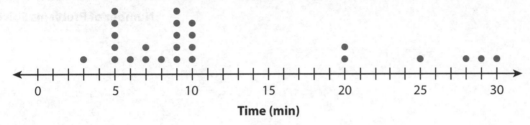

Travel Times for Mr. Shen's Students

Time (min)

 TRY IT

 Math Toolkit graph paper, number lines, sticky notes

DISCUSS IT

Ask: How did you decide which measure of center to use?

Share: I picked . . . because . . .

 Learning Target SMP 1, SMP 2, SMP 3, SMP 4, SMP 5, SMP 6
Summarize numerical data sets in relation to their context by relating the choice of measures of center and variability to the shape of the data distribution and the context in which the data were gathered.

CONNECT IT

1 Look Back Which measure of center do you think Mr. Shen should choose to represent the typical travel time for a student? Explain your reasoning.

2 Look Ahead Mr. Shen gives his students some math problems. The dot plot shows the number of problems each student solves.

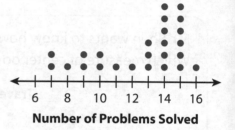

Number of Problems Solved

a. Find the median and the mean of the data set.

b. Describe the shape of the data distribution. Are there any outliers?

c. Which measure of center is more affected by the skew of the distribution? Why?

d. Would you choose the *mean* or the *median* to represent the typical number of problems a student solves. Explain your reasoning.

3 Reflect How can the shape of a data distribution affect which measure of center you choose to describe the data?

Prepare for Using Measures of Center and Variability to Summarize Data

1 Think about what you know about measures of center and variability. Fill in each box. Use words, numbers, and pictures. Show as many ideas as you can.

Word	In My Own Words	Examples
mean		
mean absolute deviation (MAD)		
median		
interquartile range (IQR)		

2 The distribution of a certain data set is perfectly symmetric. Is the mean *greater than, equal to,* or *less than* the median? Explain your reasoning.

LESSON 33 Use Measures of Center and Variability to Summarize Data   **741**

3 The dot plot shows the masses of female wolf pups in a Minnesota forest.

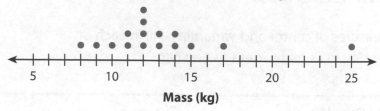

Mass (kg)

a. A forest ranger wants to report the mass of a typical female wolf pup. Which measure of center do you think she should choose to represent the typical mass? Explain your reasoning.

b. Check your answer to problem 3a. Show your work.

Develop Choosing Measures of Center and Variability

➤ **Read and try to solve the problem below.**

Two Double-Dutch teams practice for a competition. The goal is to get the greatest number of jumps possible in 2 min. The lists show their practice scores in number of jumps.

Pink Team: 430, 422, 424, 410, 396, 401, 432, 420, 412, 424, 406, 427

Green Team: 411, 409, 402, 420, 418, 411, 406, 421, 415, 414, 417, 412

Use the data sets to support an argument that one team is more likely than the other to win in a competition.

TRY IT   **Math Toolkit** graph paper, number lines, sticky notes

DISCUSS IT

Ask: How can you explain what the problem is asking in your own words?

Share: The problem is asking . . .

➤ **Explore different ways to choose measures of center and variability.**

Two Double-Dutch teams practice for a competition. The goal is to get the greatest number of jumps possible in 2 min. The lists show their practice scores in number of jumps.

Pink Team: 430, 422, 424, 410, 396, 401, 432, 420, 412, 424, 406, 427

Green Team: 411, 409, 402, 420, 418, 411, 406, 421, 415, 414, 417, 412

Use the data sets to support an argument that one team is more likely than the other to win in a competition.

Model It

You can use a data display to compare the shapes of the distributions.

Practice Scores

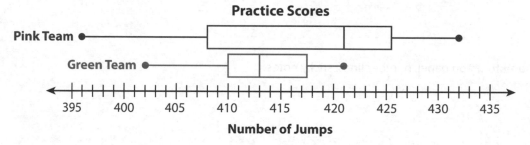

The box plots show that the median of the Pink Team's scores is greater than the median of the Green Team's scores. However, the Green Team's scores are less variable than the Pink Team's scores.

Analyze It

You can use measures of center and variability to compare the data sets.

Compare the medians, ranges, and IQRs for the two teams' scores.

	Pink Team's Scores	Green Team's Scores
Median	421	413
Range	432 − 396 = **36**	421 − 402 = 19
IQR	425.5 − 408 = **17.5**	417.5 − 410 = **7.5**

➤ **Use the problem from the previous page to help you understand how to choose measures of center and variability.**

1 Look at the values of the medians shown in **Analyze It**. Which team has the greater median? How is this relationship shown in the box plot?

2 Look at the IQRs in the table. An IQR of **17.5** is more than two times an IQR of **7.5**. How is this relationship shown in the box plots? What does this tell you?

3 How can you use the data to argue that the Green Team is more likely to win?

4 Look at the box plots. The line inside the box for the Pink Team lines up with the right-most point of the Green Team's plot. How could you use this to support an argument that the Pink Team is more likely to win in a competition?

5 How can you choose measures of center and variability to describe data sets?

6 **Reflect** Think about all the models and strategies you have discussed today. Describe how one of them helped you better understand how to solve the **Try It** problem.

LESSON 33 Use Measures of Center and Variability to Summarize Data

Apply It

➤ **Use what you learned to solve these problems.**

7 A competitive wood chopper keeps track of how long it takes to chop a log in half during 13 competitions. The list shows his results. Would you choose the IQR or the MAD to summarize the variability of the times? Answer without finding the IQR or MAD. Explain your reasoning.

Log Chop Times (seconds)
12, 13, 14, 15, 15, 15, 16,
17, 18, 18, 19, 20, 42

8 The histograms show quiz scores of the students in Ms. Shaw's class. Is the range the most appropriate measure of variability for comparing the data sets? Explain.

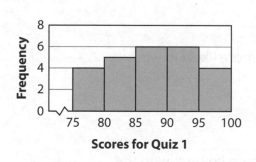

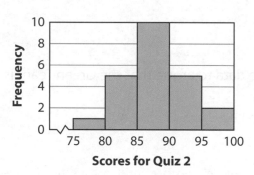

9 The lists show the number of grams of fat in the subs sold at two sandwich shops.

Juan's Subs: 24, 5, 52, 12, 15, 10, 4, 26, 45, 6

Efia's Subs: 28, 13, 18, 12, 13, 15, 16, 18, 10, 7

How can you use the data to support the argument that the subs at Efia's shop have less fat than the subs at Juan's?

Practice Choosing Measures of Center and Variability

➤ **Study the Example showing how to choose measures of center and variability. Then solve problems 1–4.**

Example

Button and Fluffy are popular cats online. The lists show the number of "likes," in thousands, each of their last 16 photos received.

Button: 27, 21, 21, 29, 20, 15, 17, 20, 19, 29, 18, 28, 28, 29, 21, 26

Fluffy: 19, 21, 10, 26, 24, 19, 25, 25, 24, 10, 25, 24, 24, 22, 28, 10

Based on this data, which cat would you say is more popular?

You can display the data to see the shape of each distribution.

You can argue that Fluffy is more popular than Button because the median number of likes for his photos is greater than for Button's.

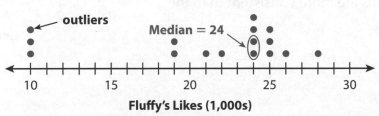

1 Use the data in the Example to argue that Button is more popular than Fluffy.

2 The table shows the daily attendance for a swimming pool over a period of 2 weeks.

The pool manager wants to determine the typical daily attendance. Which measure should the manager find and why?

Daily Attendance						
269	282	52	216	239	264	210
242	285	54	259	259	252	197

A The mean, because it is influenced by outliers

B The median, because it is not affected by a few outliers

C The interquartile range, because it gives the range of the middle 50% of the attendance values

D The mean absolute deviation, because it gives the average distance of the attendance values from the middle

3 The box plots show the number of goals scored by two hockey teams in their first 20 games of a season. Use the data to support the argument that the Sea Lions are more consistent than the Lightning Bolts.

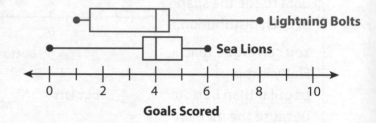

4 An employee at a seafood market tries to measure portions of shrimp that weigh exactly 20 oz each. The list shows the initial measurements, in ounces, of five portions.

20.1, 20.4, 30.2, 20.2, 20.2

Decide whether the *interquartile range* or the *mean absolute deviation* is a better measure of variability. Do this without making any calculations. Explain your reasoning.

Refine Using Measures of Center and Variability to Summarize Data

➤ **Complete the Example below. Then solve problems 1–8.**

Example

The list shows the combined scores for a diver. Athletes with the highest typical scores are allowed to compete for the championship.

67.5, 68.2, 81.0, 81.6, 83.2, 84.8, 84.8, 91.2, 91.2

Which measure would the diver likely prefer to use to describe her diving scores, the mean or the median? Explain.

Look at how you could choose an appropriate measure of center.

Mean:
$$\frac{67.5 + 68.2 + 81 + 81.6 + 83.2 + 2 \cdot 84.8 + 2 \cdot 91.2}{9} = \frac{733.5}{9} = 81.5$$

Median:
67.5, 68.2, 81.0, 81.6, (83.2) 84.8, 84.8, 91.2, 91.2

The mean of the diver's scores is 81.5, and the median is 83.2.

SOLUTION _____

_____

CONSIDER THIS . . .
How is this question different from the question *Which measure of center best represents the data?*

PAIR/SHARE
What measure of center might a competitor prefer to use to describe this diver's scores? Why?

Apply It

1 The list shows the daily attendance at a skate park for 1 week.

23, 27, 20, 92, 88, 94, 90

Would you choose the *mean* or the *median* as a measure of the center of the data set? Explain your reasoning.

CONSIDER THIS . . .
Does the data set have outliers? How do you know?

PAIR/SHARE
Would your answer change if you wanted to argue that attendance at the skate park is high? Explain.

2 The students in Ms. Díaz's class want to answer this statistical question: *What is a typical number of raisins in a snack-size box?*

Each student counts the number of raisins in a different box. The dot plot shows their results. Based on the data, what is the answer to the students' question? Explain your reasoning.

CONSIDER THIS . . .
How could you use the shape of the distribution to find the mean and median without doing any calculations?

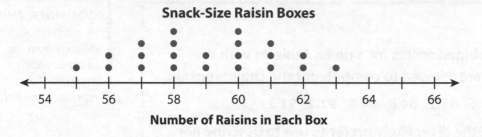

Snack-Size Raisin Boxes

Number of Raisins in Each Box

PAIR/SHARE
Why are the mean and median both appropriate measures for describing the data set?

3 Grace and Maria are practicing for a fitness test. Each day, they do as many curl-ups as they can in 1 min.

CONSIDER THIS . . .
What does a greater mean absolute deviation tell you about a data set?

	Mean	MAD	Min	Q1	Median	Q3	Max
Grace	36	3.25	30	32.5	37	38.5	43
Maria	38	4.5	24	35.5	39	42.5	45

Which measures could **best** be used to argue that Maria is better at doing curl-ups than Grace is?

A The mean and median

B The median and interquartile range

C The mean and mean absolute deviation

D The mean absolute deviation and the maximum

Alec chose D as the correct answer. How might he have gotten that answer?

PAIR/SHARE
Which measures can you use to argue that Grace is better at doing curl-ups than Maria? Explain.

4 The table shows the heights of the red oak trees in a park.

a. Make a data display to show the distribution of the data.

Heights of Red Oak Trees (ft)				
69	64	9	67	23
20	60	8	15	53
14	59	23	13	18
65	62	54	19	65

b. The mean and median are not good measures of the typical height of the red oak trees in the park. Explain why.

5 Daniel and Elena play a card game. The goal is to get the lowest score possible. The lists show their scores over the course of 10 games.

Daniel: 29, 30, 7, 26, 30, 33, 5, 8, 28, 4

Elena: 24, 19, 24, 20, 23, 20, 12, 33, 17, 18

Which measure could **best** be used to argue that Daniel is the better player?

A The mean

B The range

C The median

D The mean absolute deviation

6 Tell whether a measure of *center* or a measure of *variability* would be more appropriate for answering each question.

	Center	Variability
a. How many hours of sleep do students at Lincoln Middle School usually get?	○	○
b. How much do the weights of the dogs at an animal shelter differ from each other?	○	○
c. Do the tomato plants in the garden each have about the same number of tomatoes?	○	○

7 The wind speed in a city was measured each hour on March 18. The histogram shows the results.

a. The possible values for the median wind speed

are _____, _____, or _____ miles per hour.

b. Is the mean wind speed *less than, approximately equal to,* or *greater than* the median wind speed? How do you know?

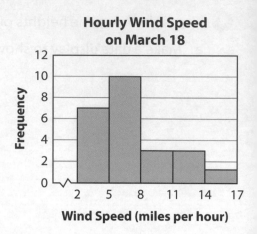

Hourly Wind Speed on March 18

Frequency vs. Wind Speed (miles per hour)

c. Which measure of center better represents the typical wind speed in the city on March 18? Explain.

8 **Math Journal** The box plot represents weights of a rancher's cows. Based on the box plot, Kiara says that the mean is likely to be a good measure of the typical weight of the cows. Is Kiara correct? Explain.

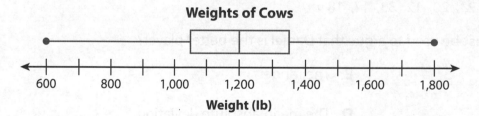

Weights of Cows

Weight (lb)

✔ End of Lesson Checklist

☐ **INTERACTIVE GLOSSARY** Write a new entry for *argument*. Tell what you do when you use data to support an argument.

☐ **SELF CHECK** Go back to the Unit 7 Opener and see what you can check off.

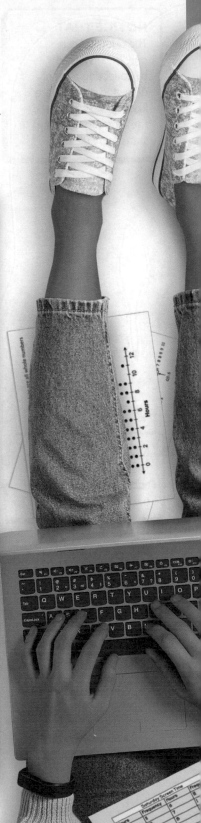

Math IN Action

SMP 1 Make sense of problems and persevere in solving them.

Study an Example Problem and Solution

➤ **Read this problem involving statistical questions and measures of center and variability. Then look at one student's solution to this problem on the following pages.**

Reporting on Data

Claudia is the data reporter for her school's online newspaper. Read this email from her teacher, and help her complete her next assignment.

Delete   Archive | Reply   Reply All   Forward

To: Claudia
Subject: Next assignment: data article

Hi Claudia,

Your next article should involve an investigation of a statistical question.

Start by coming up with a question you can answer by surveying your classmates. Your article should include a data display, so be sure to use a statistical question that involves numerical data. Here are some example questions, so you know what I am looking for:

How many hours last week did my classmates spend outdoors?

On a scale of 1 to 10, how do my classmates rate the cafeteria food?

How many movies have my classmates watched in the last 12 months?

After you collect and analyze a data set to answer your question, write an article to summarize your results.

IN YOUR ARTICLE, PLEASE INCLUDE:

- the statistical question you set out to answer.
- an appropriate display of the data you collect.
- a description of the data using an appropriate measure of center and measure of variability.
- a statement that answers your statistical question based on the data.

Thanks!

Ms. Gordon

One Student's Solution

First, I have to come up with a statistical question.

I think Claudia should write an article about students' screen time. A statistical question she could ask is, "How many hours did my classmates spend using screens last Saturday?"

Next, I need to collect a data set.

Since I cannot survey Claudia's classmates, I will survey my own classmates. I will ask each student how many hours he or she spent using screens last Saturday. Then I will record their answers in a frequency table.

Saturday Screen Time												
Hours	0	1	2	3	4	5	6	7	8	9	10	11
Frequency	II	III	‖‖‖	IIII	II	II	III	I	II	I		I

Then, I will make the data display to go with the article.

The data values are all whole numbers. The number of different data values is fairly small, and the frequencies are fairly low. These things make a dot plot an appropriate display for this data set. Plus, a dot plot makes it easy to see the shape of the distribution.

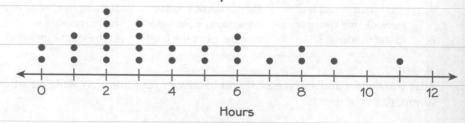

Saturday Screen Time

Hours

Now, I will calculate a measure of center and measure of variability for the data.

The dot plot shows that the distribution of the data is skewed right. The smaller number of higher data values will tend to affect the mean and MAD more than the median and IQR. I will use the median to describe the center of the data and the IQR to describe the variability.

0 0 1 1 1 2 2 2 2 2 3 3 3 3 4 4 5 5 6 6 6 7 8 8 9 11

Q1 = 2   median = 3   Q3 = 6

IQR = 6 − 2 = 4

> **NOTICE THAT . . .**
> If the distribution were more symmetric, the mean and the MAD would be appropriate measures for describing the data set.

Next, I will write the text of the article.

Have you ever wondered how much time students spend staring at a screen each day? Well, this reporter decided to find out. The dot plot shows the survey results of 26 students at our school. Each student was asked how much time he or she spent using screens on Saturday.

Based on the survey, the median amount of screen time was 3 hours. So, about half the students used screens 3 hours or less and about half used screens 3 hours or more.

> **NOTICE THAT . . .**
> The article helps readers understand what the median represents.

As you can see from the dot plot, the screen times varied from 0 hours to a nearly unbelievable 11 hours! The middle half of the data set ranged from 2 hours of screen time to 6 hours of screen time.

In conclusion, the surveyed students typically spent about 3 hours on Saturday staring at screens, but there was quite a bit of variability in their screen use.

Finally, I will check that I met the requirements of the article.

The first paragraph includes my statistical question, I made a dot plot to display the data, I described the data using the median and IQR, and the last paragraph answers the statistical question.

Try Another Approach

➤ **There are many ways to solve problems. Think about how you might solve the Reporting on Data problem in a different way.**

Reporting on Data

Claudia is the data reporter for her school's online newspaper. Read this email from her teacher, and help her complete her next assignment.

To: Claudia
Subject: Next assignment: data article

Hi Claudia,

Your next article should involve an investigation of a statistical question.

Start by coming up with a question you can answer by surveying your classmates. Your article should include a data display, so be sure to use a statistical question that involves numerical data. Here are some example questions, so you know what I am looking for:

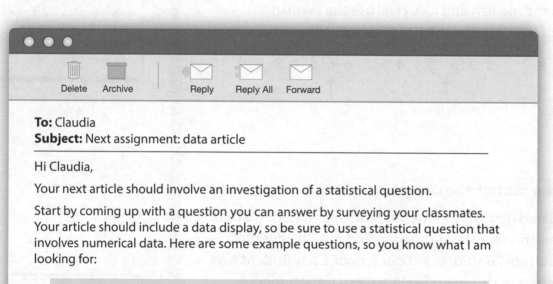

How many hours last week did my classmates spend outdoors?

On a scale of 1 to 10, how do my classmates rate the cafeteria food?

How many movies have my classmates watched in the last 12 months?

After you collect and analyze a data set to answer your question, write an article to summarize your results.

IN YOUR ARTICLE, PLEASE INCLUDE:
- the statistical question you set out to answer.
- an appropriate display of the data you collect.
- a description of the data using an appropriate measure of center and measure of variability.
- a statement that answers your statistical question based on the data.

Thanks!

Ms. Gordon

Plan It

➤ **Answer these questions to help you start thinking about a plan.**

a. What statistical question will you ask?

b. What data will you collect to answer your statistical question?

Solve It

➤ **Find a different solution for the Reporting on Data problem. Show all your work on a separate sheet of paper. You may want to use the Problem-Solving Tips to get started.**

PROBLEM-SOLVING TIPS

 Math Toolkit connecting cubes, grid paper, number lines, sticky notes

Key Terms

statistical question	measure of variability	range
distribution	mean	interquartile range
measure of center	median	mean absolute deviation (MAD)

Sentence Starters

- I know my question is a statistical question because . . .
- I will display my data set with a . . . because . . .

Reflect

Use Mathematical Practices As you work through the problem, discuss these questions with a partner.

- **Use a Model** What can the readers of your article learn by looking at your data display?

- **Use Structure** How can the shape of the data distribution help you decide which measure of center and variability to use for your article?

Discuss Models and Strategies

➤ **Read the problem. Write a solution on a separate sheet of paper. Remember, there can be lots of ways to solve a problem.**

Investigating Weights of Backpacks

For her next assignment, Claudia will be working on a team with two other reporters from the school newspaper, Caleb and Ichiro. Read this email, and help Claudia provide the information they need.

Delete   Archive   Reply   Reply All   Forward

To: Claudia
Subject: Backpack article

Hey Claudia,

Caleb and I are planning to write an article on the weights of students' backpacks. We think it is important for teachers and family members to know how much we carry each day.

Yesterday, we measured the weights of 40 students' backpacks. Here is our data set.

Weights of Backpacks (lb)							
12.9	9.1	9.6	12.2	9.2	14.3	12.9	10.0
10.3	10.7	15.3	10.3	11.6	8.2	9.9	23.7
12.1	13.4	25.6	13.8	11.7	9.7	13.3	28.1
11.1	11.8	24.9	11.8	11.4	26.3	11.9	11.9
12.4	12.3	11.9	12.3	11.6	14.6	13.3	12.6

WHAT WE NEED YOUR HELP WITH:
• Make an appropriate data display for the article.
• Calculate a value for the typical weight of a student's backpack.
• Tell which measure of center you used for the typical weight and why you chose that measure.

Thanks, Claudia!

Ichiro

Plan It and Solve It

➤ **Find a solution to the Investigating Weights of Backpacks problem.**

Write a detailed plan and support your answer. Be sure to include:

- an appropriate data display for the weights of the backpacks.

- the typical weight of a backpack based on the data set.

- an explanation of which measure of center you used for the typical weight and why you chose that measure.

PROBLEM-SOLVING TIPS

 Math Toolkit connecting cubes, grid paper, number lines, sticky notes

Key Terms

box plot	cluster	dot plot
gap	histogram	mean
median	outlier	peak

Questions

- Why is a dot plot probably not the best way to display the weights of the backpacks?

- How would you describe the shape of the distribution of the weights?

Reflect

Use Mathematical Practices As you work through the problem, discuss these questions with a partner.

- **Make Sense of Problems** What statistical question were Caleb and Ichiro most likely trying to answer with the data they collected? How do you know?

- **Make an Argument** Suppose you want to use the article to persuade readers that students' backpacks are too heavy. Would this affect the measure of center you use to describe the data set? Explain.

It is suggested that a backpack be no more than 10%–15% of a person's body weight.

Persevere On Your Own

Problem-Solving Checklist

- [ ] Tell what is known.
- [ ] Tell what the problem is asking.
- [ ] Show all your work.
- [ ] Show that the solution works.

➤ **Read the problem. Write a solution on a separate sheet of paper.**

Analyzing the Spelling Bee

Claudia's school recently held a spelling bee, and she was asked to write an article about it. Read this email from her teacher, and help her come up with a response.

Delete   Archive | Reply   Reply All   Forward

To: Claudia
Subject: Spelling bee article

Hi Claudia,

We are hearing rumors that the words in this year's spelling bee were more difficult than in last year's spelling bee. People are saying that too many students were eliminated in the first round. I would like you to do an article about it.

Longer words are probably more difficult to spell, so compare the word lengths in the first round of both spelling bees.

Length of First Round Words (letters)	Frequency This Year	Frequency Last Year
5						
6																											
7																														
8																							
9												
10									
11						
12			

WHAT I NEED YOU TO DO:
- Make data displays for the two sets of word lengths. The displays will be included in your article.
- Use a measure of center and a measure of variability to draw a conclusion about the word lengths.
- Write a paragraph for your article that supports your conclusion.

Thanks!

Ms. Gordon

Solve It

➤ **Find a solution to the Analyzing the Spelling Bee problem.**

- Make appropriate data displays for the two sets of word lengths. Use the same type of display for each data set.

- Calculate a measure of center and a measure of variability for each data set. Use the measures to draw a conclusion about whether the words in the first round of this year's spelling bee were longer than last year's words.

- Write a paragraph for an article that supports your conclusion.

Reflect

Use Mathematical Practices After you complete the problem, choose one of these questions to discuss with a partner.

- **Reason Mathematically** How are the two sets of word lengths the same? How are they different?

- **Critique Reasoning** What did your partner conclude about the word lengths in the first round of both spelling bees? Is your partner's conclusion supported by the data sets? Explain.

The longest word in the English language is the name for the protein titin. Its chemical name has 189,819 letters.

In this unit you learned to . . .

Skill	Lesson
Represent data in a frequency table, dot plot, and histogram.	29, 30
Describe a set of data by its center, spread, and overall shape.	29, 30
Summarize data by describing how the data were measured and their units of measurement.	30
Represent data in a box plot.	31
Calculate median and IQR of a data set, then interpret them in different contexts.	31
Calculate the mean and MAD of a data set, then interpret them in different contexts.	32
Compare measures of center and variability, then choose measures of center and variability to summarize the data set.	33
Use math vocabulary and precise language to describe sets of data.	29–33

Think about what you have learned.

➤ **Use words, numbers, and drawings.**

1 The most important topic I learned is _____ because . . .

2 The hardest thing I learned to do is _____ because . . .

3 I still need to work on . . .

➤ **Review the unit vocabulary. Put a check mark by items you can use in speaking and writing. Look up the meaning of any terms you do not know.**

Math Vocabulary

☐ **interquartile range (IQR)**

☐ **lower quartile**

☐ **mean**

☐ **mean absolute deviation (MAD)**

☐ **median**

☐ **outlier**

☐ **range**

☐ **upper quartile**

Academic Vocabulary

☐ **interval**

☐ **maximum**

☐ **minimum**

☐ **summarize**

➤ **Use the unit vocabulary to complete the problems.**

1 Label parts of the box plot. Use at least five math or academic vocabulary terms.

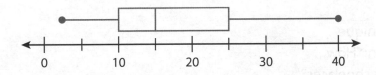

2 Which terms name measures of center? Which terms name measures of variability?

3 Look at the data for number of daily customers at a store. Which measure of variability would you choose to summarize the data? Explain your reasoning.

13, 46, 52, 59, 43, 53, 55, 61, 50

4 Look at the data for a student's test scores. Explain which measure of center the student would likely prefer to summarize the test scores.

80, 75, 90, 92, 85, 100, 70, 88

➤ **Use what you have learned to complete these problems.**

1 The histogram shows the ages of the cast of a new play. Is the mean a good measure of the typical age for a member of the cast? Explain your reasoning.

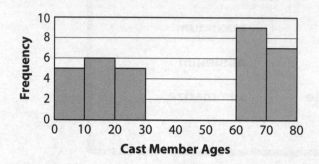

Cast Member Ages

SOLUTION _____

_____

_____

_____

2 The dot plot shows the data Monique collected to answer this question: "How quickly can Lester tie both of his shoelaces?" Which statement describes the distribution of Monique's data set?

Tying Both Shoelaces

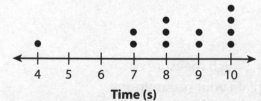

Time (s)

A A typical time is 7 s.

B The distribution is spread from 4 s to 10 s.

C The range is 14 s.

D The distribution is skewed right.

3 A coach asks, "How many minutes did you practice last week?" The answers are shown in the table. Draw a histogram with the same data. Show your work.

Minutes Spent Practicing							
4	10	24	25	19	3	12	20
29	27	9	22	12	18	18	27

4 Sia sells bracelets for $20 per bracelet and tracks how much she earns each week. The box plot displays Sia's data. What does the IQR show about the data?

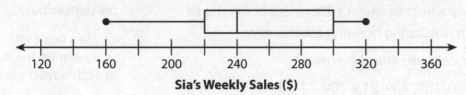

Sia's Weekly Sales ($)

A The IQR is 80, so 50% of customers spend $80.

B The IQR is 80, so 50% of weekly sales are within an $80 range.

C The IQR is 240, so 50% of weekly sales are less than $240.

D The IQR is 240, so 50% of weekly sales are within a $160 range.

5 Beck and Mandi collect donations for a fundraiser. They make a dot plot to show the shape of the distribution. Beck says they received 15 donations. This is not correct. What error might he have made, and what is the correct number of donations received? Explain your reasoning.

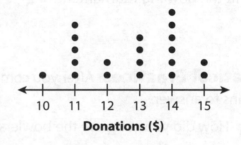

Donations ($)

SOLUTION _____

_____

_____

6 The weights of the lamps for sale at an online auction, in pounds, are 5, 8, 8, 12, 11, 6, 10, 6, 6, and 48. The 48-pound lamp is an outlier. What is the MAD of the weights, in pounds, when this outlier is left out of the data set? Record your answer on the grid. Then fill in the bubbles.

Performance Task

➤ **Answer the questions and show all your work on separate paper.**

Felix and Crystal are coworkers who are both on their company's bowling team. Their company wants to select either Felix or Crystal to represent the company in an upcoming bowling tournament.

The recent scores for the bowlers are found below.

- Felix: 194, 197, 215, 185, 220, 180, 209, 214, 200, 211, 199

- Crystal: 202, 195, 188, 195, 190, 231, 213, 177, 190, 185, 211, 211, 170, 228, 170

The company asks you to recommend the bowler that has the best chance of winning the tournament. Determine the mean and MAD for each data set. Round your calculations to the nearest whole number. Draw a box plot to represent the bowlers' scores. Then use your data to explain why the company should select that bowler to represent the company at the bowling tournament.

Reflect

Use Mathematical Practices   After you complete the task, choose one of the following questions to answer.

- **Use Reasoning**   How did you compare the bowlers' scores when each data set had a different number of values?

- **Argue and Critique**   Was a measure of center or a measure of variability more important when selecting the bowler you think has the best chance of winning the tournament?

Data Sets

Unit 7

LESSON 30 | SESSION 1 ■ □ □ □

Try It

Ages in Years				
10	6	8	8	14
10	9	7	11	10
13	3	9	8	5
6	9	6	7	11
14	11	10	9	8
10	5	4	7	12
16	8	9	12	15
8	9	12	6	10
15	14	5	10	17
6	10	8	9	6

Data Sets

Unit 7

LESSON 30 | SESSION 2 ■ ■ ☐ ☐

Try It

Points Scored	
Date	**Points**
Oct 16	81
Oct 19	88
Oct 21	91
Oct 24	102
Oct 26	97
Oct 28	124
Oct 30	122
Nov 1	101
Nov 3	108
Nov 5	102
Nov 7	114
Nov 10	106
Nov 12	107
Nov 14	101
Nov 16	135
Nov 19	109
Nov 20	110
Dec 1	117
Dec 3	118
Dec 4	110
Dec 6	112
Dec 8	118
Dec 11	106
Dec 13	115
Dec 15	116

Points Scored	
Date	**Points**
Dec 20	112
Dec 22	115
Dec 23	121
Dec 25	128
Dec 29	124
Dec 30	120
Jan 3	121
Jan 5	133
Jan 7	120
Jan 10	99
Jan 12	125
Jan 13	126
Jan 15	121
Jan 17	128
Jan 20	141
Jan 22	120
Jan 25	124
Jan 27	125
Jan 30	122
Feb 2	97
Feb 4	108
Feb 6	135
Feb 10	140
Feb 12	141
Feb 14	129

Set 1 Rates and Unit Rates

➤ **Fill in the blank with the unit rate.**

1 Liam spends $4 for 2 pounds of grapes. The grapes sell at a rate of $_____ per pound.

2 Latasha reads 9 pages in 3 minutes. Latasha reads at a rate of _____ pages

per minute. She reads at a rate of _____ minute per page.

3 A package of 6 pencils costs $3. The cost per pencil is $_____ .

4 A pizza dough recipe has a ratio of 5 cups of flour to 2 cups of water. There are

_____ cups of flour per cup of water.

Set 2 Solve Unit Rate Problems

➤ **Solve the problems. Show your work.**

1 Maximo can hike 2 miles in 30 minutes. At this rate, how long will it take him to complete a 7-mile hike?

2 Emma has 200 pages of her book left to read. In 4 minutes, she reads 6 pages. At this rate, can she finish her book in 2 hours?

3 It takes a printer 6 minutes to print 40 pages. At this rate, how many pages will it print in 15 minutes?

Set 3 Convert Measurements

➤ **Solve the problems. Show your work.**

1 The table shows the prices of two types of juice. How much does each type of juice cost per gallon? There are 4 quarts in a gallon.

Juice	Price	Volume
Orange	$3.25	0.5 gallon
Peach	$4.50	1.5 quarts

2 Luna is 5 feet tall. How tall is she in centimeters? There are about 2.5 centimeters in an inch.

Set 4 Percents

➤ **Fill in the blanks for problems 1–3.**

1 35% of 100 is _____.

2 80% of 400 is _____.

3 90% of 20 is _____.

➤ **Solve problems 4 and 5. Show your work.**

4 Jaylon has 20 math problems for homework. He has completed 60% of the problems so far. How many problems has he completed?

5 Fai spends $9 on his lunch. This is 30% of the money he had in his wallet. How much money did Fai have in his wallet?

Cumulative Practice

Name: _____

Set 5 Equivalent Ratios

➤ **Fill in the missing values in the table. Plot the values on the coordinate plane.**

1 There are 4 grams of protein for every serving of broccoli.

Servings	1	2	3	4
Grams of Protein				

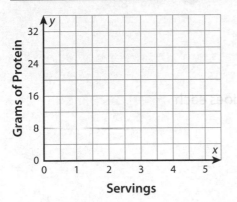

2 The floor of a school has 3 blue tiles for every 7 green tiles.

Blue Tiles	3	6	9	
Green Tiles	7			28

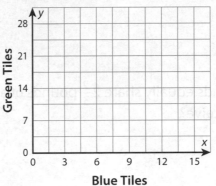

Set 6 Part-to-Part and Part-to-Whole Ratios

➤ **Fill in the missing values in the tables. Then solve the problems.**

1 A movie theater sold 4 adult tickets for every 2 child tickets. The theater sold 32 adult tickets. How many tickets did it sell in all?

Adult tickets	Child tickets	Total tickets
4	2	
32		

2 Mila and Ben use red and orange beads to make bracelets with 60 beads each. Mila uses 2 red beads for every 3 orange beads. Ben uses 5 red beads for every 7 orange beads. Who uses more orange beads?

Mila		
Red	Orange	Total
2	3	
		60

Ben		
Red	Orange	Total
5	7	
		60

Set 7 Divide with Fractions

➤ **Divide. Show your work.**

1 $\frac{3}{4} \div \frac{2}{3}$

2 $\frac{4}{5} \div 6$

3 $4 \div \frac{8}{5}$

4 $1\frac{7}{8} \div \frac{5}{6}$

5 $2\frac{3}{4} \div \frac{9}{4}$

6 $4\frac{1}{5} \div \frac{7}{8}$

7 Four friends equally share $2\frac{2}{3}$ pounds of apples. How much does each friend receive?

Set 8 Evaluate Algebraic Expressions

➤ **Evaluate the expressions. Show your work.**

1 $3x^3 + 4$ when $x = 5$

2 $4(m - 2)^2$ when $m = 11$

3 $12 - 4a^2$ when $a = \frac{1}{4}$

4 $\frac{h^2}{2}$ when $h = 3$

5 $6x + 2y^5$ when $x = 10$ and $y = 10$

6 $6(x^3 + 4)$ when $x = 2$

Cumulative Practice

Name:

Set 1 Write Equivalent Expressions

➤ **Solve the problems.**

1 Rewrite the expression $3(4w + 2)$ as a sum. Show your work.

2 Write an expression equivalent to $15m + 1 + 3m$ with exactly two terms. Show your work.

3 Write a whole number in each blank to show an expression that is equivalent to $12n - 8$.

_______ • $n + 5n -$ _______

Set 2 Identify Equivalent Expressions

➤ **Solve the problems.**

1 Are the expressions $2x + 3(x + y) + 4$ and $5x + y + 2(y + 2)$ equivalent? Show your work.

2 Circle all the expressions equivalent to $6d + 10$.

$3d + 10 + 3d$	$2(3d + 5)$	$3(3d + 7)$
$6(d + 1) + 4$	$4d + 10 + 2d$	$4(d + 2) + 2(d + 1)$

Set 3 Solutions of Equations

➤ **Solve the problems. Show your work.**

1 Use substitution to determine if 2 is a solution of the equation $3x = 12$.

2 Use substitution to determine if 5 is a solution of the equation $10 = 2x$.

Set 4 Solve One-Variable Equations

➤ **Solve each equation for *x*. Show your work.**

1 $24 = 4x$

2 $8 + x = 10$

3 $2x = 40$

Set 5 Convert Measurements

➤ **Solve the measurement conversion problems. Show your work.**

1 If you travel 60 feet in 4 seconds, how fast are you going in yards per minute?

2 If you travel 20 kilometers in 29 minutes, how fast are you going in meters per second?

Set 6 Write Equations in Two Variables

➤ **Solve the problem. Show your work.**

1 The total weight of a package is equal to the weight of the empty box plus the weight of the contents of the box. The contents of the box weigh 12 lb.

   a. Write an equation that shows how to use the total weight of the package, t, in pounds, to find the weight of the empty box, b, in pounds.

   b. Which is the independent variable in your equation? _____

   c. Which is the dependent variable in your equation? _____

Set 7 Solve Unit Rate Problems

➤ **Solve the problems. Show your work.**

1 Bus fare costs $45 for 20 trips. At this rate, how much do 6 trips on the bus cost?

2 Mikey collects beach glass. In the first 6 days, he finds 15 pieces of beach glass. At this rate, how many pieces of beach glass will Mikey have on day 28?

3 Paula reads 360 pages of a book over 8 nights. At this rate, how many pages will she read over 100 nights?

Set 8 Percents

➤ **Solve the problems. Show your work.**

1 What is 75% of 600?

2 5% of what number is 20?

3 What is 20% of 80?

4 25% of what number is 40?

Set 9 Evaluate Algebraic Expressions

➤ **Solve the problems. Show your work.**

1 Evaluate $5n + 2m - 5$ for $n = 2$ and $m = 4$.

2 Evaluate $500g + 120{,}000$ for $g = 11$.

3 Evaluate $3a + 2b - c$ for $a = 5$, $b = 1$ and $c = 8$.

4 Evaluate $200 - 5w$ for $w = 26$.

Set 1 Positive and Negative Numbers

➤ **Solve the problems.**

1 Plot and label each of the following rational numbers as a point on the number line:

$-1\frac{1}{3}, 0, \frac{2}{3}$.

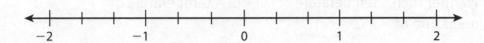

2 Plot and label the opposite of each number in problem 1 on the number line.

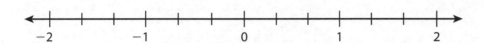

3 What is the opposite of −14? How many units away from 0 is its location on a horizontal number line and in which direction?

4 What is the opposite of 14? How many units away from 0 is its location on a horizontal number line and in which direction?

5 What number is the opposite of the opposite of −14? Show your work.

Set 2 Interpret Statements of Inequality

➤ **Write <, >, or = in each circle to make a true statement. For each statement of inequality, circle the value located farther to the right on the number line.**

1 5 ◯ −12

2 −32 ◯ −14

3 $\frac{2}{6}$ ◯ $\frac{2}{4}$

4 $2\frac{1}{4}$ ◯ $-2\frac{1}{4}$

5 $-4\frac{2}{3}$ ◯ $-5\frac{1}{4}$

6 $5\frac{1}{8}$ ◯ $5\frac{1}{4}$

7 7 ◯ $\frac{26}{4}$

8 $-\frac{14}{5}$ ◯ −3.2

9 6.7 ◯ $\frac{52}{8}$

Set 3 Write Statements of Order

➤ **Write an inequality to express each relationship.**

1 A depth of 10 ft is lower than a depth of 6 ft. An elevation of 7 ft is higher than an elevation of 4 ft.

2 A temperature of −4°C is warmer than a temperature of −11°C. A temperature of −12°C is colder than a temperature of −7°C.

3 A bank balance of $1,500 is more than a bank balance of $150. A bank balance of −$100 is more than a bank balance of –$200.

Set 4 Absolute Value

➤ **Write <, >, or = in each circle to make a true statement.**

1 −2 ◯ 7 and $|-2|$ ◯ $|7|$ **2** −8 ◯ 4 and $|-8|$ ◯ $|4|$

3 −9 ◯ −1 and $|-9|$ ◯ $|-1|$ **4** 11 ◯ 7 and $|11|$ ◯ $|7|$

5 12 ◯ −17 and $|12|$ ◯ $|-17|$ **6** 22 ◯ −21 and $|22|$ ◯ $|-21|$

Set 5 Identify Solutions of Inequalities

➤ **Solve the problems.**

1 Circle the values that are solutions of the inequality −10 > m.

   −5   −10   5   20   −20   −50

2 Circle the values that are solutions of the inequality h ≤ −6.

   −8   −2   8   2   10   −6

3 Circle the values that are solutions of the inequality 17 ≥ g.

   20   10   −20   −10   17   0

Set 6 Write and Graph Inequalities

➤ **Write and graph an inequality to show each situation.**

1 The temperature is at most 8 degrees Celsius.

2 Mary's elevation is more than −10 feet.

3 Deion is less than 5 feet above sea level.

Set 7 The Four-Quadrant Coordinate Plane

➤ **Use the coordinate plane to solve the problems.**

1 The coordinate plane shows points *P*, *Q*, *R* and *S*. Write the coordinates for each point.

P(_____) Q(_____) R(_____) S(_____)

2 Point *E* is a reflection of point *D* across the *x*-axis. Plot and label point *E*.

3 Plot and label each point on the coordinate plane.

A(1, 4)   B(3, −2)   C(−1, 3)   D(−2, −4)

4 In which quadrant would you plot the point (7, −10)?

_____

5 In which quadrant would you plot the point (−8, 8)?

_____

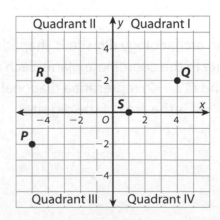

Set 8 Solve Problems in the Coordinate Plane

➤ **Solve the problems. Show your work.**

1 What is the distance between point $F(-5, 2)$ and point $G(-1, 2)$?

2 A map of a dog park is laid out in a coordinate plane. Distances on the map are in yards. A dog starts at a fountain at $(2, -2)$. He then runs to catch a ball at $(2, 5)$, brings the ball back to his owner at $(5, 5)$, and then walks over to greet another dog at $(5, -4)$. What is the total distance the dog travels? Show your work.

3 Cyril walks south from his house to a park. He spends 0.5 hour at the park and then walks home. His walking speed is 2.5 miles per hour. Distances on the map are in miles. For how many hours is Cyril away from home?

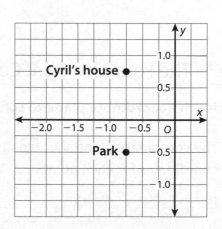

4 An archaeology dig site is shaped like a square. The archaeologists make a map of the site in the coordinate plane. Each unit on the map represents 1 ft. Vertices $A(2, 3)$ and $C(7, -2)$ represent a diagonal of the square. Vertices B and D are not yet mapped. What is the area of the dig site?

Interactive Glossary/Glosario interactivo

English/Español	Example/Ejemplo	Notes/Notas

Aa

absolute value a number's distance from 0 on the number line. Absolute value is never negative.

$|-3| = 3$
$|3| = 3$

valor absoluto distancia de un número desde 0 en la recta numérica. El valor absoluto nunca es negativo.

acute angle an angle that measures more than 0° but less than 90°.

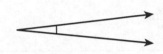

ángulo agudo ángulo que mide más de 0° pero menos de 90°.

acute triangle a triangle that has three acute angles.

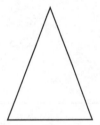

triángulo acutángulo triángulo que tiene tres ángulos agudos.

additive inverses two numbers whose sum is zero. The additive inverse of a number is the opposite of that number, i.e., the additive inverse of a is $-a$.

-2 and 2
$\frac{1}{2}$ and $-\frac{1}{2}$

inverso aditivo dos números cuya suma es cero. El inverso aditivo de un número es el opuesto de ese número; por ejemplo, el inverso aditivo de a es $-a$.

algorithm a set of routine steps used to solve problems.

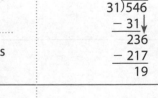

algoritmo conjunto de pasos rutinarios que se siguen para resolver problemas.

angle a geometric shape formed by two rays, lines, or line segments that meet at a common point.

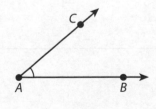

ángulo figura geométrica formada por dos semirrectas, rectas o segmentos de recta que se encuentran en un punto común.

English/Español	Example/Ejemplo	Notes/Notas

area the amount of space inside a closed two-dimensional figure. Area is measured in square units such as square centimeters.

área cantidad de espacio dentro de una figura bidimensional cerrada. El área se mide en unidades cuadradas, como los centímetros cuadrados.

6 units

Area = 30 units² 5 units

---

associative property of addition regrouping the terms does not change the value of the expression.

propiedad asociativa de la suma reagrupar los términos no cambia el valor de la expresión.

$(a + b) + c = a + (b + c)$

$(2 + 3) + 4 = 2 + (3 + 4)$

---

associative property of multiplication regrouping the terms does not change the value of the expression.

propiedad asociativa de la multiplicación reagrupar los términos no cambia el valor de la expresión.

$(a \cdot b) \cdot c = a \cdot (b \cdot c)$

$(2 \cdot 3) \cdot 4 = 2 \cdot (3 \cdot 4)$

---

axis a horizontal or vertical number line that determines a coordinate plane. The plural form is *axes*.

eje recta numérica horizontal o vertical que determina un plano de coordenadas.

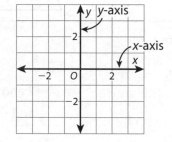

Bb

balance point the point that represents the center of a data set. In a two-variable data set, the coordinates of the balance point are the mean of each variable.

punto de equilibrio punto que representa el centro de un conjunto de datos. En un conjunto de datos de dos variables, las coordenadas del punto de equilibrio son la media de cada variable.

Data set: (1, 1), (3, 4), (5, 6), (7, 8)

$$\frac{1 + 3 + 5 + 7}{4} = 4$$

$$\frac{1 + 4 + 6 + 8}{4} = 4.75$$

Balance point: (4, 4.75)

---

base (of a parallelogram) a side of a parallelogram from which the height is measured.

base (de un paralelogramo) lado de un paralelogramo desde el que se mide la altura.

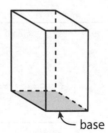

---

base (of a power) in a power, the number that is used as a repeated factor.

base (de una potencia) en una potencia, el número que se usa como factor que se repite.

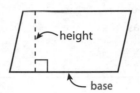

8^2

base

---

base (of a three-dimensional figure) a face of a three-dimensional figure from which the height is measured.

base (de una figura tridimensional) cara de una figura tridimensional desde la que se mide la altura.

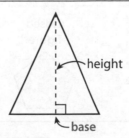

base

---

base (of a triangle) a side of a triangle from which the height is measured.

base (de un triángulo) lado de un triángulo desde el que se mide la altura.

height

base

box plot a visual display of a data set on a number line that shows the minimum, the lower quartile, the median, the upper quartile, and the maximum. The sides of the box show the lower and upper quartiles and the line inside the box shows the median. Lines connect the box to the minimum and maximum values.

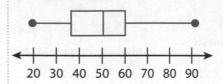

diagrama de caja representación visual de un conjunto de datos en una recta numérica que muestra el mínimo, el cuartil inferior, la mediana, el cuartil superior y el máximo. Los lados de la caja muestran los cuartiles inferior y superior y la recta del centro muestra la mediana. Las rectas conectan la caja con los valores mínimo y máximo.

Cc

closed figure a two-dimensional figure that begins and ends at the same point.

Closed figure   Open figure

figura cerrada figura bidimensional que comienza y termina en el mismo punto.

cluster a group of data points that are close to each other.

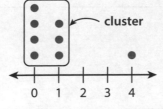

cluster

agrupación conjunto de datos que están cerca unos de otros.

English/Español	Example/Ejemplo	Notes/Notas
coefficient a number that is multiplied by a variable.		
coeficiente número que se multiplica por una variable.	$5x + 3$ coefficient	
common denominator a number that is a common multiple of the denominators of two or more fractions.	A common denominator for $\frac{1}{2}$ and $\frac{3}{5}$ is 10 because $2 \cdot 5 = 10$.	
denominador común número que es múltiplo común de los denominadores de dos o más fracciones.		
commutative property of addition changing the order of the addends does not change the sum.	$a + b = b + a$ $4.1 + 7.5 = 7.5 + 4.1$	
propiedad conmutativa de la suma cambiar el orden de los sumandos no cambia el total.		
commutative property of multiplication changing the order of the factors does not change the product.	$ab = ba$ $4(7.5) = 7.5(4)$	
propiedad conmutativa de la multiplicación cambiar el orden de los factores no cambia el producto.		
compare to describe the relationship between the value or size of two numbers or quantities.	$-4 < 8.5$	
comparar describir la relación que hay entre el valor o el tamaño de dos números o cantidades.		
compose to make by combining parts. You can put together numbers to make a greater number or put together shapes to make a new shape.		
componer formar al combinar partes. Se pueden unir números para hacer un número mayor o unir figuras para formar una figura nueva.		

English/Español	Example/Ejemplo	Notes/Notas
composite number a number that has more than one pair of whole number factors.	16 is a composite number because 1 • 16, 2 • 8, and 4 • 4 all equal 16.	
número compuesto número que tiene más de un par de números enteros como factores.		
convert to write an equivalent measurement using a different unit.	60 in. is the same as 5 ft.	
convertir escribir una medida equivalente usando una unidad diferente.		
coordinate plane a two-dimensional space formed by two perpendicular number lines called *axes*.		
plano de coordenadas espacio bidimensional formado por dos rectas numéricas perpendiculares llamadas ejes.		
corresponding terms terms that have the same position in two related patterns. For example, the second term in one pattern and the second term in a related pattern are corresponding terms.	Pattern A: 12, 18, 24, **30**	
términos correspondientes términos que tienen la misma posición en dos patrones relacionados. Por ejemplo, el segundo término en un patrón y el segundo término en un patrón relacionado son términos correspondientes.	Pattern B: 6, 9, 12, **15**	
cube a rectangular prism in which each face of the prism is a square.	1 unit 1 unit 1 unit	
cubo prisma rectangular en el que cada cara del prisma es un cuadrado.		

Dd

data a set of collected information. Often numerical information such as a list of measurements.

datos conjunto de información reunida. Con frecuencia, información numérica como una lista de medidas.

Commute length (mi):

15, 22, 10.5, 21, 9.5

---

decimal a number containing a decimal point that separates a whole from fractional place values (tenths, hundredths, thousandths, and so on).

decimal número que tiene un punto decimal que separa un entero de los valores posicionales fraccionarios (décimas, centésimas, milésimas, etc.).

1.293

---

decompose to break into parts. You can break apart numbers and shapes.

descomponer separar en partes. Se puede separar en partes números y figuras.

---

degree (°) a unit used to measure angles.

grado (°) unidad que se usa para medir ángulos.

There are 360° in a circle.

---

denominator the number below the line in a fraction that tells the number of equal parts in the whole.

denominador número debajo de la línea en una fracción que indica el número de partes iguales que hay en el entero.

$\dfrac{3}{4}$

---

dependent variable a variable whose value depends on the value of a related independent variable.

variable dependiente variable cuyo valor depende del valor de una variable independiente relacionada.

$y = 5x$

The value of y depends on the value of x.

---

difference the result of subtraction.

diferencia resultado de la resta.

$$\begin{array}{r} 16.75 \\ -\ 15.70 \\ \hline 1.05 \end{array}$$

English/Español	**Example**/Ejemplo	**Notes**/Notas

digit a symbol used to write numbers.

dígito símbolo que se usa para escribir números.

The digits are 0, 1, 2, 3, 4, 5, 6, 7, 8, and 9.

---

dimension length in one direction. A figure may have one, two, or three dimensions.

dimensión longitud en una dirección. Una figura puede tener una, dos o tres dimensiones.

5 in.

2 in.

3 in.

---

distribution a representation that shows how often values in a data set occur.

distribución representación que muestra la frecuencia con la que ocurren los valores en un conjunto de datos.

Pet	Frequency
Bird	7
Cat	12
Dog	8
Snake	3

---

distributive property multiplying each term in a sum or difference by a common factor does not change the value of the expression.

propiedad distributiva multiplicar cada término de una suma o diferencia por un factor común no cambia el valor de la expresión.

$a(b + c) = ab + ac$

$5(4 + 2) = 5(4) + 5(2)$

---

dividend the number that is divided by another number.

dividendo número que se divide por otro número.

$22.5 \div 3 = 7.5$

---

divisor the number by which another number is divided.

divisor número por el que se divide otro número.

$22.5 \div 3 = 7.5$

GL8 **Interactive Glossary**/Glosario interactivo

©Curriculum Associates, LLC   Copying is not permitted.

English/**Español**	**Example**/Ejemplo	**Notes**/Notas
dot plot a data display that shows data as dots above a number line. A dot plot may also be called a *line plot*.	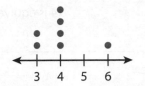	
diagrama de puntos representación de datos que muestra datos como puntos sobre una *recta numérica*.		

Ee

edge a line segment where two faces meet in a three-dimensional shape.	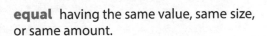 edge	
arista segmento de recta en el que dos caras se unen en una figura tridimensional.		
equal having the same value, same size, or same amount.	$50 - 20 = 30$	
igual que tiene el mismo valor, el mismo tamaño o la misma cantidad.	$50 - 20$ **is equal to** 30.	
equation a mathematical statement that uses an equal sign (=) to show that two expressions have the same value.	$x + 4 = 15$	
ecuación enunciado matemático que tiene un signo de igual (=) para mostrar que dos expresiones tienen el mismo valor.		
equilateral triangle a triangle that has all three sides the same length.	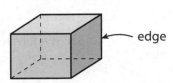	
triángulo equilátero triángulo que tiene los tres lados de la misma longitud.		

Interactive Glossary/Glosario interactivo

English/Español	Example/Ejemplo	Notes/Notas
equivalent having the same value.		
equivalente que tiene el mismo valor.	4 is equivalent to $\frac{8}{2}$.	
equivalent expressions two or more expressions in different forms that always name the same value.		
expresiones equivalentes dos o más expresiones en diferentes formas que siempre nombran el mismo valor.	$2(x + 4)$ is equivalent to $2x + 2(4)$ and $2x + 8$.	
equivalent fractions two or more different fractions that name the same part of a whole or the same point on the number line.	$-\frac{5}{10}$ $\frac{4}{8}$ $-\frac{1}{2}$ $\frac{1}{2}$	
fracciones equivalentes dos o más fracciones diferentes que nombran la misma parte de un entero o el mismo punto en la recta numérica.		
equivalent ratios two ratios that express the same comparison. Multiplying both numbers in the ratio $a : b$ by a nonzero number n results in the equivalent ratio $na : nb$.		
razones equivalentes dos razones que expresan la misma comparación. Multiplicar ambos números en la razón $a : b$ por un número distinto de cero n da como resultado la razón equivalente $na : nb$.	$6 : 8$ is equivalent to $3 : 4$	
estimate (noun) a close guess made using mathematical thinking.	$28 + 21 = ?$	
estimación suposición aproximada que se hace por medio del razonamiento matemático.	$30 + 20 = 50$ 50 is an estimate of $28 + 21$.	
estimate (verb) to give an approximate number or answer based on mathematical thinking.		
estimar dar un número o respuesta aproximada basados en el razonamiento matemático.	$28 + 21$ is about 50.	

English/Español	Example/Ejemplo	Notes/Notas
evaluate to find the value of an expression. **evaluar** hallar el valor de una expresión.	The expression $4.5 \div (1 + 8)$ has a value of 0.5.	
exponent in a power, the number that shows how many times the base is used as a factor. **exponente** en una potencia, el número que muestra cuántas veces se usa la base como factor.	8^2 exponent	
exponential expression an expression that includes an exponent. **expresión exponencial** expresión que tiene un exponente.	$3x^3$	
expression a group of numbers, variables, and/or operation symbols that represents a mathematical relationship. An expression without variables, such as $3 + 4$, is called a *numerical expression*. An expression with variables, such as $5b^2$, is called an *algebraic expression*. **expresión** grupo de números, variables y/o símbolos de operaciones que representa una relación matemática. Una expresión sin variables, como $3 + 4$, se llama *expresión numérica*. Una expresión con variables, como $5b^2$, se llama *expresión algebraica*.	$\dfrac{32 - 4}{7}$ $3x + y - 9$	

Ff

face a flat surface of a solid shape.

cara superficie plana de una figura sólida.

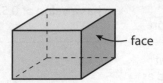
face

---

factor a number, or expression with parentheses, that is multiplied.

factor número, o expresión entre paréntesis, que se multiplica.

$4 \times 5 = 20$

factors

---

factor pair two numbers that are multiplied together to give a product.

par de factores dos números que se multiplican para dar un producto.

$4 \times 5 = 20$

factor pair

---

factors of a number whole numbers that multiply together to get the given number.

factores de un número números enteros que se multiplican para obtener el número dado.

$4 \times 5 = 20$

4 and 5 are factors of 20.

---

formula a mathematical relationship that is expressed in the form of an equation.

fórmula relación matemática que se expresa en forma de ecuación.

$A = \ell w$

---

fraction a number that names equal parts of a whole. A fraction names a point on the number line and can also represent the division of two numbers.

fracción número que nombra partes iguales de un entero. Una fracción nombra un punto en la recta numérica y también puede representar la división de dos números.

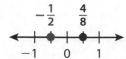

English/Español	Example/Ejemplo	Notes/Notas

frequency a numerical count of how many times a data value occurs in a data set.

frecuencia conteo numérico de cuántas veces ocurre un valor en un conjunto de datos.

Data set: 12, 13, 12, 15, 12, 13, 15, 14, 12, 12

Data Value	Frequency
12	5
13	2
14	1
15	2

Gg

gap an interval of the number line for which a distribution has no data values.

espacio intervalo de la recta numérica para el que una distribución no tiene valores.

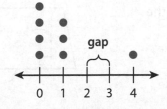

greatest common factor (GCF) the greatest factor two or more numbers have in common.

máximo común divisor (M.C.D.) el mayor factor que dos o más números tienen en común.

GCF of 20 and 30: **2 · 5, or 10**

20 = **2 · 2 · 5**

30 = **2 · 3 · 5**

English/Español	Example/Ejemplo	Notes/Notas
grouping symbol a symbol, such as braces {}, brackets [], or parentheses (), used to group parts of an expression that should be evaluated before others.	$3 \div (7 - 2) = 3 \div 5$ $\dfrac{3}{7 - 2} = \dfrac{3}{5}$	
símbolo de agrupación símbolo, como las llaves {}, los corchetes [] o los paréntesis (), que se usa para agrupar partes de una expresión que deben evaluarse antes que otras.		

Hh

height (of a parallelogram) the perpendicular distance from a base to the opposite side.	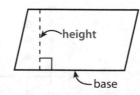	
altura (de un paralelogramo) distancia perpendicular desde una base hasta el lado opuesto.		
height (of a prism) the perpendicular distance from a base to the opposite base.	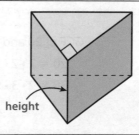	
altura (de un prisma) distancia perpendicular desde una base hasta la base opuesta.		

English/Español	Example/Ejemplo	Notes/Notas
height (of a triangle) the perpendicular distance from a base to the opposite vertex.		
altura (de un triángulo) distancia perpendicular desde una base hasta el vértice opuesto.	height — base	
hexagon a polygon with exactly 6 sides and 6 angles.		
hexágono polígono que tiene exactamente 6 lados y 6 ángulos.		
histogram a data display similar to a bar graph. A histogram groups the data into equal-size intervals. The height of each bar represents the number of data points in that group.		
histograma presentación de datos parecida a una gráfica de barras. Un histograma agrupa los datos en intervalos de igual tamaño. La altura de cada barra representa el número de datos que hay en ese grupo.		

Ii

identity property of multiplication
any number multiplied by 1 is itself.

$3 \cdot 1 = 3$

**propiedad de identidad de la
multiplicación** cualquier número
multiplicado por 1 es el mismo número.

independent variable a variable
whose value is used to find the value of
another variable. An independent variable
determines the value of a dependent
variable.

$y = 5x$

The value of x is used to find
the value of y.

variable independiente variable cuyo
valor se usa para hallar el valor de otra
variable. Una variable independiente
determina el valor de una variable
dependiente.

inequality a mathematical statement
that uses an inequality symbol
($<, >, \leq, \geq$) to show the relationship
between values of expressions.

$4{,}384 > 3{,}448$

$x \geq -2$

desigualdad enunciado matemático
que muestra con un símbolo de
desigualdad ($<, >, \leq, \geq$) la relación que
existe entre los valores de las expresiones.

integers the set of whole numbers and
their opposites.

$-3, -1, 0, 2, 3$

enteros (positivos y negativos)
conjunto de números enteros y sus
opuestos.

interquartile range (IQR) the
difference between the upper quartile and
lower quartile.

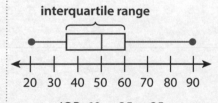

interquartile range

IQR: $60 - 35 = 25$

rango entre cuartiles (REC) diferencia
entre el cuartil superior y el cuartil inferior.

English/Español	Example/Ejemplo	Notes/Notas
inverse operations operations that undo each other. For example, addition and subtraction are inverse operations, and multiplication and division are inverse operations.	$300 \div 10 = 30$ $30 \times 10 = 300$	
operaciones inversas operaciones que se cancelan entre sí. Por ejemplo, la suma y la resta son operaciones inversas, y la multiplicación y la división son operaciones inversas.		
isosceles triangle a triangle that has at least two sides the same length.	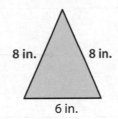	
triángulo isósceles triángulo que tiene al menos dos lados de la misma longitud.	8 in. 8 in. 6 in.	

Ll

English/Español	Example/Ejemplo	Notes/Notas
least common multiple (LCM) the least multiple shared by two or more numbers.	LCM of 20 and 30: $2 \cdot 2 \cdot 3 \cdot 5$, or 60 $20 = 2 \cdot 2 \cdot 5$ $30 = 2 \cdot 3 \cdot 5$	
mínimo común múltiplo (m.c.m.) el menor múltiplo que comparten dos o más números.		
like terms two or more terms that have the same variable factors.	$2x^2$ and $4x^2$ 1.2 and 5.1 $6xy$ and xy	
términos semejantes dos o más términos que tienen los mismos factores variables.		

English/Español	Example/Ejemplo	Notes/Notas
line a straight row of points that goes on forever in both directions.		
recta línea recta de puntos que continúa infinitamente en ambas direcciones.		
line of symmetry a line that divides a shape into two mirror images.		
eje de simetría línea que divide a una figura en dos imágenes reflejadas.		
line segment a straight row of points between two endpoints.		
segmento de recta fila recta de puntos entre dos extremos.	A ●————————● B	
lower quartile the middle number between the minimum and the median in an ordered set of numbers. The lower quartile is also called the 1st quartile or Q1.	lower quartile	
cuartil inferior el número del medio entre el mínimo y la mediana en un conjunto ordenado de números. El cuartil inferior también se llama primer cuartil, o Q1.	20 30 40 50 60 70 80 90	

Mm

English/Español	Example/Ejemplo	Notes/Notas
maximum (of a data set) the greatest value in a data set.	Data set: 9, 10, 8, 9, 7	
máximo (de un conjunto de datos) mayor valor en un conjunto de datos.		
mean the sum of a set of values divided by the number of values. This is often called the *average*.	Data set: 9, 10, 8, 9, 7 $$\text{Mean: } \frac{9 + 10 + 8 + 9 + 7}{5} = 8.6$$	
media suma de un conjunto de valores dividida por el número de valores. Suele llamarse *promedio*.		
mean absolute deviation (MAD) the sum of the distances of each data point from the mean of the data set divided by the number of data points. It is always positive.	Data set: 9, 10, 8, 9, 7 Mean: 8.6 MAD: $$\frac{0.4 + 1.4 + 0.6 + 0.4 + 1.7}{5} = 0.9$$	
desviación media absoluta (DMA) suma de las distancias de cada dato desde la media del conjunto de datos dividido por el número de datos. Siempre es positiva.		
measure of center a single number that summarizes what is typical for all the values in a data set. Mean and median are measures of center.	Data set: 9, 10, 8, 9, 7 Mean: 8.6 Median: 9	
medida de tendencia central único número que resume qué es típico para todos los valores en un conjunto de datos. La media y la mediana son medidas de tendecia central.		
measure of variability a single number that summarizes how much the values in a data set vary. Mean absolute deviation and interquartile range are measures of variability.	Data set: 9, 10, 8, 9, 7 MAD: 0.9 IQR: 1	
medida de variabilidad único número que resume cuánto varían los valores en un conjunto de datos. La desviación media absoluta y el rango entre cuartiles son medidas de variabilidad.		

English/Español	Example/Ejemplo	Notes/Notas
median the middle number, or the halfway point between the two middle numbers, in an ordered set of values.	Data set: 9, 10, 8, 9, 7 7, 8, 9, 9, 10	
mediana el número del medio, o punto intermedio entre los dos números del medio, de un conjunto ordenado de valores.		
minimum (of a data set) the least value in a data set.	Data set: 9, 10, 8, 9, 7	
mínimo (de un conjunto de datos) valor mínimo en un conjunto de datos.		
multiple the product of a given number and any other whole number.	4, 8, 12, 16 are multiples of 4.	
múltiplo producto de un número dado y cualquier otro número entero.		
multiplicative comparison a comparison that tells how many times as many.	$\frac{1}{2} \times 6 = 3$ tells that 3 is $\frac{1}{2}$ times as many as 6 and that 3 is 6 times as many as $\frac{1}{2}$.	
comparación multiplicativa comparación que indica cuántas veces más.		
multiplicative inverse a number is the multiplicative inverse of another number if the product of the two numbers is 1.	3 and $\frac{1}{3}$	
inverso multiplicativo un número es el inverso multiplicativo de otro número si el producto de los dos números es 1.		

Nn

negative numbers numbers that are less than 0. They are located to the left of 0 on a horizontal number line and below 0 on a vertical number line.

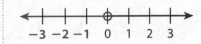

números negativos números que son menores que 0. Se ubican a la izquierda del 0 en una recta numérica horizontal y debajo del 0 en una recta numérica vertical.

---

net a flat, "unfolded" representation of a three-dimensional shape.

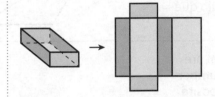

modelo plano representación plana "desplegada" de una figura tridimensional.

---

numerator the number above the line in a fraction that tells the number of equal parts that are being described.

$\frac{3}{4}$

numerador número que está sobre la línea en una fracción y que indica el número de partes iguales que se describen.

Oo

obtuse angle an angle that measures more than 90° but less than 180°.

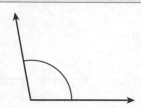

ángulo obtuso ángulo que mide más de 90° pero menos de 180°.

obtuse triangle a triangle that has one obtuse angle.

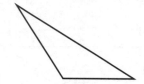

triángulo obtusángulo triángulo que tiene un ángulo obtuso.

opposite numbers numbers that are the same distance from 0 on the number line but in opposite directions. Opposite numbers have the same numeral, but opposite signs.

-3 and 3

$-\frac{8}{15}$ and $\frac{8}{15}$

números opuestos números que están a la misma distancia del 0 en la recta numérica pero en direcciones opuestas. Los números opuestos son el mismo número, pero con el signo opuesto.

Order of Operations a set of rules that state the order in which operations should be performed to evaluate an expression.

Working from left to right:

1. Grouping symbols
2. Exponents
3. Multiplication/Division
4. Addition/Subtraction

orden de las operaciones conjunto de reglas que establecen el orden en el que deben hacerse las operaciones para evaluar una expresión.

ordered pair a pair of numbers, (x, y), that describes the location of a point in the coordinate plane. The x-coordinate gives the point's horizontal distance from the y-axis, and the y-coordinate gives the point's vertical distance from the x-axis.

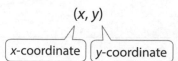

par ordenado par de números, (x, y), que describen la ubicación de un punto en el plano de coordenadas. La coordenada x da la distancia horizontal del punto desde el eje y, y la coordenada y da la distancia vertical del punto desde el eje x.

English/Español	Example/Ejemplo	Notes/Notas

origin the point (0, 0) in the coordinate plane where the *x*-axis and *y*-axis intersect.

origen el punto (0, 0) en el plano de coordenadas donde el eje *x* y el eje *y* se intersecan.

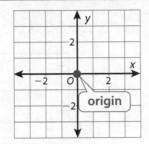

outlier a data value that is much greater or much less than most of the other values in the data set. An outlier seems to not quite fit with the rest of the data points.

valor atípico dato que es mucho mayor o mucho menor que la mayoría de los otros valores del conjunto de datos. Un valor atípico parece no ajustarse al resto de los datos.

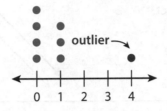

Pp

parallel (||) always the same distance apart and never meeting.

paralelos (||) que están siempre a la misma distancia y nunca se encuentran.

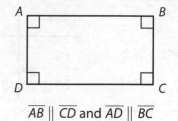

$\overline{AB} \parallel \overline{CD}$ and $\overline{AD} \parallel \overline{BC}$

parallel lines lines that are always the same distance apart and never intersect.

rectas paralelas rectas que siempre están a la misma distancia y nunca se intersecan.

parallelogram a quadrilateral with opposite sides parallel and equal in length.

paralelogramo cuadrilátero que tiene lados opuestos paralelos y de la misma longitud.

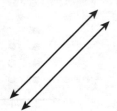

partial products the products you get in each step of the partial-products strategy. You use place value to find partial products.

productos parciales productos que se obtienen en cada paso de la estrategia de productos parciales. Se usa el valor posicional para hallar productos parciales.

218×6
Partial products:
6×200, or 1,200,
6×10, or 60, and
6×8, or 48

partial quotients the quotients you get in each step of the partial-quotient strategy. You use place value to find partial quotients.

cocientes parciales cocientes que se obtienen en cada paso de la estrategia de cocientes parciales. Se usa el valor posicional para hallar cocientes parciales.

$2,124 \div 4$
Partial quotients:
$2,000 \div 4$, or 500,
$100 \div 4$, or 25, and
$24 \div 4$, or 6

partial sums the sums you get in each step of the partial-sums strategy. You use place value to find partial sums.

sumas parciales totales que se obtienen en cada paso de la estrategia de sumas parciales. Se usa el valor posicional para hallar sumas parciales.

$124 + 234$
Partial sums:
$100 + 200$, or 300,
$20 + 30$, or 50, and
$4 + 4$, or 8

English/Español	Example/Ejemplo	Notes/Notas
partial-products strategy a strategy used to multiply multi-digit numbers.	$\begin{array}{r} 218 \\ \times\ \ \ 6 \\ \hline 48 \\ 60 \\ +\ 1{,}200 \\ \hline 1{,}308 \end{array}$ (6 × 8 ones) (6 × 1 ten) (6 × 2 hundreds)	
estrategia de productos parciales estrategia que se usa para multiplicar números de varios dígitos.		

| **partial-quotients strategy** a strategy used to divide multi-digit numbers.

estrategia de cocientes parciales estrategia que se usa para dividir números de varios dígitos. | $\begin{array}{r} 6 \\ 25 \\ 500 \\ 4\overline{)2{,}125} \\ -\ 2{,}000 \\ \hline 125 \\ -\ 100 \\ \hline 25 \\ -\ 24 \\ \hline 1 \end{array}$

The quotient 531 is the sum of partial quotients (**6**, **25**, and **500**) and the remainder (**1**). | |

| **partial-sums strategy** a strategy used to add multi-digit numbers.

estrategia de sumas parciales estrategia que se usa para sumar números de varios dígitos. | Add the hundreds. Add the tens. Add the ones. $\begin{array}{r} 312 \\ +\ 235 \\ \hline 500 \\ 40 \\ +\ \ \ \ 7 \\ \hline 547 \end{array}$ | |

| **peak** in a distribution, the shape formed when many data points are at one value or group of values.

pico en una distribución, la figura que se forma cuando los puntos de muchos datos están en un valor o grupo de valores. | peak | |

| **pentagon** a polygon with exactly 5 sides and 5 angles.

pentágono polígono que tiene exactamente 5 lados y 5 ángulos. | | |

| **per** *for each* or *for every*. The word *per* can be used to express a rate, such as $2 per pound.

por *por cada*. La palabra *por* se puede usar para expresar una tasa, como $2 por libra. | A price of $2 per pound means for every pound, you pay $2. | |

percent per 100. A percent is a rate per 100. A percent can be written using the percent symbol (%) and represented as a fraction or decimal.

porcentaje por cada 100. Un porcentaje es una tasa por cada 100. Un porcentaje se puede escribir usando el símbolo de porcentaje (%) y se representa como fracción o decimal.

15% can be represented as $\frac{15}{100}$ or 0.15.

perimeter the distance around a two-dimensional shape. The perimeter is equal to the sum of the lengths of the sides.

perímetro distancia alrededor de una figura bidimensional. El perímetro es igual a la suma de las longitudes de los lados.

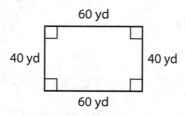

60 yd

40 yd   40 yd

60 yd

Perimeter: 200 yd
(60 yd + 40 yd + 60 yd + 40 yd)

perpendicular (⊥) meeting to form right angles.

perpendicular (⊥) unión donde se forman ángulos rectos.

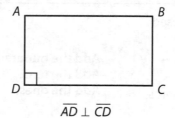

$\overline{AD} \perp \overline{CD}$

perpendicular lines two lines that meet to form a right angle, or a 90° angle.

rectas perpendiculares dos rectas que se encuentran y forman un ángulo recto, o ángulo de 90°.

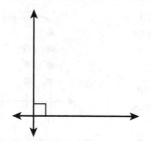

place value the value of a digit based on its position in a number.

valor posicional valor de un dígito que se basa en su posición en un número. Por ejemplo, el 2 en 3.52 está en la posición de las centésimas y tiene un valor de 2 centésimas, o 0.02.

The 2 in 3.52 is in the hundredths place and has a value of **2 hundredths** or 0.02.

English/Español	Example/Ejemplo	Notes/Notas
plane figure a two-dimensional figure, such as a circle, triangle, or rectangle. **figura plana** figura bidimensional, como un círculo, un triángulo o un rectángulo.		
point a single location in space. **punto** ubicación única en el espacio.	*A* ●	
polygon a two-dimensional closed figure made with three or more straight line segments that meet only at their endpoints. **polígono** figura bidimensional cerrada formada por tres o más segmentos de recta que se encuentran solo en sus extremos.		
positive numbers numbers that are greater than 0. They are located to the right of 0 on a horizontal number line and above 0 on a vertical number line. **números positivos** números que son mayores que 0. Se ubican a la derecha del 0 en una recta numérica horizontal y sobre el 0 en una recta numérica vertical.	−3 −2 −1　0　1　2　3	
power an expression with a base and an exponent. **potencia** expresión que tiene una base y un exponente.	8^2	
power of 10 a number that can be written as a product of 10s. **potencia de 10** número que se puede escribir como el producto de 10.	100 and 1,000 are powers of 10 because $100 = 10 \times 10$ and $1,000 = 10 \times 10 \times 10$.	

English/Español	**Example/Ejemplo**	**Notes/Notas**
prime number a whole number greater than 1 whose only factors are 1 and itself. **número primo** número entero mayor que 1 cuyos únicos factores son 1 y sí mismo.	2, 3, 5, 7, 11, 13	
prism a three-dimensional figure with two parallel bases that are the same size and shape. The other faces are parallelograms. A prism is named by the shape of the base. **prisma** figura tridimensional que tiene dos bases paralelas que tienen el mismo tamaño y la misma forma. Las otras caras son paralelogramos. La base determina el nombre del prisma.		
product the result of multiplication. **producto** resultado de la multiplicación.	$3 \cdot 5 = 15$	

Qq

quadrants the four regions of the coordinate plane that are formed when the *x*-axis and *y*-axis intersect at the origin. **cuadrantes** las cuatro regiones del plano de coordenadas que se forman cuando los ejes *x* y *y* se intersecan en el origen.		

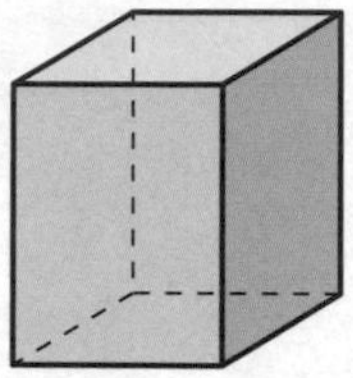

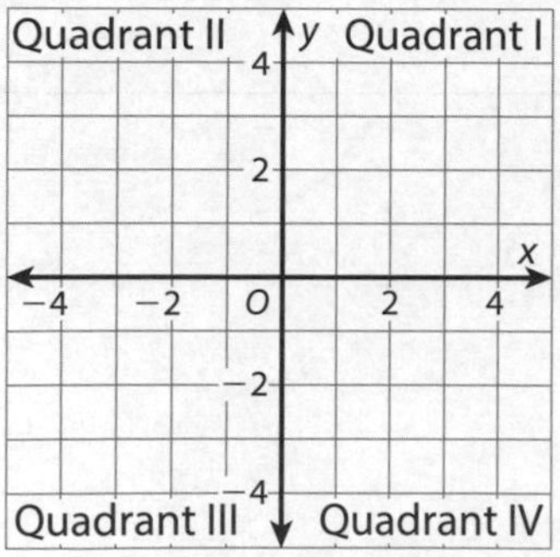

English/Español	Example/Ejemplo	Notes/Notas
quadrilateral a polygon with exactly 4 sides and 4 angles.		
cuadrilátero polígono que tiene exactamente 4 lados y 4 ángulos.		
quotient the result of division.	$22.5 \div 3 = 7.5$	
cociente resultado de la división.		

Rr

range the difference between the greatest value (maximum) and the least value (minimum) in a data set.	Data set: 9, 10, 8, 9, 7 Range: $10 - 7 = 3$	
rango diferencia entre el mayor valor (máximo) y el menor valor (mínimo) en un conjunto de datos.		
rate a ratio tells the number of units of one quantity for 1 unit of another quantity. Rates are often expressed using the word *per*.	5 miles per hour 2 cups for every 1 serving	
tasa razón que indica el número de unidades de una cantidad para 1 unidad de otra cantidad. Las razones suelen expresarse usando la palabra *por*.		
ratio a way to compare two quantities when there are *a* units of one quantity for every *b* units of the other quantity. You can write the ratio in symbols as *a* : *b* and in words as *a to b*.	4 circles : 2 triangles	
razón manera de comparar dos cantidades cuando hay *a* unidades de una cantidad por cada *b* unidades de la otra cantidad. Se puede escribir la razón en símbolos como *a* : *b* y en palabras como *a a b*.		

English/Español	Example/Ejemplo	Notes/Notas

rational number a number that can be expressed as the fraction $\frac{a}{b}$ or the opposite of $\frac{a}{b}$ where a and b are whole numbers and $b \neq 0$. Rational numbers can also be expressed as a decimal.

número racional número que se puede expresar como la fracción $\frac{a}{b}$ o la opuesta a $\frac{a}{b}$ en la que a y b son números enteros y $b \neq 0$. Los números racionales también se pueden expresar

$\frac{3}{4}, -\frac{1}{8}, -3, 0, 1.2$

ray a part of a line that has one endpoint and goes on forever in one direction.

semirrecta parte de una recta que tiene un extremo y continúa infinitamente en una dirección.

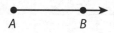

A   B

reciprocal for any nonzero number a, the reciprocal is $\frac{1}{a}$. The reciprocal of any fraction $\frac{a}{b}$ is $\frac{b}{a}$. Zero does not have a reciprocal. The reciprocal of a number is also called the *multiplicative inverse* of that number.

recíproco para cualquier número a distinto de cero, el recíproco es $\frac{1}{a}$. El recíproco de cualquier fracción $\frac{a}{b}$ es $\frac{b}{a}$. El cero no tiene recíproco. El recíproco de un número también se llama *inverso multiplicativo* de ese número.

The reciprocal of $\frac{4}{5}$ is $\frac{5}{4}$.

The reciprocal of $\frac{1}{6}$ is 6.

The reciprocal of -8 is $-\frac{1}{8}$.

rectangle a quadrilateral with 4 right angles. Opposite sides of a rectangle are the same length.

rectángulo cuadrilátero que tiene 4 ángulos rectos. Los lados opuestos de un rectángulo tienen la misma longitud.

rectangular prism a prism where the bases are rectangles.

prisma rectangular prisma en el que las bases son rectángulos.

reflection a transformation that flips (reflects) a figure across a line to form a mirror image.

reflexión transformación que gira (refleja) una figura del otro lado de una línea para formar una imagen reflejada.

A   B

remainder the amount left over when one number does not divide another number a whole number of times.

residuo cantidad que queda cuando un número no divide a otro un número entero de veces.

$$7 \div 2 = 3 \, R \, 1$$

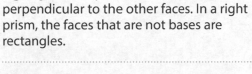

remainder

rhombus a quadrilateral with all sides the same length.

rombo cuadrilátero que tiene todos los lados de la misma longitud.

right angle an angle that measures 90°.

ángulo recto ángulo que mide 90°.

right prism a prism where each base is perpendicular to the other faces. In a right prism, the faces that are not bases are rectangles.

prisma recto prisma en el que cada base es perpendicular a las otras caras. En un prisma recto, las caras que no son bases son rectángulos.

English/Español	Example/Ejemplo	Notes/Notas

right rectangular prism a right prism where the bases and other faces are all rectangles.

prisma rectangular recto prisma recto en el que las bases y las otras caras son rectángulos.

right triangle a triangle with one right angle.

triángulo rectángulo triángulo que tiene un ángulo recto.

right triangular prism a right prism where the bases are triangles and the other faces are rectangles.

prisma triangular recto prisma recto en el que las bases son triángulos y las otras caras son rectángulos.

round to approximate the value of a number by finding the nearest ten, hundred, or other place value.

48 rounded to the nearest ten is 50.

redondear aproximar el valor de un número hallando la decena, la centena u otro valor posicional más cercano.

English/Español	Example/Ejemplo	Notes/Notas

Ss

scale (on a graph) the value represented by the distance between one tick mark and the next on a number line.

escala (en una gráfica) valor representado por la distancia que hay entre una marca y la siguiente en una recta numérica.

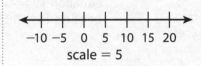

scale = 5

scalene triangle a triangle that has no sides the same length.

triángulo escaleno triángulo que no tiene lados de la misma longitud.

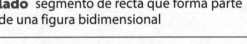

side a line segment that forms part of a two-dimensional shape.

lado segmento de recta que forma parte de una figura bidimensional

side

skewed left when most of the data points of a distribution are clustered near the greater values.

asimétrica a la izquierda cuando la mayoría de los datos de una distribución se agrupan cerca de los valores más altos.

Skewed Left

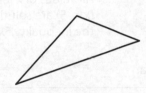

skewed right when most of the data points of a distribution are clustered near the lesser values.

asimétrica a la derecha cuando la mayoría de los datos de una distribución se agrupan cerca de los valores más bajos.

Skewed Right

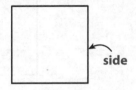

English/Español	Example/Ejemplo	Notes/Notas
solution of an equation a value that can be substituted for a variable to make an equation true. **solución de una ecuación** valor que puede sustituir a una variable para hacer que una ecuación sea verdadera.	The value 5 is the solution of the equation $19 = 4x - 1$ because $19 = 4(5) - 1$.	
solution of an inequality a value that can be substituted for a variable to make an inequality true. **solución de una desigualdad** valor que puede sustituir a una variable para hacer que una desigualdad sea verdadera.	All values of x less than 5 ($x < 5$) are solutions of the inequality $5x < 25$.	
square a quadrilateral with 4 right angles and 4 sides of equal length. **cuadrado** cuadrilátero que tiene 4 ángulos rectos y 4 lados de la misma longitud.		
statistical question a question that can be answered by collecting data that are expected to vary. **pregunta estadística** pregunta que se puede responder reuniendo datos que se espera que varíen.	What is the typical amount of rain in April?	
sum the result of addition. **total** resultado de la suma.	 $24 + 35 = 59$	
surface area the sum of the areas of all the faces of a three-dimensional figure. **área total** suma de las áreas de todas las caras de una figura tridimensional.	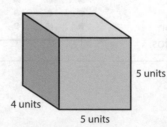 5 units 4 units 5 units Surface Area: $2(4)(5) + 2(4)(5) + 2(5)(5) = 130$ units^2	

symmetric when a distribution has the same shape on both sides of a middle point.

simétrico cuando una distribución tiene la misma forma en ambos lados de un punto que está en el medio.

Symmetric

Tt

term a number, a variable, or a product of numbers, variables, and/or expressions. A term may include an exponent.

término número, variable o el producto de números, variables y/o expresiones. Un término puede tener un exponente.

$$4x + 9 + y^2$$

term

three-dimensional solid, or having length, width, and height. For example, a cube is three-dimensional.

tridimensional sólido, o que tiene longitud, ancho y altura. Por ejemplo, un cubo es tridimensional.

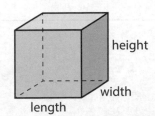

height

width

length

trapezoid (exclusive) a quadrilateral with exactly one pair of parallel sides.

trapecio (exclusivo) cuadrilátero que tiene exactamente un par de lados paralelos.

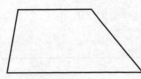

English/Español	Example/Ejemplo	Notes/Notas
trapezoid (inclusive) a quadrilateral with at least one pair of parallel sides.		
trapecio (inclusivo) cuadrilátero que tiene al menos un par de lados paralelos.		
triangle a polygon with exactly 3 sides and 3 angles.		
triángulo polígono que tiene exactamente 3 lados y 3 ángulos.		
triangular prism a prism where the bases are triangles.		
prisma triangular prisma en el que las bases son triángulos.		
two-dimensional flat, or having measurement in two directions, like length and width. For example, a rectangle is two-dimensional.	width length	
bidimensional plano, o que tiene medidas en dos direcciones, como longitud y ancho. Por ejemplo, un rectángulo es bidimensional.		

Uu

unit fraction a fraction with a numerator of 1. Other fractions are built from unit fractions.

fracción unitaria fracción que tiene un numerador de 1. Otras fracciones se construyen a partir de fracciones unitarias.

$$\frac{1}{5}$$

unit rate the numerical part of a rate. For the ratio $a : b$, the unit rate is the quotient $\frac{a}{b}$.

tasa por unidad parte numérica de una tasa. Para la razón $a : b$, la tasa por unidad es el cociente $\frac{a}{b}$.

Rate: 3 miles per hour

Unit rate: 3

unknown the value you need to find to solve a problem.

incógnita valor que hay que hallar para resolver un problema.

$$20.5 + x = 30$$

upper quartile the middle number between the median and the maximum in an ordered set of numbers. The upper quartile is also called the 3rd quartile or Q3.

cuartil superior número del medio entre la mediana y el máximo en un conjunto ordenado de números. El cuartil superior también se llama tercer cuartil, o Q3.

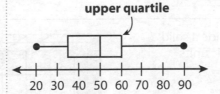

upper quartile

20 30 40 50 60 70 80 90

Vv

variability how spread out or close together values in a data set are.

variabilidad la dispersión o cercanía de los valores en un conjunto de datos.

Gavin's Handstand Times

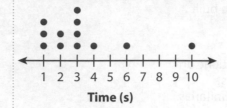

Time (s)

There is high variability in Gavin's handstand times.

---

variable a letter that represents an unknown number. In some cases, a variable may represent more than one number.

variable letra que representa un número desconocido. En algunos casos, una variable puede representar más de un número.

$$3x + 9 = 90$$

---

vertex the point where two rays, lines, or line segments meet to form an angle.

vértice punto en el que dos semirrectas, rectas o segmentos de recta se encuentran y forman un ángulo.

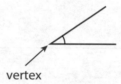

vertex

---

volume the amount of space inside a solid figure. Volume is measured in cubic units such as cubic inches.

volumen cantidad de espacio dentro de una figura sólida. El volumen se mide en unidades cúbicas como las pulgadas cúbicas.

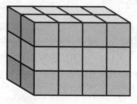

volume: 24 units³

English/Español	Example/Ejemplo	Notes/Notas

Ww

whole numbers the numbers 0, 1, 2, 3, 4, . . . Whole numbers are nonnegative and have no fractional part.

0, 8, 187

números enteros los números 0, 1, 2, 3, 4, . . . Los números enteros no son negativos y no tienen partes fraccionarias.

Xx

x-axis the horizontal number line in the coordinate plane.

eje x recta numérica horizontal en el plano de coordenadas.

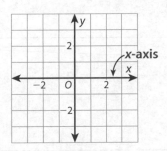

x-coordinate the first number in an ordered pair. It tells the point's horizontal distance from the y-axis.

coordenada x primer número en un par ordenado. Indica la distancia horizontal del punto al eje y.

Yy

y-axis the vertical number line in the coordinate plane.

eje y recta numérica vertical en el plano de coordenadas.

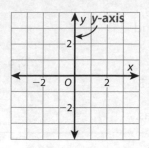

y-coordinate the second number in an ordered pair. It tells the point's vertical distance from the *x*-axis.

coordenada y el segundo número en un par ordenado. Indica la distancia vertical del punto al eje *x*.

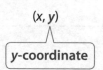

Credits

Acknowledgment

Common Core State Standards © 2010. National Governors Association Center for Best Practices and Council of Chief State School Officers. All rights reserved.

Photography Credits

Cover: Song Heming/stock.adobe.com
Back Cover: 468 Morinka/Shutterstock; 599, 600 Kenishirotie/Shutterstock; 670 Tatiana Popova/Shutterstock
Text: ii, 96 Lukiyanova Natalia frenta/Shutterstock; ii, 120 redtbird02/Shutterstock, Kriengsuk Prasroetsung/Shutterstock; iii, 161 Olga Danylenko/Shutterstock; iii, 180 Rainbow4527/Shutterstock; iii, 194 Feaspb/Shutterstock, Roman Borodaev/Shutterstock; iv, 272 Matthias G. Ziegler/Shutterstock; v, 364 Maridav/Shutterstock, Production Perig/Shutterstock; v, 410 Vaclav Volrab/Shutterstock; vi, 494 Gino Santa Maria/Shutterstock; vi, 496 Jiri Hera/Shutterstock.com; vi, 509 Mrinal Pal. Shutterstock, Robert Biedermann/Shutterstock; vii, 560 Palmer Kane LLC/Shutterstock, Dmitry Naumov/Shutterstock; vii, 582 Jojoo64/Shutterstock; vii, 590 ToffeePhoto/Shutterstock, Iryna Dobrovynska/Shutterstock; viii, 664 vnlit/Shutterstock, Scisetti Alfio/Shutterstock; viii, 689 Gerald A. DeBoer/Shutterstock; viii, 735 YP_Studio/Shutterstock; 1, 41 Comaniciu Dan/Shutterstock; 3 marekuliasz/Shutterstock; 4 Bankrx/Shutterstock; 5 Japan Stock Photography/Alamy Stock Photo; 8 adike/Shutterstock; 9 sripfoto/Shutterstock, NASA/JPL-Caltech/Space Science Institute; 12 saaton/Shutterstock, little birdie/Shutterstock; 13 foto-select/Shutterstock.com; 19 IROOM STOCK/Shutterstock; 20, 229 chinasong/Shutterstock; 21 Krasovski Dmitri/Shutterstock; 24 7Crafts/Shutterstock; 25 I.B.Me/Shutterstock; 31 CD Lenzen/Shutterstock; 32 Jozef Sowa/Shutterstock; 42 Chonlawut/Shutterstock; 43 GoWithLight/Shutterstock; 47 Andrey Starostin/Shutterstock; 52 alleski/Shutterstock; 54 yanik88/Shutterstock, 3DMAVR/Shutterstock; 61 Lorena Huerta/Shutterstock; 63 Artbox/Shutterstock; 64 goir/Shutterstock; 65 Arthur Salimullin/Shutterstock; 69 Brent Hofacker/Shutterstock; 70 AGCuesta/Shutterstock; 72 AS Food Studio/Shutterstock; 74, 201 lzf/Shutterstock; 75 Den Rozhnovsky/Shutterstock; 76 Vladyslav Danlin/Shutterstock; 80 Tony Savino/Shutterstock; 83 chuckchee/Shutterstock; 85 Mikadun/Shutterstock; 87 Kathrin Richter/FOAP/Getty Images; 90 PolyPloiid/Shutterstock; 97 Eleni Mavrandoni/Shutterstock; 98 Sirin_bird/Shutterstock; 108 An Nguyen/Shutterstock; 109 FabrikaSimf/Shutterstock, stefanphotozemun/Shutterstock; 112 trabantos/Shutterstock.com; 113 David Fine/FEMA; 114 Jason Yoder/Shutterstock; 116 Nadezhda Nesterova/Shutterstock; 119, 129, 362, 366 Eric Isselee/Shutterstock, 119 MuratGungut/Shutterstock; 124 OSTILL is Franck Camhi/Shutterstock; 127 Nantawat Chotsuwan/Shutterstock; 129, 132 Diane Garcia/Shutterstock; 129, 132 pfuegler-photo/Shutterstock; 129 Ljupco Smokovski/Shutterstock, LittlePerfectStock/Shutterstock, Tsekhmister/Shutterstock, Aksenova Natalya/Shutterstock; 135 RiumaLab/Shutterstock; 136 Rustic/Shutterstock, Inegvin/Shutterstock, Kovtun Dmitriy/Shutterstock, photomaster/Shutterstock; 137 PhotoSongserm/Shutterstock, Andrey Esin/Shutterstock, Alexander Baumann/Shutterstock, Anya Hess/Shutterstock; 143, 195 Ocskay Bence/Shutterstock; 145 Edy Wibowo/Shutterstock; 147 Normana Karia/Shutterstock; 150 Vaclav Hroch/Shutterstock; 151 Spiroview Inc/Shutterstock, Somchai Som/Shutterstock, Andrei Kuzmik/Shutterstock, jackhollingsworth.com/Shutterstock, Alexander Mak/Shutterstock; 154 M. Rohana/Shutterstock; 156 Suzanne Tucker/Shutterstock; 157 Rachel Moon/Shutterstock; 158 Benhamin Simeneta/Shutterstock; 160 Alexandru Chiriac/Shutterstock; 166 Oleksandr Osipov/Shutterstock; 167 Pavel1964/Shutterstock; 168 Rob Hainer/Shutterstock; 169 pelfophoto/Shutterstock; 172 Mike Flippo/Shutterstock; 173 ArliftAtoz2205/Shutterstock.com; 174 donatas1205/Shutterstock; 176 stockphoto-graf/Shutterstock; 178 welcomia/Shutterstock; 179 Roberto Galan/Shutterstock.com; 185 evrymmnt/Shutterstock; 186, 672 sirtravelalot/Shutterstock, 186 theerapol sri-in/Shutterstock; 188, 476, 737 Brocreative/Shutterstock; 190 MiVa/Shutterstock; 197 RG-vc/Shutterstock; 198 Adcharin Chitthammachuk/Shutterstock; 200 Graeme Dawes/Shutterstock, ZaZa Studio/Shutterstock; 203 Rachel Juliet Lerch/Shutterstock; 204 Slavica Stajic/Shutterstock; 206 kosam/Shutterstock, Tiger Images/Shutterstock; 207 A_stockphoto/Shutterstock; 208 MaxyM/Shutterstock; 209 KREUS/Shutterstock, Evgeny Prokofyev/Shutterstock; 212 akiyoko/Shutterstock, Andrzej Rostek/Shutterstock; 213 Tippman98x/Shutterstock.com, Diana Johanna Velasquez/Alamy Stock Photo; 214 iStock.com/Bastiaan Slabbers; 216 Arina P Habich/Shutterstock; 218 irin-k/Shutterstock, Erkki Makkonen/Shutterstock; 219 Moonborne/Shutterstock; 220 Tsekhmister/Shutterstock; 223 DONOT6_STUDIO/Shutterstock, Daniel Prudek/Shutterstock; 224 Cultura Creative (RF)/Alamy Stock Photo; 230 cybrain/Shutterstock; 231 lucadp/Shutterstock; 234 luskiv/Shutterstock; 235, 236 Cathy Keifer/Shutterstock; 235 Leonardo Garofalo/Shutterstock; 239 iStock.com/EdwardMosser, Rashevskyi Viacheslav/Shutterstock; 241 Viktor1/Shutterstock; 242 iStock.com/evemilla; 250 Microgen/Shutterstock;

Data Sets

660 https://quake.utah.edu/special-events/2019-bluffdale-earthquake-sequence-faq; 694 https://www.washingtonpost.com/news/the-switch/wp/2018/03/02/why-almost-no-one-is-making-a-living-on-youtube/?noredirect=on; 699 https://www.weather-atlas.com/en/australia/darwin-climate